AMC'S BEST DAY HIKES NEAR
NEW YORK CITY

Four-Season Guide to 50 of the Best Trails
in New York, Connecticut, and New Jersey

DANIEL CASE

Appalachian Mountain Club Books
Boston, Massachusetts

The AMC is a nonprofit organization and sales of AMC books fund our mission of protecting the Northeast outdoors. If you appreciate our efforts and would like to make a donation to the AMC, contact us at Appalachian Mountain Club, 5 Joy Street, Boston, MA 02108.

http://www.outdoors.org/publications/books/

Distributed by The Globe Pequot Press, Guilford, Connecticut.

Front cover photographs © (top) Greg Miller Photography, (bottom) Ned Frisk Photography/
    Brand X/Corbis
Back cover photographs © (l-r) iStockphoto, Appalachian Mountain Club, iStockphoto
All interior photographs © Daniel Case
Maps by Ken Dumas, © Appalachian Mountain Club
Book design by Eric Edstam

Library of Congress Cataloging-in-Publication Data
Case, Dan.
  AMC's best day hikes near New York City : four-season guide to 50 of the best trails in New York, Connecticut, and New Jersey / Dan Case.
    p. cm.
  Includes bibliographical references and index.
  ISBN 978-1-934028-38-4 (alk. paper)
  1. Hiking—New York Region—Guidebooks. 2. Trails—New York Region—Guidebooks. 3. New York Region—Guidebooks. I. Appalachian Mountain Club. II. Title. III. Title: Appalachian Mountain Club's best day hikes near New York City. IV. Title: Best day hikes near New York City.
  GV199.42.N64C37 2010
  796.5109747'1—dc22
                    2009053603

The paper used in this publication meets the minimum requirements of the American National Standard for Information Sciences-Permanence of Paper for Printed Library Materials, ANSI Z39.48-1984. ∞

Outdoor recreation activities by their very nature are potentially hazardous. This book is not a substitute for good personal judgment and training in outdoor skills. Due to changes in conditions, use of the information in this book is at the sole risk of the user. The author and the Appalachian Mountain Club assume no liability for accidents happening to, or injuries sustained by, readers who engage in the activities described in this book.

Interior pages contain 30% post-consumer recycled fiber.
Cover contains 10% post-consumer recycled fiber.
Printed in the United States of America,
using vegetable-based inks.

Mixed Sources
Product group from well-managed forests, controlled sources and recycled wood or fiber
www.fsc.org   Cert no. SCS-COC-002464
©1996 Forest Stewardship Council
FSC

10 9 8 7 6 5 4 3 2 1   10 11 12 13 14 15 16 17

To the late Barbara McMartin, whom I never met, but who served as an example for anyone who writes hiking guide books—not just in New York, but anywhere.

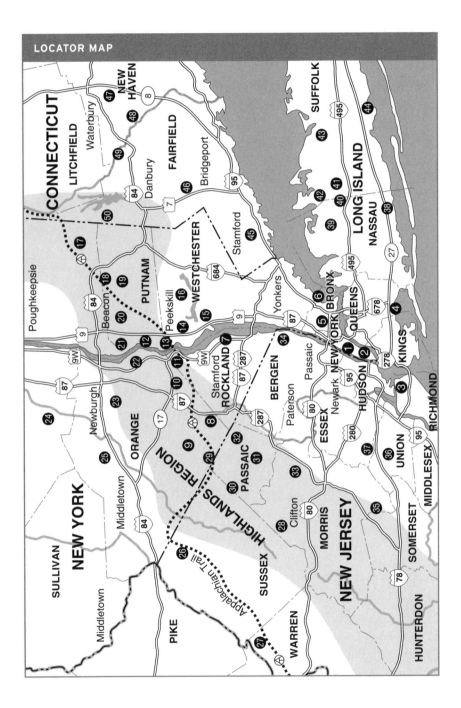

CONTENTS

Locator Map . . . . **iv**

At-a-Glance Trip Planner. . . . . **viii**

Preface . . . .**xvii**

Acknowledgments . . . . **xix**

Introduction . . . . **xxi**

How to Use This Book . . . . **xxiii**

Trip Planning and Safety . . . . **xxv**

Leave No Trace . . . . **xxix**

SECTION 1: NEW YORK CITY AND THE LOWER HUDSON VALLEY

❶ Central Park 3

❷ High Line 10

❸ Staten Island Greenbelt. 15

❹ West Pond Loop. 20

❺ New York Botanical Garden—Native Forest 24

❻ Pelham Bay Park 28

7 Hook Mountain State Park. 32

8 Tuxedo Loop 37

9 Bellvale Mountain 41

10 Sugarloaf South 45

11 Harriman State Park—Long Mountain 50

12 Bear Mountain. 55

13 Manitoga/The Russel Wright Design Center. 60

14 Blue Mountain Reservation 64

15 Teatown Lake Reservation 69

16 Turkey Mountain Nature Preserve 73

17 Pawling Nature Reserve 77

18 Ward Pound Ridge Reservation 82

19 Nimham Mountain State Forest 87

20 Clarence Fahnestock State Park—Canopus Lake 91

21 Hudson Highlands State Park—Breakneck Ridge and Bull Hill. 96

22 Black Rock Forest 102

23 Stewart State Forest. 107

24 Shawangunk Grasslands National Wildlife Refuge 111

25 Highland Lakes State Park 117

SECTION 2: NORTHERN NEW JERSEY

26 High Point 123

27 Rattlesnake Swamp Loop 127

28 Mahlon Dickerson Reservation. 133

29 Bearfort Mountain. 137

30 Abraham S. Hewitt State Forest—Terrace Pond 142

31 Assiniwikam Mountain 147

32 Ringwood State Park. 151

33 Pyramid Mountain Natural Historic Area. 156

34 Palisades Interstate Park. 160

35 Great Swamp National Wildlife Refuge 166

36 Watchung Reservation 170

37 South Mountain Reservation. 175

SECTION 3: LONG ISLAND AND CONNECTICUT

38 Massapequa Preserve 183

39 Muttontown Preserve 187

40 Manetto Hills 191

41 West Hills County Park 195
42 Uplands Farm Sanctuary to Cold Spring Harbor State Park.......... 199
43 Nissequogue River State Park 204
44 Connetquot River State Park Preserve 209
45 Mianus River Park... 214
46 Devil's Den Preserve 218
47 Naugatuck State Forest 223
48 Lower Paugusett State Forest 227
49 Upper Paugusett State Forest.................................... 232
50 Pootatuck State Forest.. 236

NATURE AND HISTORY ESSAYS

Robert Moses: Urban Planner Extraordinaire......................... 9
The Fall and Rise of the White-Tailed Deer 36
The Hudson Highlands and the American Revolution 54
The Wild Turkey 68
The Chestnut Oak.. 81
Saving Storm King 101
The Short-Eared Owl 116
Tocks Island Dam 132
AMC and the Highlands Conservation Act 141
The Legends of Clinton Road 146
The Geology of the Palisades.................................... 165
Snapping Turtles 208
The Threatened Hemlock 231
The Mountain Laurel 240

APPENDICES

A: Critical Treasures of the Highlands........................... 241
B: Resources... 244
C: Further Reading 245

Index.. 247
About the Author 253
Appalachian Mountain Club..................................... 254
About the AMC in New York 255
AMC Books Updates 255

AT-A-GLANCE TRIP PLANNER

#	Trip	Page	Location (Town)	Rating	Distance and Elevation Gain
NEW YORK CITY AND LOWER HUDSON VALLEY					
1	Central Park	3	New York, NY	Easy	3.0 mi, 70 ft
2	High Line	10	New York, NY	Easy	0.8 mi, 30 ft
3	Staten Island Greenbelt	15	Staten Island, NY	Difficult	7.0 mi, 540 ft
4	West Pond Loop	20	Broad Channel, NY	Easy	1.8 mi, 20 ft
5	New York Botanical Garden–Native Forest	24	Bronx, NY	Easy	1.5 mi, 20 ft
6	Pelham Bay Park	28	Bronx, NY	Easy	2.0 mi, 20 ft
7	Hook Mountain State Park	32	Upper Nyack, NY	Moderate	2.3 mi, 420 ft

Estimated Time	Fee	Good for Kids	Dogs Allowed	Public Transit	X-C Skiing	Snow-shoeing	Trip Highlights
1.5 hrs		✓	✓	✓	✓	✓	New York City's iconic park
0.5 hr		✓		✓			Elevated park on old rail line
5.0 hrs		✓	✓	✓	✓	✓	Largest tract of undeveloped land in city
1.0 hr		✓		✓	✓	✓	Popular birding spot
1.0 hr	$	✓		✓			Only remaining tract of original forest in the city
1.0 hr		✓	✓	✓	✓	✓	Largest New York City park
1.5 hr		✓	✓		✓	✓	Views of Tappan Zee Bridge

#	Trip	Page	Location (Town)	Rating	Distance and Elevation Gain
8	Tuxedo Loop	37	Tuxedo, NY	Difficult	5.3 mi, 900 ft
9	Bellvale Mountain	41	Bellvale, NY	Moderate	3.6 mi, 440 ft
10	Sugarloaf South	45	Garrison, NY	Moderate	3.2 mi, 530 ft
11	Harriman State Park–Long Mountain	50	Fort Montgomery, NY	Moderate	1.6 mi, 320 ft
12	Bear Mountain	55	Bear Mountain, NY	Difficult	4.5 mi, 1,130 ft
13	Manitoga / The Russel Wright Design Center	60	Garrison, NY	Moderate	2.2 mi, 500 ft
14	Blue Mountain Reservation	64	Peekskill, NY	Moderate	4.0 mi, 630 ft
15	Teatown Lake Reservation	69	Ossining, NY	Moderate	1.7 mi, 220 ft
16	Turkey Mountain Nature Preserve	73	Yorktown, NY	Moderate	1.8 mi, 400 ft
17	Pawling Nature Reserve	77	Pawling, NY	Difficult	5.9 mi, 858 ft
18	Ward Pound Ridge Reservation	82	Cross River, NY	Moderate	3.1 mi, 680 ft
19	Nimham Mountain State Forest	87	Kent Lakes, NY	Moderate	1.5 mi, 520 ft
20	Clarence Fahnestock State Park–Canopus Lake	91	Carmel, NY	Moderate	4.6 mi, 420 ft
21	Hudson Highlands State Park–Breakneck Ridge and Bull Hill	96	Cold Spring, NY	Difficult	5.9 mi, 1,250 ft

Estimated Time	Fee	Good for Kids	Dogs Allowed	Public Transit	X-C Skiing	Snow-shoeing	Trip Highlights
6.0 hrs		✓	✓	✓	✓	✓	Challenging hike from train station
2.0 hrs		✓	✓	✓	✓	✓	Short trip to two vistas
3.0 hrs		✓	✓	✓	✓	✓	Small mountain with views of West Point
1.0 hr		✓	✓		✓	✓	Spectacular view
4.0 hrs	$		✓	✓		✓	Challenging hike with sweeping views
1.5 hrs		✓	✓	✓	✓	✓	Trails laid out by a master American designer
3.0 hrs		✓	✓	✓	✓	✓	Dramatic post-glacial landscape
1.0 hr		✓	✓		✓	✓	Lakeside circuit at nature preserve
1.5 hrs	$	✓	✓	✓	✓	✓	Small local mountain with big views
5.0 hrs			✓	✓	✓		Diverse nature reserve accessible from train station
2.0 hrs	$	✓	✓	✓	✓	✓	Westchester County's largest park
1.0 hr		✓	✓		✓	✓	Tallest fire tower in New York
3.5 hrs			✓		✓	✓	Scenic lake view
7.0 hrs			✓	✓		✓	Classic Hudson Highlands hike

#	Trip	Page	Location (Town)	Rating	Distance and Elevation Gain
22	Black Rock Forest	102	Cornwall, NY	Difficult	4.3 mi, 868 ft
23	Stewart State Forest	107	New Windsor, NY	Moderate	4.2 mi, 380 ft
24	Shawangunk Grasslands National Wildlife Refuge	111	Wallkill, NY	Easy	3.1 mi, Level
25	Highland Lakes State Park	117	Scotchtown, NY	Easy	3.5 mi, 90 ft

NORTHERN NEW JERSEY

#	Trip	Page	Location (Town)	Rating	Distance and Elevation Gain
26	High Point	123	Montague, NJ	Moderate	2.8 mi, 380 ft
27	Rattlesnake Swamp Loop	127	Blairstown, NJ	Moderate	4.6 mi, 400 ft
28	Mahlon Dickerson Reservation	133	Jefferson, NJ	Moderate	4.4 mi, 300 ft
29	Bearfort Mountain	137	West Milford, NJ	Difficult	4.3 mi, 780 ft
30	Abraham S. Hewitt State Forest–Terrace Pond	142	Upper Greenwood Lake, NJ	Moderate	3.1 mi, 260 ft
31	Assiniwikam Mountain	147	West Milford, NJ	Moderate	2.2 mi, 200 ft
32	Ringwood State Park	151	Ringwood, NJ	Moderate	3.5 mi, 400 ft
33	Pyramid Mountain Natural Historic Area	156	Montville, NJ	Moderate	2.2 mi, 320 ft
34	Palisades Interstate Park	160	Alpine, NJ	Easy	1.5 mi, 100 ft
35	Great Swamp National Wildlife Refuge	166	Meyersville, NJ	Easy	3.0 mi, 20 ft

Estimated Time	Fee	Good for Kids	Dogs Allowed	Public Transit	X-C Skiing	Snow-shoeing	Trip Highlights
5.0 hrs			🐕		✓	✓	Sustainable buildings and sweeping views
2.5 hrs		✓	🐕		✓	✓	Expansive fields and nice view
2.0 hrs		✓			✓	✓	Old airport with views of Shawangunks
2.5 hrs		✓	🐕		✓	✓	Old country roads in a quiet woodland
1.5 hrs		✓	🐕		✓	✓	Highest point in New Jersey
3.5 hrs		✓	🐕			✓	View of Delaware Water Gap region
3.0 hrs		✓	🐕		✓	✓	Highest point in Morris County
4.0 hrs			🐕	🚌		✓	Views over Greenwood Lake
3.5 hrs		✓	🐕		✓		Popular and scenic glacial pond
1.5 hrs		✓	🐕			✓	Wild views from high in the Wyanokies
2.5 hrs	$		🐕			✓	State botanical garden, woods, and lake
1.5 hrs		✓	🐕			✓	Small hill with interesting rock formations
1.0 hr		✓	🐕	🚌	✓	✓	Views over Hudson River from cliff edges
1.5 hrs		✓			✓	✓	Only federal wilderness area in northern New Jersey

#	Trip	Page	Location (Town)	Rating	Distance and Elevation Gain
36	Watchung Reservation	170	Mountainside, NJ	Moderate	3.8 mi, 150 ft
37	South Mountain Reservation	175	Millburn, NJ	Moderate	5.2 mi, 350 ft

LONG ISLAND AND CONNECTICUT

#	Trip	Page	Location (Town)	Rating	Distance and Elevation Gain
38	Massapequa Preserve	183	Massapequa, NY	Easy	2.0 mi, Level
39	Muttontown Preserve	187	East Norwich, NY	Easy	1.5 mi, 30 ft
40	Manetto Hills	191	Plainview, NY	Moderate	3.5 mi, 160 ft
41	West Hills County Park	195	Melville, NY	Moderate	4.0 mi, 220 ft
42	Uplands Farm Sanctuary to Cold Spring Harbor State Park	199	Cold Spring Harbor, NY	Moderate	3.5 mi, 200 ft
43	Nissequogue River State Park	204	Kings Park, NY	Easy	3.0 mi, 50 ft
44	Connetquot River State Park Preserve	209	Oakdale, NY	Moderate	3.8 mi, 15 ft
45	Mianus River Park	214	Greenwich and Stamford, CT	Easy	2.2 mi, 140 ft
46	Devil's Den Preserve	218	Weston, CT	Difficult	7.0 mi, 450 ft
47	Naugatuck State Forest	223	Beacon Falls, CT	Moderate	1.0 mi, 400 ft
48	Lower Paugussett State Forest	227	Newtown, CT	Moderate	2.0 mi, 270 ft
49	Upper Paugussett State Forest	232	Newtown, CT	Moderate	2.4 mi, 450 ft
50	Pootatuck State Forest	236	New Fairfield, CT	Moderate	3.1 mi, 600 ft

Estimated Time	Fee	Good for Kids	Dogs Allowed	Public Transit	X-C Skiing	Snow-Shoeing	Trip Highlights
3.0 hrs		✓	✓		✓	✓	Suburban nature preserve with historic sights
4.0 hrs			✓	✓	✓	✓	Scenic waterfall
1.0 hr		✓	✓		✓	✓	Only pine barrens left in Nassau County
1.0 hr		✓	✓		✓	✓	Small untouched piece of Long Island's North Shore
2.0 hrs		✓	✓		✓	✓	Wooded loop
2.5 hrs		✓	✓	✓	✓	✓	Highest point on Long Island
2.5 hrs		✓	✓	✓	✓	✓	Short but challenging hike to quaint small town
2.0 hrs		✓			✓	✓	Views of Long Island Sound
2.5 hrs		✓		✓	✓	✓	Large expanse of pine barrens
1.0 hr		✓	✓		✓	✓	Suburban preserve on picturesque river
3.5 hrs					✓	✓	Popular nature preserve
1.0 hr		✓	✓	✓	✓	✓	View of Naugatuck Valley
1.0 hr		✓	✓		✓	✓	Walk along wooded shoreline
2.0 hrs		✓	✓			✓	Exciting, roller-coaster-like trail
2.5 hrs		✓	✓		✓	✓	Cascades and views of Candlewood Lake

PREFACE

THERE WERE ALWAYS WOODS NEARBY IN THE TOWNS in northeastern New Jersey where I grew up, and my friends and I had parents who were willing to let us spend hours after school and on weekends exploring them unsupervised. These journeys weren't intended to be nature walks, unless you count searches for the perfect slopes to roll a bunch of rocks down or a place to do stunts on dirt bikes, which requires a very broad definition of "nature walk."

We learned things in the woods nevertheless: how to follow a trail, blazed or (usually) not; how to get home in a hurry; and how to be independent. The best lesson of all was the one we didn't realize we were learning: how to appreciate the woods. This kind of knowledge has become less common as parents have grown less willing to leave children to their own devices. On my own, I'd often venture into the woods just to explore trails for their own sake. Where, I would wonder, did this trail ultimately go?

I kept all that in mind when I got older and went to summer camp in the mountainous regions of northern New England. There I translated what I had learned in the suburban forests into the skills of a hiker, with help, of course, from the counselors who led us into the boreal reaches of New Hampshire and Maine.

As I grew up, that part of my life was in the past—something I had once done but still loved. High school sports took over, and in college I found other pursuits as well. It wasn't until I moved back to the New York area in the late 1990s that I rediscovered hiking on the trails of the Catskills, when my wife and I lived in the region briefly and I didn't have much else to do on weekends at the time.

I climbed all 35 of the Catskill High Peaks, but didn't stop there. I soon realized that the Hudson Valley has many great places to hike within a short drive. I became interested in climbing the high points of other counties in the region as well, which took me north to the Adirondacks, south into New Jersey and Connecticut, and eventually down to Long Island.

In the course of doing all this, I learned to really appreciate the outdoors. Often hikers look forward to a view of something from somewhere, a sight like a waterfall or lake, or claiming a difficult summit. I had those experiences, but I realized along the way that the journey itself is also a destination, and that sometimes the woods themselves are what you remember most.

After a while, I didn't just hike—I became involved. I joined several different hiking organizations and took an active role in them. I went on maintenance trips and became a regular trail maintainer.

Everywhere I went I discovered something interesting and memorable, whether it involved a major expedition or a short walk. Some of those hikes are in this book, but many were also new to me. On them, I felt the same sense of joy at the discovery of new sights and experiences that I did on my first hikes.

Whether you recently started hiking, or have done so for a long time, I hope this book brings you the same joy I felt, and that it takes you to the same places inside, as well as outside, that it did for me.

ACKNOWLEDGMENTS

AS FUN AS IT SOUNDS TO BE ASKED TO GO OUT INTO THE WOODS, do some hikes and walks, and write a guidebook about them, it *is* work and can be quite demanding, especially when done over a very broad region. I could never have completed this project without a lot of support and help from many different people, both on and off the trails.

First and foremost have been the two other people in my own house—my family. My wife, Elizabeth, made time for me to go out into the deep reaches of the tri-state area and kept dinner warm. My son, Anguel, not only went on some of these trips with me, but also put up with some stiff climbs, boots that were getting too small, and the attention of too many insects.

I also cannot forget to thank both of my parents. My mother let my son and me use her home in New Jersey as a base for some of our hikes. My father was always encouraging, and helped plan the Central Park trip.

No book can go anywhere without its editor, especially for a first-time writer. Dan Eisner at AMC Books was very understanding and supportive throughout many phone conversations and email exchanges. I could not have asked for a better editor. There are too many places in this book where his suggestions and comments improved things. Publisher Heather Stephenson, my initial contact with AMC, was supportive as well. Stacy Gould from AMC's New York–North Jersey Chapter suggested some hikes, in particular Teatown

Lake, which enhanced this book. Mike Urban made the initial introductions, and Marshall Nicolson at AMC's Mohican Outdoor Center was helpful in suggesting a route in the Delaware Water Gap.

Outside of AMC, but within the hiking world, thanks go to Dan Chazin, all-around helpful person at the New York–New Jersey Trail Conference and a frequent writer of local guidebooks, some of which were useful in planning this one. Dan gave me my first opportunity to work on hiking guidebooks years ago, when I revised and expanded the Catskill sections of the *New York Walk Book*, and without him I never would have had this opportunity.

The list of people to thank does not end with those I can name, and includes anyone who has maintained a trail or section of trail covered by this book. As a former trail maintainer myself, I can appreciate what a difficult and thankless job it is. Most hikers don't notice trail maintenance except when it isn't done, but those of us who have packed loppers and shovels along on hikes do, and greatly appreciate it.

Thanks also go to the many people I met along the trails during the summer of 2009. Foremost among them are the people who accepted my invitation to pose for pictures and signed releases allowing their publication. But I'd also like to thank the people who stopped and chatted with me. The Appalachian Trail thru-hikers, particularly the one who helped me with the vending machine at the top of Bear Mountain, cannot go unmentioned either. I hope you all were able to make it to Katahdin or, in a few cases, Springer. Also from Bear Mountain, I'd like to thank the visiting family from Texas that let me have a spare bottle of water.

Last but not least, thank you to anyone involved in putting useful information for these hikes on the Internet. You know who you are.

INTRODUCTION

EARLY IN MY REDISCOVERY OF HIKING, I made a difficult winter ascent of Blackhead Mountain in the northern Catskills. It involved a much longer approach than usual to the mountain, over which I had to break trail and make two stiff climbs. It acquired epic dimensions. For the first time I began to understand that you must climb mountains inside yourself as well as outside. To me, that day, I might as well have been in the Himalayas.

But unlike the Mallories, Hillaries, or Messners of the world, I came home that night and slept in my own warm bed. As I drifted off to sleep, I recall feeling struck by the extremes I had traversed, from falling face first into a snow bank near a wilderness summit almost 4,000 feet above the Hudson, to the warm, dry sheets and blankets that surrounded me mere hours later.

I've had some variation of that feeling on the many day hikes I've done since. It stretches the range of possibilities in our day to gaze out from the heights, to look back at a distant peak on the drive home, and to think, "I was on top of that a few hours ago." I have done overnight backpacks into the woods since then, of course, but to me a day hike makes the experience of wildness more special. When you know you aren't staying in the woods, the sense of removal from the everyday world is that much stronger, and nature's fragility and ephemerality is that much more evident. All of the hikes in this book will stretch the boundaries of your day in some way. You can start from your home, touch the wild eternal, and then return to where you began.

One main consideration guiding route selection was to make sure the city and all its suburban areas were covered, going as far as the Delaware Water Gap to the west, the Harlem and Naugatuck valleys to the north, and the central South Shore on the east. I chose some popular areas and classic routes that you would expect to see in a hiking guidebook covering areas within the city or a day's reach away, such as Palisades Park and the Hudson Highlands, whose trails are busy on any nice, warm weekend. I added some lesser-known sites that are worthy of hiker attention, like Assiniwikam and Pootatuck State Forest. Newer areas not previously covered in other guidebooks are included as well, such as Stewart State Forest and the High Line. The latter, along with Central Park, stretches the definition of a day hike to include long walks through urban parks.

Another major principle guiding the selection of hikes for this book was that about half of them should be accessible via public transportation. In an age when climate change is a growing public concern, hikers should be doing what they can to reduce their carbon footprint (for that reason, there are no car-shuttle hikes). New York's excellent network of bus, subway, and commuter rail systems makes even a hike as distant as Pawling reachable without a vehicle, and those willing to use bicycles or car-sharing services may find they can extend the reach of the MTA, NJ Transit, or ConnDOT even farther than mentioned here.

HOW TO USE THIS BOOK

WITH 50 HIKES TO CHOOSE FROM, you may wonder how to decide where to go. The locator map at the front of this book will help you narrow down the trips by location, and the At-a-Glance Trip Planner will provide more information to guide you toward a decision.

Once you settle on a destination and turn to a trip in this guide, you will find a series of icons that indicate whether the hike is good for kids, if dogs are permitted, if you can go snowshoeing or cross-country skiing, and whether there are fees. This information is also covered in the At-a-Glance Trip Planner.

Information on the basics follows: location, rating, distance, elevation gain, estimated time, and maps. The ratings are based on the author's perception and are estimates of what the average hiker will experience. However, you may find the hikes to be easier or more difficult than stated. The estimated time is also based on the author's perception. Consider your own pace when planning a trip.

The elevation gain is calculated by subtracting the elevation of the trip's lowest point from the elevation of the trip's highest point. It does not account for every dip and rise along the route. Information is included about the relevant USGS maps, as well as about where you can find trail maps. The bolded summary provides a basic overview of what you will see on your hike.

The Directions section explains how to reach the trailhead by car and, for some trips, public transportation. GPS coordinates for the parking lots are also included. If you don't own a GPS device, it is wise to consult an atlas before leaving home.

In the Trail Description, you will find instructions on which trails to hike and where to turn. You will also learn about the history of the area and the flora, fauna, landmarks, and other points of interest you may encounter.

The trail maps that accompany each trip will help guide you along your hike, but it would be wise to also take an official trail map with you. They are often—but not always—available online, at the trailhead, or at the office or visitor center.

Each trip ends with a More Information section that provides details about the location of bathrooms, access times and fees, the property's rules and regulations, and contact information for the agency that manages the land where you will be hiking.

TRIP PLANNING AND SAFETY

HIKES IN THE NEW YORK METROPOLITAN AREA RANGE FROM GENTLE WALKS in the park to rugged mountains in remote hinterlands. While they are not deep wilderness expeditions, it is still possible to have adverse outcomes if you are not well prepared and careful in your planning.

You will be more likely to have an enjoyable, safe hike if you take the proper precautions. Before heading out for your hike, please consider the following:

- Select a hike that everyone in your group is comfortable taking. Match the hike to the abilities of the least capable person in the group. If anyone in your group is uncomfortable with the weather or is tired, turn around and complete the hike another day.
- Plan to be back at the trailhead before dark. Before beginning your hike, determine a turnaround time and don't change it, even if you have not reached your destination.
- Check the weather. If you are planning a ridge or summit hike, especially in summer, get an early start so you will be off the exposed area before the afternoon hours when thunderstorms most often strike. In the New York area, this is most likely to be in July and August when the weather is hot and humid. Late afternoon is the most common time for thunderstorms, but they can occur in the morning if conditions are right.

- Bring a pack with the following items:
  - ✓ Water: Two quarts per person is usually adequate, depending on the weather and length of the trip.
  - ✓ Food: Even if you are planning only a one-hour hike, bring some high-energy snacks such as nuts, dried fruit, or snack bars. Pack a lunch for longer trips.
  - ✓ Map and compass: Be sure you know how to use them. A handheld GPS may also be helpful, but such devices are not always reliable.
  - ✓ Headlamp or flashlight, with spare batteries
  - ✓ Extra clothing: Rain gear, wool or fleece sweater, hat, and mittens
  - ✓ First-aid kit: Adhesive bandages, gauze, nonprescription painkiller, moleskin
  - ✓ Pocketknife or multitool
  - ✓ Waterproof matches (coated with wax and kept in a jar) or a lighter
  - ✓ Trash bag to carry out waste
  - ✓ Toilet paper
  - ✓ Whistle
  - ✓ Insect repellent
  - ✓ Sunscreen
  - ✓ Sunglasses
  - ✓ Cell phone: Be aware that cell phone service is unreliable in rural areas and may not be available. If you are receiving a signal, use only for emergencies to avoid disturbing the backcountry experience for other hikers.
  - ✓ Binoculars (optional)
  - ✓ Camera (optional)
  - ✓ This guide
- Wear appropriate footwear and clothing. Wool or synthetic hiking socks will keep your feet dry and help prevent blisters from forming, and comfortable, waterproof hiking boots will provide ankle support and good traction. Avoid wearing cotton clothing, which absorbs sweat and rain and contributes to an unpleasant and sometimes dangerous hiking experience. Polypropylene, fleece, silk, and wool all do a good job of wicking moisture away from your body and keeping you warm in wet or cold conditions.
- When you are in front of the rest of your hiking group, wait at all trail junctions until the others catch up. This avoids confusion and helps keep people in your group from getting lost or separated.

- If you see downed wood that appears to be purposely covering a trail, it probably means the trail is closed due to overuse or hazardous conditions.

- If a trail is muddy, walk through the mud or on rocks, never on trees, roots, or plants. Having waterproof boots will keep your feet comfortable, and by staying in the center of the trail you will keep it from eroding into a wide hiking highway. Similarly, on steep rocky trails where you may find yourself scrambling, try not to use adjacent shrubs as handholds. Stay low and close to the surface to minimize the risk of falling, and turn your feet sideways to better brace yourself if you slip.

- Leave your itinerary and the time you expect to return with someone you trust. If you see a logbook at a trailhead, be sure to sign in when you arrive and sign out when you finish your hike.

- To avoid bites from bugs, you may want to wear pants and a long-sleeved shirt. After you complete your hike, check for deer ticks, which carry dangerous Lyme disease. This is especially important in low, grassy areas such as those near the sea on Long Island. There is no safe time of year; ticks live through all seasons.

- Poison ivy is always a threat when hiking. To identify the plant, look for clusters of three leaves that shine in the sun but are dull in the shade. If you do come into contact with poison ivy, wash the affected area with soap and water as soon as possible.

- Wear blaze-orange items in hunting season if you choose to hike in an area where firearm hunting of large game (such as bears and deer) is permitted. New York's season starts on the third Saturday in November and runs for 23 days, with a nine-day muzzleloader season following immediately thereafter. Harriman and Bear Mountain state parks prohibit all hunting, but it is allowed in portions of all of other state parks and all state forests. Westchester County does not have a firearm deer season. Suffolk County permits firearm deer hunting only by special permit throughout most of January, and no hunting at all is permitted in the city and Nassau County. New Jersey's deer season varies by year; usually with only certain days (which never include Sundays) in November and December set aside. Check the state Department of Environmental Protection's (DEP) website (www.state.nj.us/dep/fgw/hunting.htm, then click Deer under Rules and Regulations) for the upcoming year's season. Connecticut sets aside a period in late November to late December, with an earlier start permitted on private lands that allow hunting (The Nature Conservancy does not yet permit hunting at Devil's Den).

- Encounters between humans and bears have become more frequent in northwestern New Jersey in the last decade. You can help avoid them by making noise in areas where you could expect to see them, wearing a bear bell, talking with your companions, or banging poles together if you have them, all of which let the bears know humans are in the vicinity. You may see their scat or sometimes smell or hear them (they make noises similar to humans and deer moving through underbrush, but are not as fast as the latter). If you happen upon a black bear, remain calm but respect it. While it is true that bears may be as scared as you and run away, they sometimes respond aggressively, by snorting or banging the ground in front of them. In those instances, back away. New Jersey's DEP has further information at www.state.nj.us/dep/fgw/bearfacts_safetytips.htm, and distributes literature you may find at trailheads in the region.
- Seven hikes in this book utilize, in whole or part, segments of the Appalachian Trail. If hiking during late June or July, it is quite possible that you will meet some northbound thru-hikers going the distance from Springer Mountain in Georgia to Mount Katahdin in Maine (similarly, in August and early September, you may meet some "southbounders"). You can usually identify them by their clothes and heavy packs. Extend them every courtesy you can—it is appreciated. If you are on your return leg, consider being a "trail angel" and offering them any leftover water or snacks that you have.
- Despite the best efforts of trail builders and maintainers, sometimes the way forward is not always obvious. If you think you have lost a trail, first look backward and see if there is a blaze or marker for hikers going the other way. Look around on the ground—sometimes the blaze may be on a tree that has been blown down. If this still doesn't work, backtrack to the last place you were on a certain path or saw a blaze. Look around carefully—a turn may not have been indicated properly. Scout the neighboring woods for places where the trail may reappear. If you have completely lost the trail and can't find your way back to where it was, *don't panic*. Three blasts of a whistle, a shout, or a flash of light will signal anyone who sees or hears it that you need help. A map can help you find your way out to another trail or a road. Streams will always lead you to civilization. If you find yourself trapped in the dark without a headlamp or other light source, use the warm clothing you should have brought with you to prepare a bivouac. Make a small fire, taking care to keep it under control by clearing the adjacent ground and using rocks to reflect the heat.

LEAVE NO TRACE

THE APPALACHIAN MOUNTAIN CLUB is a national educational partner of Leave No Trace, a nonprofit organization dedicated to promoting and inspiring responsible outdoor recreation through education, research, and partnerships.  The Leave No Trace program seeks to develop wild land ethics—ways in which people think and act in the outdoors to minimize their impact on the areas they visit and to protect our natural resources for future enjoyment. Leave No Trace unites four federal land management agencies— the U.S. Forest Service, National Park Service, Bureau of Land Management, and U.S. Fish and Wildlife Service—with manufacturers, outdoor retailers, user groups, educators, organizations such as AMC and the National Outdoor Leadership School (NOLS), and individuals.

The Leave No Trace ethic is guided by these seven principles:

1. **Plan ahead and prepare.** Know the terrain and any regulations applicable to the area you're planning to visit, and be prepared for extreme weather or other emergencies. This will enhance your enjoyment and ensure that you've chosen an appropriate destination. Small groups have less effect on resources and the quality of experience for other backcountry visitors.

2. **Travel and camp on durable surfaces.** Travel and camp on established trails and campsites, rock, gravel, dry grasses, or snow. Good campsites are found, not made. Camp at least 200 feet from lakes and streams, and focus activities on areas where vegetation is absent. In pristine areas, disperse use to prevent the creation of campsites and trails.

3. **Dispose of waste properly.** Pack it in, pack it out. Inspect your camp for trash or food scraps. Deposit solid human waste in catholes dug 6 to 8 inches deep, at least 200 feet from water, camp, and trails. Pack out toilet paper and hygiene products. To wash yourself or your dishes, carry water 200 feet away from streams or lakes and use small amounts of biodegradable soap. Scatter strained dishwater.

4. **Leave what you find.** Cultural or historic artifacts, as well as natural objects such as plants or rocks, should be left as found.

5. **Minimize campfire impacts.** Cook on a stove. Use established fire rings, fire pans, or mound fires. If a campfire is built, keep it small and use dead sticks found on the ground.

6. **Respect wildlife.** Observe wildlife from a distance. Feeding wildlife alters their natural behavior. Protect wildlife from your food by storing rations and trash securely.

7. **Be considerate of other visitors.** Be courteous, respect the quality of other visitors' backcountry experience, and let nature's sounds prevail.

The AMC is a national provider of the Leave No Trace Master Educator course. The AMC offers this five-day course, designed especially for outdoor professionals and land managers, as well as the shorter two-day Leave No Trace Trainer course, at locations throughout the Northeast.

For Leave No Trace information and materials, contact Leave No Trace Center for Outdoor Ethics, P.O. Box 997, Boulder, CO 80306; toll-free 800-332-4100, or locally 303-442-8222; fax: 303-442-8217; www.lnt.org.

1

NEW YORK CITY AND THE LOWER HUDSON VALLEY

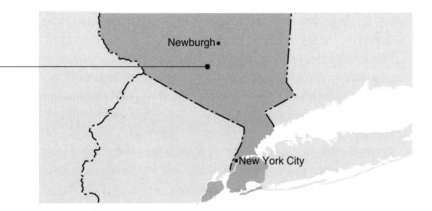

BEFORE HUMANITY EVER CAME ON THE SCENE, New York City, or at least the land it would come to be on, was a meeting place. The glaciers that shaped the landscape during the last Ice Age, thousands of years ago, got as far as central Brooklyn, Queens, and Staten Island, where they would leave their terminal ridges, called "moraines" by geologists, on the Paleozoic bedrock. The particularly strong rock that forms Manhattan would become an ideal foundation for the city's skyscrapers.

The glacial moraines guaranteed that the future city would be the place where the Atlantic coast would change from the generally rocky shores of New England to the sandy barrier beaches of the Jersey Shore and south. Pelham Bay recalls the former, West Pond the latter.

The lands that were there when the Dutch bought Manhattan from the local American Indians had a geography slightly different from today's. Manhattan itself was not an island—it was a peninsula joined to the mainland where the Harlem River Ship Canal now cuts through. Lower Manhattan was narrower; it would be some time before the marshes were filled in to make its coastline consistent with the rest of the island. Those marshes bordered forests similar to those still seen on Long Island—great forests of oak and maple, with some southern or lowland species like sweetgum and sassafras mixed in. In the seventeenth century, the experience of walking along the American Indian trail that became Broadway was similar to what you can still experience today in the Native Forest and Staten Island Greenbelt.

It was not quite obvious during the colonial period that this city would eventually become the largest on the continent. New York played nearly no role in the prelude to the American Revolution. The city was a Tory hotbed, occupied by the British throughout the war. The last shot of the war was fired in New York Harbor, when a British sailor, irritated by crowds taunting his retreating ship, aimed a cannonball in their direction (it landed harmlessly in the water).

However, the city received a gift from the glaciers that Boston and Philadelphia did not: the Hudson River. Despite the frustration Henry Hudson felt when he reached Glens Falls and realized he had not found the passage between oceans he sought, the Hudson's estuary was, and remains, navigable all the way to Troy, 120 miles to the north. It provided access via the Mohawk Valley to the interior beyond the Appalachians—the geographic niche that Thomas Jefferson promised would make New York the "seat of empire."

The Hudson, sometimes called "America's Rhine," defines its valley as few other rivers do. It swells to over 3 miles wide at Haverstraw, then merely 20 miles upriver narrows into the only genuine fjord on the east coast of North America, with water depths reaching 200 feet off West Point in the Hudson Highlands where the river breaches the Appalachian Mountains.

Geologically, the lower valley starts off as a contrast between the exposed bedrock of the Palisades and the softer rocks of the lowlands: Mesozoic sandstones and shales on the Rockland County side, and marble and gneiss in Westchester. Some of the tougher sections of the latter create the rolling landscape of the Ward Pound Ridge and Teatown Lake reservations.

The Ramapo Fault, running roughly from Suffern to Peekskill, marks the boundary between these sedimentary formations and the tougher Precambrian granite gneiss of the Hudson Highlands. This rock is highly resistant to erosion, leading to the exposed outcrops at Bear Mountain and Black Rock Forest. Its gneiss results in the northeast–southwest orientation of the ridges, visible from Harriman State Park on the west to Fahnestock State Park on the east.

For those interested in hikes farther up the Hudson Valley and into the Catskill Mountains, refer to *AMC's Best Day Hikes in the Catskills and Hudson Valley* by Peter Kick.

TRIP 1
CENTRAL PARK

Location: New York, NY
Rating: Easy
Distance: 3.0 miles
Elevation Gain: 70 feet
Estimated Time: 1.5 hours
Maps: USGS Central Park; trail map available online at Central Park Conservancy website

Climb a summit boulder, take in the view over a reservoir, and walk through history and greenery in this crossing of one of the world's greatest urban parks.

DIRECTIONS

Merchants' Gate, the southeast entrance to Central Park, is located at Columbus Circle, Central Park West, and 59th Street. *GPS coordinates*: 40° 46.090' N, 73° 58.858' W.

Parking is available on the nearby streets, though it is hard to find; there are some paid parking garages in the area. The 59th Street–Columbus Circle Subway station is located adjacent to it; the MTA M5, M7, M10, M20, and M104 bus routes also stop there.

TRAIL DESCRIPTION

Walk in Central Park on any beautiful summer Saturday, and you really would think it was the Fourth of July: "People dancing, people laughing . . . a real celebration." Robert Lamm of the band Chicago wrote that song after coming back from just such a trip, penning lyrics that joined the public energy he'd witnessed to his own hopes for social progress.

Frederick Law Olmsted and Calvert Vaux didn't live long enough to hear "Saturday in the Park," but they would have been glad to hear what their work inspired. The park they created, the city's "green lung," has become a National Historic Landmark and an indispensable part of New York City for visitors and residents alike, redolent with history. The Central Park Conservancy, a private nonprofit, maintains and improves the park on the city's behalf.

This walk goes along the slightly less-developed west side of the park, a bit truer to Olmsted and Vaux's original design. It begins at Merchants' Gate on

CENTRAL PARK SOUTH

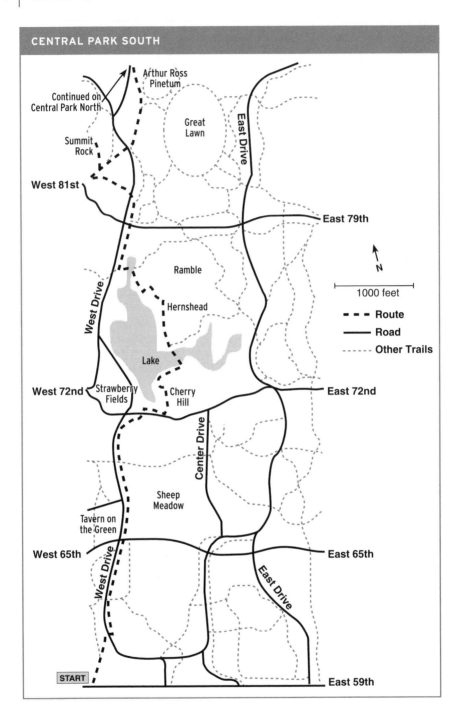

Arthur Ross Pinetum

Continued on Central Park North

Great Lawn

East Drive

Summit Rock

West 81st

East 79th

Ramble

West Drive

Hernshead

N

1000 feet

- - - Route
—— Road
---- Other Trails

Lake

West 72nd Strawberry Fields Cherry Hill

East 72nd

Center Drive

Sheep Meadow

Tavern on the Green

West 65th

West Drive

East 65th

East Drive

START

East 59th

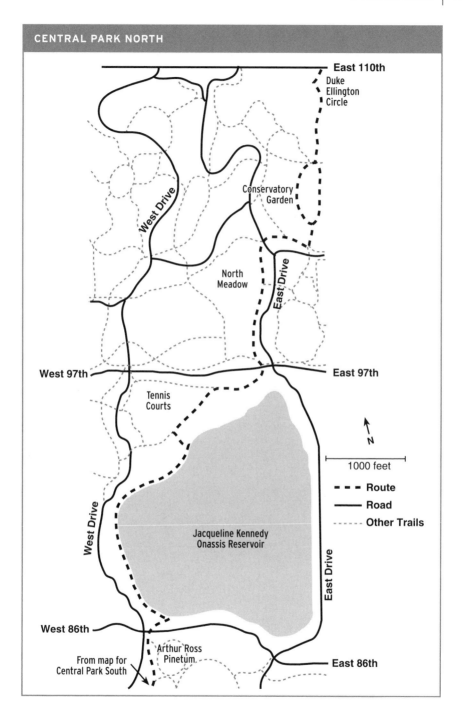

CENTRAL PARK NORTH

East 110th
Duke Ellington Circle

West Drive

Conservatory Garden

North Meadow

East Drive

West 97th

East 97th

Tennis Courts

N

1000 feet

- - - Route
——— Road
·····— Other Trails

West Drive

Jacqueline Kennedy Onassis Reservoir

East Drive

West 86th

Arthur Ross Pinetum

From map for Central Park South

East 86th

Columbus Circle, the most ornate entrance to the park. From there, bear left and follow the paved path down through a rock cleft toward West Drive, one of the park's interior roads (closed to traffic on weekends). Cross it and continue past the ballfields to the left, parallel to the road, on another paved path. The skyline of the East Side rises above the trees beyond the fields, centered on the recently renovated Plaza (another National Historic Landmark).

Pass a stand of trees, cross 65th Street, and Sheep Meadow opens up to the left. It isn't just a name—sheep actually grazed here until the 1930s, when it was feared that during the Great Depression destitute New Yorkers would poach and eat them. To the west is the finish line for the annual New York City Marathon.

The path continues to 72nd Street, marked by the Gothic peaked roofs of the Dakota apartment building, also a National Historic Landmark, on Central Park West, just to the left. Roman Polanski used this distinctive exterior as the setting for the movie *Rosemary's Baby*. It was also the home of John Lennon, who was killed there as he returned on the night of December 7, 1980. The city named the small patch of land just across 72nd Street Strawberry Fields in his memory, after one of his best-known songs from his career with the Beatles; it has a memorial mosaic in the center.

Keep following the path on the left side of the road as it bends past the lake. Here you can appreciate the curving paths, one hallmark of Olmsted's parks. The stone bridges (no two of them are alike anywhere in the park, as intended by Vaux, who handled most of the architecture while Olmsted designed the landscapes) and the trees and shrubbery that screen the roads were meant to create the impression of a rural landscape.

Central Park was not part of the original 1811 Commissioners' Plan, which laid out Manhattan's grid system of streets. But as the city's population quadrupled in the ensuing decades, more and more residents began calling for some land to be set aside for a park. In 1853, a 700-acre parcel between 59th and 106th streets was designated as Central Park (it was later extended to 110th Street, adding 143 acres more). Olmsted, who had been impressed by parks he had seen on a trip to England, was aware of the importance of the project, calling it "a democratic development of the highest significance." Nevertheless, he fought bitterly with city officials over its construction, and the battles may have contributed to his mental decline late in life.

Cross the Terrace Traverse Road and turn right onto the paralleling path. Take the next major path left, to Cherry Hill. Continue across the fountain plaza to the path along the shore of the lake, which winds around to Bow

People often gather on Sheep's Meadow, where real sheep grazed until the Great Depression.

Bridge. After crossing the lake at its narrowest point, bear left at the fork along its shore.

The rocky, wooded area along your left is the Ramble, meant by Vaux to be a "wild garden" without paths. The path rises to the Hernshead, a rocky point graced by the Women's Shelter, a pavilion for the ladies of the era to relax in after their walks in the park. It was moved here from the Merchants' Gate after the monument to the *Maine*, the U.S. battleship whose 1898 sinking started the Spanish–American War, was installed in its place.

When you reach the bridge over the small northern inlet of the Lake, turn left, cross it, and return to West Drive, this time following the path along the west side of the street. Turn right and continue to the north, crossing the 79th Street Traverse Road and passing the Swedish Cottage, home to one of the country's few marionette theater companies. Past the Shakespeare Garden, bear left away from the road, toward the Museum of Natural History. When you have almost left the park, make a sharp right toward the Diana Ross Playground. After passing it, follow the stone stairway uphill to the meadow around Summit Rock, the highest point in Central Park. There is a limited view toward New Jersey down 83rd Street from the west side of the rock.

Off to the east is the Great Lawn, added to the park in 1934 by Robert Moses, then citywide Parks Commissioner, as part of a general cleanup and restoration of the park. Baseball fields were built and it has become a popular picnic spot and site for free concerts in the summertime.

Go back to the playground and turn left on the path that leads toward the lawn. Cross West Drive again and turn left. Continue north past the Arthur Ross Pinetum and its two dozen conifer species to the running path around the Jacqueline Kennedy Onassis Reservoir, Manhattan's largest body of water, practically filling the park east to west at this point with its 106 acres.

Follow the reservoir shoreline 0.4 mile to the path to the tennis courts and turn left. At the courts themselves, turn right again and follow the path to the 97th Street Traverse, after which you should bear right onto the path along the North Meadow, another area with baseball diamonds and soccer fields. At the north end of the meadow, bear right and cross the East Drive.

At the last intersection of paths before you reach the 102nd Street gate, turn left. This brings you right through the middle of the 6-acre Conservatory Garden, the only formal garden in Central Park, on the site of a former conservatory. Either of the two forks allows you to take in different aspects of the garden's three sections before the paths reunite to take you along the east edge of the Harlem Meer to Frawley Circle, the junction of Fifth Avenue and 110th Street at the park's northwest corner.

From here you can go back the way you came, or find your own route back. The 110th Street Station on the 5 line is a few blocks to the east at Lexington Avenue. The M1, M2, M3, and M4 lines stop here on their way downtown and on Madison Avenue, a block east, uptown.

MORE INFORMATION

Restrooms are available at Merchants' Gate, Tavern on the Green, and the Conservatory Garden. Dogs must be leashed from 9 A.M. to 9 P.M. on bridle paths, when passing through the Ramble, and whenever ordered by a park employee. See centralparkpaws.org for more information about dogs in the park. Central Park Conservancy, 14 East 60th St., New York, NY, 10022; 212-310-6600; www.centralparknyc.org.

ROBERT MOSES: URBAN PLANNER EXTRAORDINAIRE

The park system on Long Island and the surrounding roads that are used to get to it are almost exclusively the work of one man: Robert Moses. In the 1950s, he held thirteen jobs with the city and state of New York, none elected and most with no compensation other than an expense account. What he built, and what he destroyed, explains why he is both admired and reviled today.

Moses began as a Progressive-era government-reform activist in the 1910s. His proposed reforms of city government were often frustrated by popular opposition and the city's Tammany Hall political machine. He learned how to never let that happen again.

After hiking and boating all over Long Island, he came up with a plan for a system of parks and the parkways to get to these recreational areas. Brilliant and ruthless, when he was appointed the first head of the Long Island State Parks Commission by Governor Al Smith in 1924, he wrote laws to give him and him alone control of the parks and parkways. Within a decade he had built much of what he had originally envisioned.

In New York City during the Depression, he cleaned up and expanded the parks and directed the construction of hundreds of playgrounds. He built many of the bridges within the city. For this he was lionized by an adoring public long accustomed to officials who had promised these things but failed to deliver.

His critics blame his roads for destroying neighborhoods and promoting suburban sprawl on Long Island. His defenders note that what he built is still in good shape today and did not cause the city's decline all by itself.

The critics were largely muted until the 1960s, when the public was growing more skeptical of the value of large public-works projects, particularly roads. In 1967, then-Governor Nelson Rockefeller maneuvered Moses out of his last public job, director of the Triborough Bridge Authority. It became clear that it and Moses's other authorities were designed to be completely unaccountable to anyone despite a budget of billions of public dollars.

While a road and state park on Long Island are named after Moses, there are only two memorials to him: at Fordham University, which he had helped to expand, and at Babylon village hall on Long Island, where he lived. His epitaph might be the same as that of British architect Christopher Wren: "If you would seek his monument, look around you."

TRIP 2
HIGH LINE

Location: New York, NY
Rating: Easy
Distance: 0.8 mile
Elevation Gain: 30 feet
Estimated Time: 0.5 hour
Maps: USGS Central Park; trail map available at Friends of the High Line website

Enjoy the Lower West Side cityscape from one of Manhattan's newest attractions.

DIRECTIONS

The High Line's southern terminus is at the junction of Gansevoort and Washington streets in Manhattan's Meatpacking District, a block east of the West Side Highway (Route 9A). *GPS coordinates:* 40° 44.364′ N, 74° 00.489′ W.

Parking is available on the nearby streets for free, or in local parking garages and lots for a fee.

If coming by subway, the closest stop is the 8th Avenue–14th Street station on the A, C, E, and L lines. From that intersection, walk south on 8th Avenue one block to 13th Street and turn right. At Notre Dame School, bear left onto Gansevoort and continue two blocks to Washington Street.

The MTA M11 and M14 bus routes serve the area. The former has a scheduled stop at Hudson and Bethune streets several blocks away, but also passes within a block of the trailhead on Greenwich Street if you want to make a request stop.

TRAIL DESCRIPTION

To most people, hiking means that you pull up to a trailhead in an unpaved lot somewhere at the edge of the woods, lace up your boots, throw on your pack, and start ambling down a dusty path through towering trees with the intention of reaching a rewarding vista or other scenery that puts you in close touch with nature. It doesn't have to. Hiking can mean taking public transportation in your sandals or old sneakers, with nothing but a water bottle, and taking in the beauty of the built environment, where the variety of the architecture offers as

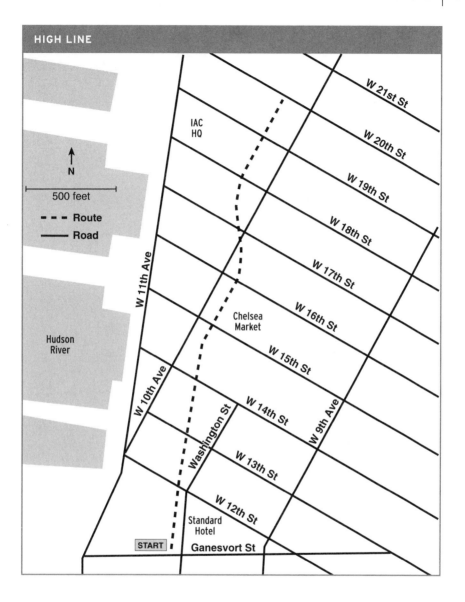

interesting a view as a mountain range or river. Of course, you'd probably like to have some greenery to pass by and stand amidst just the same.

In the summer of 2009, New York City's Parks Department opened up the first segment of the long-awaited High Line, a former rail viaduct, on the western edge of Greenwich Village. It was an instant hit. The *New York Times* called it "almost a small town in the air." This elevated park, only the second of its kind in the world, gives you that urban hiking experience.

At the corner of Gansevoort and Washington streets, you'll climb up the stairs to the south end of the line. This takes care of most of the vertical. You will find yourself standing on a deck of long, concrete planks from which several benches and water fountains rise discreetly. Rails can still be seen poking through, and there are pockets of wildflowers and scrubby trees, most notably a grove of birches around the staircase.

If there are other people there, and there usually are, most will be walking north toward the impressive new Standard Hotel, which dominates the view. Built by hotelier Andre Balazs in the modernist International Style usually associated with the 1960s, the Standard, its two sections slightly askew like a wide-open book, straddles the High Line on two concrete pillars. This way you can appreciate the building's massive form as you walk beneath it through the Washington Grassland. Once through the Grassland, the High Line continues, bending slightly to the west as it crosses Little West 12th and 13th streets, indicated by signs on either side of the crossings.

The trail then crosses under another building, with the walking deck remaining on the higher of two levels. The lower level, to the left side, is an overgrown railroad track, recalling the state of the High Line for much of the late twentieth century.

New York Central Railroad built the High Line in the 1930s, which moved tracks inland to clear the way for Riverside Park. This section served the warehouses of the meatpacking district and the Bell Telephone Laboratories complex (now the Westbeth artists' community) south of Gansevoort Street.

The High Line survived the railroad's demise in the early 1970s, and Conrail, the federally created company that took over the operations of many failed Northeastern railroads that decade, continued to operate trains along it until 1980. After that, it fell into disuse, its tracks becoming overgrown while the supporting viaduct remained structurally sound.

In the 1990s, the city decided to demolish it. However, before they were able to, younger residents of the area, many of them the artistic types who have long been drawn to Greenwich Village and its environs, found ways to get to the abandoned track and walk it. What they found was a pleasant surprise to them—a strip of relative wilderness flourishing and elevated over a few blocks of the country's largest city.

They told their friends about the area, and eventually started a website with photos and historical information, which led to an activist group, Friends of the High Line. Since the structure was not in danger of falling down, they asked that the area be convert into an elevated linear park, much like Paris had done with an even longer old rail line, now the *Promenade plantée*.

A walk on the High Line will give visitors a chance to see this building designed by the famous architect Frank Gehry.

Support for the idea grew and by the end of the century it was certain to happen. In 2004, the city allocated money for the renovation, and the next year the federal government allowed it to be designated as a rail trail.

The High Line crosses busy 14th Street, passing through an area with lounge chairs and fountains. Then it enters the former Nabisco plant, now the Chelsea Markets retail and dining complex, where a section is covered with tables (in warm weather) for those who wish to partake of the food and drink sold by the nearby stands. Artists also display their work here. At this point, you can leave the line and enter the market complex, or return to the street.

After a full block under one roof, the path continues along a wide section of line and veers more to the north, crossing Tenth Avenue and Seventeenth Street. North of here, over a parking lot, is a wide section that offers an excellent opportunity to appreciate the view of the city at the pace of a pedestrian rather than a passenger on an elevated section of subway. To the northeast is Midtown, centered on the Empire State Building. Off to the west is the Hudson River and the very different, twisting white forms of the InterActive

Corporation headquarters building, co-designed by deconstructivist Canadian architect Frank Gehry, his only major building in New York thus far. It is meant to evoke a ship at full sail.

The InterActive building, like the Standard, is one of many projects in the neighborhood that has been catalyzed by the High Line. The Whitney Museum is planning to build a museum of American art designed by another renowned contemporary architect, Renzo Piano, at the southern end. The High Line has inspired more than architecture, though. Residents of nearby buildings have been presenting musical and theatrical performances from their fire escapes in the evenings.

You can appreciate Gehry's work and its changing forms from different directions as you wind north through an area called the Chelsea Grassland toward the current end of the High Line at 20th Street. Through the grates you can look north to the next section under construction, which should take it to 30th Street. Eventually, it is hoped, the entire 2.3-mile High Line will be open all the way to the Javits Center at 34th Street.

MORE INFORMATION

Restrooms are available along 16th Street. No dogs. Friends of the High Line, 529 West 20th Street, Suite 8W, New York, NY 10011; 212-206-9922; www.thehighline.org.

TRIP 3
STATEN ISLAND GREENBELT

Location: Staten Island, NY
Rating: Difficult
Distance: 7.0 miles
Elevation Gain: 540 feet
Estimated Time: 5.0 hours
Maps: USGS Arthur Kill, the Narrows; trail map available online at Staten Island Greenbelt website

Explore the most extensive tract of undeveloped land in the five boroughs of New York City to the city's highest point in this epic loop.

DIRECTIONS

From the east, get off Interstate 278, the Staten Island Expressway, at Exit 11 (Bradley Avenue). Follow Gannon Avenue North (the expressway's service road) to Woolley Avenue 0.6 mile west and turn left. From the west, get off at Exit 8. Turn left on Victory Boulevard and follow it to Gannon Avenue South just before the underpass. Turn right on Woolley Avenue 1.5 miles to the east.

Woolley becomes Forest Hill Road at the Willowbrook Avenue intersection. Two miles south of Willowbrook Avenue, turn left on Richmond Hill Road. Go uphill to the golf course entry road and turn left. There is parking for 35 to 40 vehicles in the two unpaved lots on the right. *GPS coordinates:* 40° 34.534′ N, 74° 08.773′ W.

City buses do not serve the golf course, but the route is accessible at several other points. The MTA S74's Richmondtown stop, near the beginning of the Red Trail, is the closest. The S74 and S54 also stop at Meisner Avenue near Moses Mountain.

TRAIL DESCRIPTION

Staten Island, the baby sibling of the five boroughs, has the largest tract of wooded land in New York City. An X-shaped grouping of parks in the east central section of the island along its glacial moraines, the Staten Island Greenbelt has grown to 2,800 acres over the years, comparable to the large suburban reservations such as Watchung, South Mountain and Pound Ridge. Some private tracts on its borders help buffer and augment it.

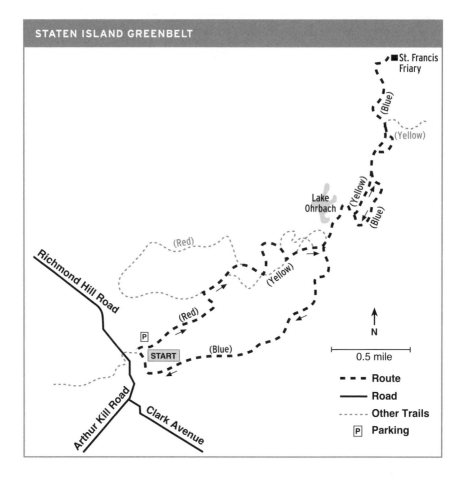

A network of four main trails goes in and out of the Greenbelt. These form the basis of a long but satisfying loop that will take you through its extremes, from deep woods where you will repeatedly remind yourself you're in New York City, to suburban streets and golf courses where you won't need to.

Opposite the parking lot is the LaTourette House, an 1830s Federal-style brick mansion now used as the clubhouse for the city-owned golf course and listed on the National Register of Historic Places. The Red Trail, on which you'll start this hike, enters the woods off to the left of LaTourette House and across the road behind it (look for the blazed tree).

At first the Red Trail meanders pleasantly in a wooded corridor between the golf course and some nearby backyards. Eventually those disappear from view, you cross some small bridges and muddy areas, and, as you ascend slightly, you find yourself in a forest dominated by tall sweetgum trees, the first of several such awe-inspiring forest-primeval groves along this hike.

This hike provides a nice view of well manicured golf courses.

The Red Trail descends off the rise slightly to a muddy area just short of a swamp where it divides into the two halves of its loop, 0.7 mile from the trailhead, concurrently blazed with the Yellow Trail. Here you'll turn right and follow the combined trails, again rising slightly, to an area of less mature trees known as Bucks Hollow, where the Yellow Trail splits off to the right. Shortly thereafter, it is replaced by the White Trail, coming in from the left. A short distance later, just before Rockland Avenue, the trails again split. Turn left and follow the White Trail through a dense, shrubby area alongside the road to a bridge and then up a short rise to Meisner Avenue.

You'll be following the Yellow Trail, the Greenbelt's oldest (although extensively rerouted), for the next couple of miles. Turn left and follow it downhill to a traffic light and the Richmond Creek Bluebelt. Carefully cross Rockland to a small parking area where the well-marked Yellow Trail re-enters the woods.

Shortly after it does, you'll see an unmarked path going straight up a steep hill. Follow it to a wide path along the edge of the hill, turn left, and then follow another short unmarked path on the right up to the summit, with a sweeping view of the wooded hills to the west—a view with little evidence of civilization for an island with nearly half a million people.

The path at the summit winds back downhill. Continue past the path from the Yellow Trail as it winds gently down the east side of Moses Mountain to rejoin the Yellow Trail, just short of where it crosses Manor Road.

Follow it across the street to where the short Green Trail loop comes in and joins from the left. In 0.1 mile, after crossing a stream and its valley, you reach the High Rock Park boundary sign, with directions to nearby Greenbelt features like the mountain.

From here, the Yellow Trail meanders back and forth across the stream, its route not always clear (avoid one uphill fork left that leads back to the Green Trail). It finally climbs out of the ravine and reaches the side of one of the park's paved roads, an area with picnic tables that makes for a nice place to stop and rest. In the woods below is a successional pond (the term for a glacial pond slowly filling in with dirt), currently a marsh. Several of these ponds and marshes in various stages are found along the next section of trail. The short Lavender Trail makes a loop around the pond here.

Short paths also connect the Lavender Trail to the next section of the Yellow Trail along the chain-link fence at the back of Moravian Cemetery, where it is joined by the Blue Trail, the longest in the Greenbelt system. These two lead to the rear of the William Pouch Boy Scout Camp property, where they briefly divide near Lake Ohrbach, and then reunite to follow the lake briefly. Some of the camp's trails join them here, then split off toward the center of the camp.

The Blue and Yellow trails continue through tall maples and oaks to Pump House and Hourglass ponds. A wooden birding pavilion has been built at Pump House.

The trails split again past the two ponds as they enter the Greenbelt's wild northeastern section. Bear left onto the Yellow Trail as it ascends slightly into another stand of tall sweetgums. It descends again to be rejoined by the Blue Trail briefly, and then climbs into another impressive area of tall trees, slowly gaining elevation as it heads for Todt Hill. The woods here seem to go on forever.

The Yellow Trail joins the Blue Trail again at a gravelly path behind some backyards. Turning left, the two trails continue to the end of unpaved Helga Road, where the Yellow Trail goes right while the Blue Trail, which you want to follow, continues ahead into the woods. The climb continues steadily but gently to a large shelter run by Camp Kauffmann. The trail splits again, and bears left on the Yellow Trail and into the clearing. In another 0.2 mile it rejoins the Blue Trail.

After passing some other camp facilities, the Blue Trail climbs a bit more to the dead end of Browning Avenue. The blazes tell you to turn right and follow the driveway, which leads back into the woods, alongside the property lines to Foster Avenue's dead end.

To the right, a cleared gas pipeline right-of-way, often overgrown in summer, rises gently. It was once part of the Yellow Trail, and you can still see the blazes. If you want, follow it to its height of land. The two rises on either side of the pipeline are the summits of Todt Hill. At 410 feet above sea level, this is both the highest point in New York City and on the East Coast south of Maine.

Shortly to the north, the Blue Trail reaches the intersection of Ocean Terrace and Todt Hill Road. For your return, follow the Blue Trail instead of the Yellow Trail, continuing straight ahead after Helga Road. Its deviations take you through a kettle hole near Camp Kauffmann, then alongside a fairway at Richmond Valley Country Club, where you can stop at the Joseph Holzka overlook, mirroring a view once painted by Jasper Cropsey. The Blue Trail takes the lower route back to the ponds, offering more of the tall sweetgum groves.

At High Rock Park Road, the Blue Trail leaves the Yellow Trail to go down through the Greenbelt headquarters, a section along paved roads concurrent in parts with two other trails. From there the Blue Trail goes downhill, to a section of newer woods with no understory, coming out along paved Tonking Road to another crossing of Rockland Avenue.

The Blue Trail follows Eleanor Avenue to where the White Trail comes in from the right. Both trails turn left and cross Nugent Street together. At St. George Road, follow the Blue Trail right as it begins a 1.5-mile roadwalk, detouring around a closed bridge, to a swampy area just past where the road turns left at the base of a hill. The blue blazes turn right into the woods here and join the Red Trail after 100 feet. Another right turn leads the combined trails up one final steep pitch to the parking lot.

MORE INFORMATION

Restrooms are available at LaTourette Park and Greenbelt headquarters. Dogs must be leashed. Staten Island Greenbelt Conservancy, 200 Nevada Avenue, Staten Island, NY 10306; 718-667-2165; www.sigreenbelt.org.

TRIP 4
WEST POND LOOP

Location: Broad Channel, NY
Rating: Easy
Distance: 1.8 miles
Elevation Gain: 20 feet
Estimated Time: 1.0 hour
Maps: USGS Far Rockaway; trail map available at visitor center

Feel the sea breezes and take in the view at this popular birding site in the middle of Jamaica Bay.

DIRECTIONS
Take the Belt Parkway to Cross Bay Boulevard (Exit 17 coming from the west, 17W from the east). Follow Cross Bay south through Howard Beach to the Joseph Addabbo Bridge, formerly the North Channel Bridge. After the bridge, turn right at the second traffic light into the Jamaica Bay National Wildlife Refuge Visitor Contact Station, 1.5 miles south of the bridge. There is room in the lot for about 40 vehicles. *GPS coordinates:* 40° 37.028′ N, 73° 49.471′ W.

The MTA Q21 and Q53 buses stop at the refuge entrance, a half-mile walk up Cross Bay from the Broad Channel subway station on the A train.

TRAIL DESCRIPTION
With the exception of the Bronx and Manhattan's Marble Hill neighborhood, New York is a city of islands. However, as so much of it is on the three big ones—Long, Manhattan, and Staten—it's easy to lose sight of that.

That's not the case with Jamaica Bay, the large lagoon most frequently seen by New Yorkers from the windows of planes on takeoff or landing at JFK airport. In its 39 square miles are many small islands, most of them saltmarshes barely above water level, inaccessible except by boat and restricted as part of the Jamaica Bay National Wildlife Refuge.

However, the loop trail around West Pond on the island known as Rulers' Bar Hassock is right off Cross Bay Boulevard. Here, after picking up a free permit, a map, and a brochure at the visitor center, you can start on a short loop, straddling the Brooklyn-Queens borough line, around West Pond that is one of the most popular nature walks in the city, despite (or because of) its somewhat remote location. You will probably want to bring along sunglasses,

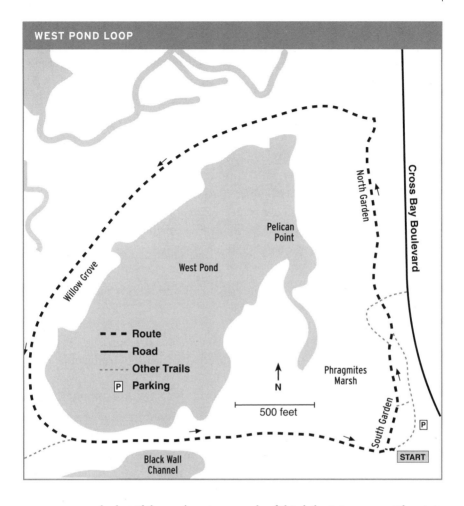

WEST POND LOOP

Pelican Point

West Pond

North Garden

Cross Bay Boulevard

Willow Grove

Phragmites Marsh

South Garden

- - - Route
——— Road
- - - - - Other Trails
P Parking

N

500 feet

Black Wall Channel

START

P

sunscreen, and a hat if the sun's out, as much of this hike is in areas with minimal shade. A windshell on cool days would be a good idea as well.

Start by turning right and heading along the north leg of the vaguely triangular loop. The gravel paths branch here. They eventually rejoin, but bear left and take the lower elevation one, as it goes through more wooded and shadier areas with tall hickory trees. Interpretive panels are found along the path, as well as numbered posts corresponding, at least part of the time, to the numbers on the map.

You will see very little of the pond itself, some distance to the west, at this point. Short paths loop down the gentle slope in that direction, allowing you to see some of the trees, shrubs, and plants more typical of the oceanfront. In one of these areas, the North Garden, there is a large clearing to the right of the trail sheltered by the tallest trees along the loop.

A short distance past here, the trail divides again briefly and makes the first corner of the loop, at its northernmost point. Turn left and follow the gravel path as the woods alongside get lower and shrubbier until they yield, on the right of the trail, to North Marsh. You can see down toward the bay, to Jamaica across it, with midtown Manhattan in the distance.

You may well see the first birds of the hike here. You will definitely see, if you crane your neck, the other "birds" that cross the sky here—the flights leaving or returning to JFK. The airport is behind the Addabbo Bridge to your right.

As you continue down the path, the gravel gives way to hard sand and dirt. The view of the bay remains open, with Black Bank Marsh just offshore as West Marsh replaces North Marsh closer to the coast. Bayberries and other scents of the sea fill the air, in season. A few short paths lead down to the pond itself, where, if you are quiet and careful, you can get close-up views of some of the larger members of the 325 different bird species that have been reported here.

The 45-acre West Pond, along with its larger neighbor on the other side of the road, is another of Robert Moses's creations. Fill from the construction of the two Cross Bay bridges was used to expand the hassock on both sides. After Moses consulted with the Fish and Wildlife Service, the ponds were then dug, replacing habitat New York City birds had lost when what was originally known as Idlewild Airport was built.

In 1953 the two ponds were opened to the public as a city park. Almost two decades later, in 1972, the land was transferred to the federal government for inclusion in the Gateway National Recreation Area, which includes seaside tracts in both New Jersey and New York. The wildlife refuge has grown to 9,155 acres, including not only all the surface saltmarsh and islands, but also the many shallow waterways between them. The area has become popular with birders, and you'll see many of them on good days along this trail, peering intently through binoculars or cameras.

The trail then climbs slightly into an area known as the Willow Grove, crossing from Queens into Brooklyn without being noted by the trail signage. Here the trail rises, allowing you to see almost the whole pond and its seagulls, herons, egrets, and swans. For this reason, you'll see a lot of the birders here as well. Some areas on the slope below are caged for research purposes (stay on the trail and leave them alone).

Just past here, at the westernmost point on the loop, is a short loop trail through the Terrapin Nesting Area. This is closed in season, which is usually most of the warm months of the year, but when it is open offers a fascinating look at one of the refuge's managed marshes.

Swans swim on a quiet corner of West Pond.

Descending again, back into Queens, the trail comes out to a narrow isthmus of low vegetation with the pond still visible inside the loop, on your left, and the bay on your left. Waves lap gently on this shore, with its view to Broad Channel nearby and Rockaway Beach in the distance. To the southwest are the high-rises of Canarsie and Bergen Beach.

Out in the bay you'll also see a nesting box for egrets. Smaller nesting boxes, with different opening sizes, are located closer to the trail and pond, and an interpretive display farther down the trail, as it re-enters the woods, explains that these are for some of the wren and sparrow species that find habitat here, but can't always make nests due to the aggressiveness of some of the other species.

Another interpretive plaque explains that piles of logs in the woods, sometimes visible from the trail, are not leftover slash but also manmade habitat, this time for rodents and snakes. From here, it's a short distance back up a slight hill to the visitor center and parking lot.

MORE INFORMATION

A free permit, available at the visitor center, is required. Open during daylight hours. Restrooms are located at the visitor center. Dogs not permitted. Jamaica Bay National Wildlife Refuge, 210 New York Avenue, Staten Island, NY, 10305; 718-318-4340; www.nyharborparks.org/visit/jaba.html.

TRIP 5
NEW YORK BOTANICAL
GARDEN–NATIVE FOREST

$ (人) (🚌)

Location: Bronx, NY
Rating: Easy
Distance: 1.5 miles
Elevation Gain: 20 feet
Estimated Time: 1.0 hour
Maps: USGS Central Park and Flushing; trail map available at entrance and at the New York Botanical Garden website

The last significant stand of untouched forest in New York City makes this a short, but fascinating, hike.

DIRECTIONS

From Exit 9 off the Major Deegan Expressway (I-87), follow Fordham Road roughly 2 miles east to Southern Boulevard (also signed as Kazimiroff Boulevard). Turn left and the entrance will be opposite the station, 0.5 mile north on your right. Parking is $12 per day; there are also privately owned parking garages in the area. If coming from the Bronx River Parkway, take Exit 7W for Fordham Road or Exit 8W for Southern Boulevard. *GPS coordinates*: 40° 52.000′ N, 73° 52.844′ W.

By train, take the Harlem Line to Metro-North's Botanical Garden station on the right. It is across the street from the Mosholu Gate. The Bx26 bus stops in front of the gate, and can be taken from Bedford Park Boulevard stations on the B, D, and 4 subway lines. If you'd rather walk from the subway, follow Bedford Park (East 200th Street) downhill approximately 0.5 mile to Southern Boulevard. Turn right and walk one block to the gate.

TRAIL DESCRIPTION

In 1979 Grandmaster Flash said the Bronx seemed "like a jungle sometimes." In the New York Botanical Garden (NYBG) some of the original wilderness is still left. One-fifth of the garden (50 acres) was set aside for a portion known as the Native Forest, which offers you the opportunity to see what New York City might have been like without the many people and buildings that are on it today. These woods haven't been cleared since before the Dutch traded beads with the American Indians.

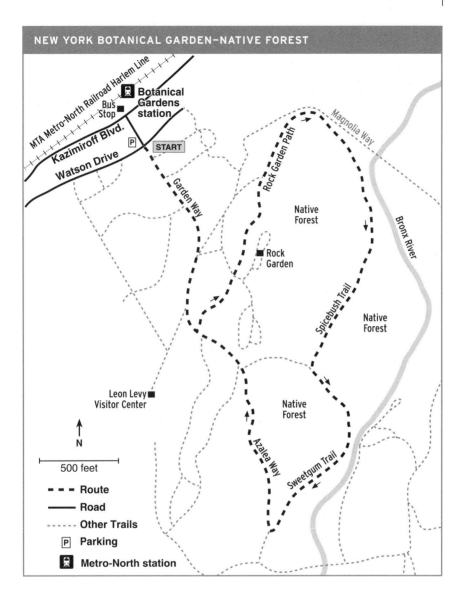

NEW YORK BOTANICAL GARDEN—NATIVE FOREST

MTA Metro-North Railroad Harlem Line

Botanical Gardens station

Bus Stop

Kazimiroff Blvd.

Watson Drive

START

Garden Way

Rock Garden Path

Magnolia Way

Native Forest

Rock Garden

Spicebush Trail

Native Forest

Bronx River

Native Forest

Leon Levy Visitor Center

Native Forest

N

Azalea Way

Sweetgum Trail

500 feet

- - - Route
—— Road
----- Other Trails
P Parking
Metro-North station

One of the garden's most attractive features is the ease of getting there without a vehicle. You'll want to make your way to the garden's Mosholu Gate, just opposite the train station on a stretch of Southern Boulevard named for Dr. Theodore Kazimiroff, an important amateur naturalist and conservationist who worked to protect open space in the borough.

Maps are available at the admissions booth, where you will be charged a fee. Then walk down Garden Way, the broad paved path past Mertz Library on the left. Rows of poplar trees were planted to frame the library along the lawn.

The path continues past one of the tram stops, where buses pick up passengers and provide transportation and tours, and gently climbs up to a junction at the reflecting pool. To your right is the Leon Levy Visitor Center.

Today, the NYBG is a National Historic Landmark. With more than 1 million plants, it is the largest botanical garden in any city in the United States and one of the most notable in the world. It is an educational and research institution, with classrooms, libraries, and herbaria (collections of preserved plant specimens) containing thousands of species. Many of these same plants are represented in the garden's meticulously landscaped trails and in its 50 curated gardens.

The main path continues, curving to the left. A narrower path to the left and slightly uphill is the Rock Garden Path. Follow it under the sycamore tree and past the large rock outcrop on the left. The trail re-enters the woods and you will see the entrance to the Rock Garden on the right. This small grotto of carefully arranged rocks and small cascades requires a separate entrance fee if you wish to see it.

The path forks just past the Rock Garden. Stay on the paved path that descends through a magnificently landscaped area of tall and short trees and goes farther down to the nearby road. As you follow it down to the corner behind the guardrail, you may think you've made a wrong turn and are somehow leaving the Botanical Garden—but you haven't.

Turn right and follow the path alongside Magnolia Way. A short distance up the street on the right, the path goes into a parking lot. At the far end you'll see a broad, wood-chip covered path with a wooden fence on one side, going uphill and turning to the right. This is the Spicebush Trail, the main route through the heart of the Native Forest. Interpretive plaques, such as the one at the start of the Spicebush Trail, identifying what you are viewing.

As you follow the path, you will see the towering oaks and maples that are similar to those that once covered all five boroughs. To the right are more scenic rock outcrops. Through the trees you may catch glimpses of the Bronx River, the only freshwater river in New York City, on the left.

This is an unusual trail, with a nice surface that is muddy in spots and occasionally interrupted by fire hydrants. It is advisable to wear boots on the chips, but you can leave hiking poles and a fully equipped backpack at home for this trip.

After 0.5 mile, the trail reaches a three-way junction. Turn right on to Azalea Way, a pleasant meandering route that takes you to the visitor center where you started this loop.

The Mertz Library, built in 1905, is home to one of the world's most important collections of books about botany.

MORE INFORMATION

Restrooms and food are located at the Leon Levy Visitor Center. Open year-round, 10 A.M. to 6 P.M., except on Mondays, Thanksgiving, and Christmas. Grounds-only admission is $6 for adults, $5 for Bronx residents, $3 for seniors, $1 for children 2–12, and free for children under 2. New York Botanical Garden, Bronx River Parkway at Fordham Road, Bronx, NY 10458; 718-817-8700; www.nybg.org.

TRIP 6
PELHAM BAY PARK

Location: Bronx, NY
Rating: Easy
Distance: 2.0 miles
Elevation Gain: 20 feet
Estimated Time: 1.0 hour
Maps: USGS Flushing; trail map available online at park website

Hike along salt marshes and through deep woods in New York City's largest park.

DIRECTIONS

Get off the Hutchinson River Parkway at Exit 5. Follow the access road to the traffic circle and turn left (north) on Elliott Road. Pass the golf course parking lot a half-mile from the circle, and turn left into the clubhouse just past it to get to the parking lot. *GPS coordinates:* 40° 52.339′ N, 73° 48.604′ W.

To get here using public transportation, take the 6 subway to its northern terminus at Pelham Bay Park station. From there, take the Westchester Bee-Line Bus Route 45 (marked on city signs sometimes as W45) to the stop near the Bartow-Pell Mansion entrance road just north of the golf course.

TRAIL DESCRIPTION

Many people assume that since Central Park is New York City's best-known park, it's also the city's largest. However, Pelham Bay Park's 2,700 acres, in the city's northeast corner, could take in Central Park three times over and still have room to spare.

After Jamaica Bay, Pelham Bay Park has the largest collection of salt marshes and other tidal wetlands in the city. Unlike Jamaica Bay, the trails here take you much closer to the salt water.

Starting from the Pelham Bay-Split Rock Golf Course parking lot, where rail fans can watch Amtrak Acelas go by on the adjacent railroad track, cross the road at the lot's south entrance (now closed to vehicles) to the yellow-blazed Siwanoy Trail, named for one of the area's original American Indian tribes, opposite the entrance to the parking lot. Turn left and follow the trail north between the road and the tall marsh grass for a few hundred feet to where it rises and enters the woods.

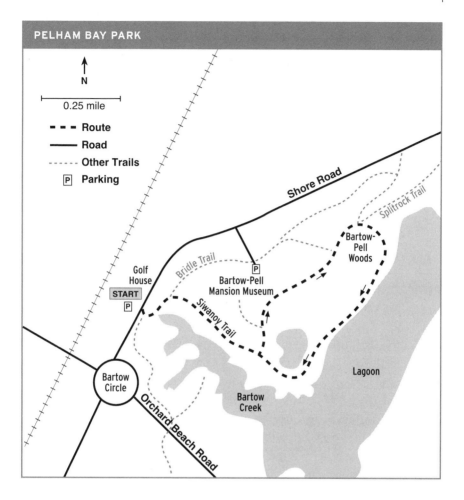

PELHAM BAY PARK

N

0.25 mile

- - - Route
——— Road
------ Other Trails
P Parking

Shore Road

Splitrock Trail

Bartow-Pell Woods

Golf House

Bridle Trail

P

Bartow-Pell Mansion Museum

START
P

Siwanoy Trail

Lagoon

Bartow Circle

Orchard Beach Road

Bartow Creek

The trail meanders slowly, with the yellow blazes continuing infrequently, through a forest dominated by bitternut hickory. The trail forks at the beginning of the loop, as it makes its way through the Bartow-Pell woods in this section of the park. Bear right and follow the shoreline. You will reach views over the marshes and inlet just to the south at clearings, some of which stretch back to the mansion property to the north.

At one of the clearings, a good path forks to the left. Stay on the trail, even though it seems fainter, as it heads out onto an elevated berm between the inlet and a marsh on the other side. The path is narrow, but it is there.

The trail turns left, following the berm, and you will have an opportunity to see views of Hunters Island and the parking lot and facilities at Orchard Beach, one of the city's most popular beaches. Before the 1930s, none of this—not the beach, the island, or even the ground you're walking on—existed.

Pelham Bay Park was created in 1888 when John Mullaly, a Bronx resident who had founded the New York Parks Association to lobby for the creation of more parks in the city, urged the association to acquire the land in the area before it was developed. The city was able to buy some of its old estates for this purpose.

For almost half a century, the park was limited to the undeveloped lands on Hunters Island, Rodman's Neck (used as a police firing range and explosive-disposal area until recently), and the areas on the shore where the golf course is now. The only facilities were a small area of Orchard Beach so poorly designed it was almost useless most of the time. It was also closed to the public due to the presence of nearby bungalows reserved for those with connections to the city's Tammany Hall political machine.

In 1934, Robert Moses, newly appointed by Mayor Fiorello La Guardia as the first citywide parks commissioner, took some of his engineers up here and showed them what he wanted done.

He instructed them to tear down everything already in place, including all 600 bungalows, without regard to cost, so that the beach could be expanded and improved. If they filled in the waters between Hunter Island and the Twin Islands to the east and Rodman's Neck to the south, they could give the city a mile-long, crescent-shaped beach with a view of Long Island Sound to the west. To make it even nicer, they brought in finer sand dredged from the oceans off the Rockaways, covering the pebbles the glaciers had left behind.

As part of the work, this berm was created, trapping a portion of the bay inland to make another salt marsh, and making the water you're looking out over into a small lagoon. You can also see the bathhouse Moses designed to lend a sense of joyfulness to beach outings.

Continuing along the trail, you will pass the marsh and reach another area where the woods come up to the shore. In some areas the path drops on to small, slightly eroded areas of beach—at high tide you will be unable to avoid getting your footwear wet, so keep that in mind when preparing for this trip.

Eventually the trail comes back into the woods and intersects the wide bridle path. Signs on the wooden barriers confirm that you are still on the Siwanoy Trail. Crossing the path takes you uphill slightly, into a stand of white pine, and then across a clearing into an area where the trail, in wet summers, can have something of a wilderness feel—heavily overgrown on the sides and blocked by occasional blowdown. The yellow markers and bare earth beneath your feet are the only things that confirm you're still on the trail.

Continuing on the Siwanoy Trail takes you to a corner of the trapped marsh, which you cross briefly on a wooden walkway, and then up into a section

You will see marshy areas such as this one on your hike in Pelham Bay Park.

where the trail is easier to follow as it crosses some of the streams that feed the marsh and reaches a small cemetery in the woods behind the mansion.

The small burial plot for members of the Pell family who lived on this property in the eighteenth and nineteenth centuries is included in the National Historic Landmark designation for the Bartow-Pell Mansion, an 1836 stone Federal-style house. It's worth taking a look at, either via the short path back to it from the trail or by driving up to it after the hike.

From the cemetery, continue down the Siwanoy Trail another 0.1 mile to the beginning of the loop, and return to your vehicle.

MORE INFORMATION

Restrooms are available in the golf clubhouse. Pelham Bay Park, Middletown Road and Bruckner Blvd., Bronx, NY 10465; 718-430-1890; www.nycgovparks .org/parks/pelhambaypark.

TRIP 7
HOOK MOUNTAIN STATE PARK

Location: Upper Nyack, NY
Rating: Moderate
Distance: 2.3 miles
Elevation Gain: 420 feet
Estimated Time: 1.5 hours
Maps: USGS Nyack; New York–New Jersey Trail Conference Hudson Palisades Trails, Map #110

Gaze at the widest section of the Hudson River, and then some, from this popular suburban summit.

DIRECTIONS
From Exit 10 on the New York State Thruway, follow North Highland Avenue (Route 9W) north 1.2 miles to the intersection with Christian Herald Road in Upper Nyack. There is parking for five to ten vehicles on the west side of the road at a dirt and gravel pullout on the left just north of the intersection. *GPS coordinates*: 41° 06.002′ N, 73° 55.654′ W.

Coach USA's buses depart from the Port Authority Bus Terminal in New York City and travel up Route 9W. You can stop at Christian Herald Road.

TRAIL DESCRIPTION
North of the Palisades, no feature on the west side of the Hudson is as distinctive as Hook Mountain, best appreciated from the small Westchester County hamlet of Scarborough, right across the river. The mountain juts out into Haverstraw Bay, the river's widest spot, just north of the Nyacks. Dutch sailors who first explored and settled the region in the seventeenth century called it "Verdrietege Hoogte," meaning tedious or troublesome point, because of the difficulty of getting around it. Its tall stone cliffs, the results of years of quarrying, are the most striking natural feature on the river south of the Hudson Highlands.

Today, that area is a group of three state parks administered by the Palisades Interstate Park Commission: Nyack Beach along the river, Rockland Lake inland, and Hook Mountain along the ridge. The second is a popular spot for swimming and picnicking, the other two for hiking and walking.

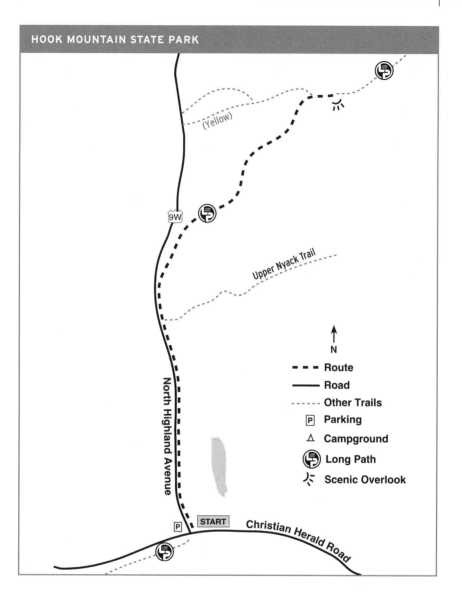

HOOK MOUNTAIN STATE PARK

(Yellow)

9W

Upper Nyack Trail

North Highland Avenue

N

- - - Route
—— Road
----- Other Trails
P Parking
△ Campground
Long Path
Scenic Overlook

START

P

Christian Herald Road

On this hike you'll follow a short section of the Long Path to Hook's open summit. It begins with a roadwalk along Route 9W north from the lot. There is plenty of room along either shoulder, but the blazes are on the right-hand side of the road as it works its way up a gentle slope as the developed area of Upper Nyack yields slowly to the woods of the state parks.

At 0.3 mile from the parking area, the trail leaves the road and enters the woods on the right, behind the guardrail. Almost immediately afterward, the white-blazed Upper Nyack Trail from Nyack Beach comes in from the right. Continue to follow the Long Path's aqua blazes straight ahead. The trail follows an old roadbed into second-growth woodland. It seems to drop as it remains close to the highway, but actually it's just climbing slowly.

When it finally gets away from Route 9W, the trail gets off the old roadbed and begins to climb into some less disturbed woods. Civilization is still near in the form of a stone wall at the back of a property to the left, but eventually that recedes as the trail begins to traverse along the slopes of Hook Mountain, winding out toward the river, gaining elevation slowly all the time. Thin, scrubby chestnut oaks begin to dominate the woods around the trail, and at some clearings in the steep woods you can begin to see a preview of the vistas that await you at the summit.

To get to the summit, the trail turns back inland, climbing some more. After a few more twists and turns, it reaches a junction with a faint yellow trail that goes back to Route 9W. Ahead, you can see the Long Path ascending through some more open areas, across bare bedrock. Follow it through them, and after two more such areas you will come out on the bare, rocky summit of Hook Mountain.

Here you have a 360-degree view of the lower Hudson Valley from 720 feet above sea level. The most notable thing you'll see is, of course, the river, and the entire 3-mile length of the Tappan Zee Bridge, the longest auto bridge in New York State. Just north of it, and below you, is Haverstraw Bay. On the other side are Tarrytown and Ossining, then the long promontory of Croton Point Park. On clear days you can make out Peekskill quite easily in front of Anthony's Nose, Bear Mountain, and the lower Hudson Highlands, with the higher peaks to the north jutting over them. Looking south along the west side of the river and the boats often moored just off it, the communities that make up the Nyacks—Nyack, Upper Nyack, Central Nyack, South Nyack, and West Nyack—are nestled neatly into the space on the west side of the bridge, between Hook and Tallman Mountain State Park to the south.

To the immediate north is High Tor, the highest point on the Palisades at 832 feet above sea level, just where the range bends inland. The large (256-acre) body of water between you and it is Rockland Lake, center of Rockland Lake State Park, the largest of the three parks on and around Hook Mountain at over a thousand acres. Its preservation history is entwined with the other two; while Hook's cliffs were being scraped in the late nineteenth century for more and more stone to face buildings in Manhattan, Rockland Lake was providing the city with a more renewable resource—ice.

The three-mile-long Tappan Zee Bridge is visible from the 720-foot summit of Hook Mountain.

For almost a century, several icehouses operated near the lake's northeast corner, harvesting blocks from the lake in winter and then using a sort of escalator to take them down to the river at Rockland Landing. In New York City's restaurants, Rockland Lake ice was highly desired, with some using no other ice to cool drinks, due to the purity of the spring-fed lake's waters.

Take as long as you want, weather permitting of course, to take this all in. Return to your vehicle the same way you came, and be careful when crossing Route 9W.

MORE INFORMATION

No restrooms are available. Rockland Lake State Park, P.O. Box 217, Congers, NY 10920; 845-268-3020; www.nysparks.com/parks/81/details.aspx.

THE FALL AND RISE OF THE WHITE-TAILED DEER

No animal has come to symbolize wildlands in America as much as the white-tailed deer. In our culture, *Odocoileus virginianus* has established itself as a national icon and has been popularized by movies such as *The Deerslayer* and *The Deer Hunter*. And like many ubiquitous American animals, it has earned this distinction for its hardiness and adaptability (and, in the case of the Bambi-like young fawns, its adorability). It flourishes almost anywhere in temperate North America east of the Rockies and as far south as Peru. It can even be found in Finland and the Czech Republic. Its four-chambered ruminant stomach, which allows it to digest a wide range of plants and fungi, and a strong sense of smell that helps it forage and sense predators, allow for its widespread range.

Deer are now abundant both inside and outside our protected parks and forests. So it may seem hard to believe that the deer was once thought of as endangered (long before the Endangered Species Act). In the late nineteenth century, New York state protected the heavily hunted species by enclosing a large area of state land near Slide Mountain in the Catskills. A herd of deer were protected while they roamed inside the enclosure until their numbers had been sufficiently restored and they were again allowed to roam naturally.

Preservation of this species has succeeded, and not just in New York. Suburbanization, whatever its other effects, was good for white-tailed deer. They found a habitat with the right balance of woodlands and grasslands and since much of the land was closed to hunters, they faced no real threat of predation (save coyotes). They were fruitful and multiplied. Now they are commonly seen poking around in the backyards of residential subdivisions. Over a million deer die in collisions with cars every year.

Even if you don't see a deer while hiking, you will probably spot signs of deer in the woods, like tracks, droppings, and the "rubs" they make against tree bark to mark territory. In some heavily populated areas, another indicator is the telltale "browse line" on the trees, which is approximately four feet off the ground. Under that line, all branches will have been thoroughly cleaned of leaves by feeding deer in the winter, when other food sources are scarce.

TRIP 8
TUXEDO LOOP

Location: Tuxedo, NY
Rating: Difficult
Distance: 5.3 miles
Elevation Gain: 900 feet
Estimated Time: 6.0 hours
Maps: USGS Sloatsburg; New York–New Jersey Trail Conference
Southern Harriman–Bear Mountain Trails, Map #118

Sweeping viewpoints, Revolutionary-era history, utility rights-of-way, and diverse forests make this a fine sampler of Harriman State Park.

DIRECTIONS

Take Route 17 to downtown Tuxedo, midway between Thruway Exits 15 and 16. Turn right on East Village Road from Route 17 just north of the train station. The main lot with space for over 100 cars, where the town prefers hikers park, is on the left about 300 feet from the intersection, just past the tracks. It is free on weekends. There is no legal parking along the 0.4 mile where the trail enters the woods. *GPS coordinates*: 41° 11.743′ N, 74° 11.035′ W.

From Hoboken or Secaucus, take the Metro-North Port Jervis Line to the Tuxedo station. The trail begins in the parking lot with three red-dot-on-white markers on a telephone pole.

TRAIL DESCRIPTION

What it lacks in elevation and wilderness compared to the Catskills, Harriman State Park makes up for in accessibility and proximity to the city. It can be said that hiking in the New York metropolitan area began here. What began as railroad magnate Edward Harriman's Arden estate is now approximately 47,000 acres of Orange and Rockland counties.

Here, in New York's second-largest state park, the first section of the Appalachian Trail was cleared and blazed. Many residents of suburb and city alike came here to go on their first real hike. Trail-building activities of various hiking clubs started here in the 1920s and were documented in Raymond Torrey's *New York Post* columns. This later led to the reestablishment of the New York–New Jersey Trail Conference.

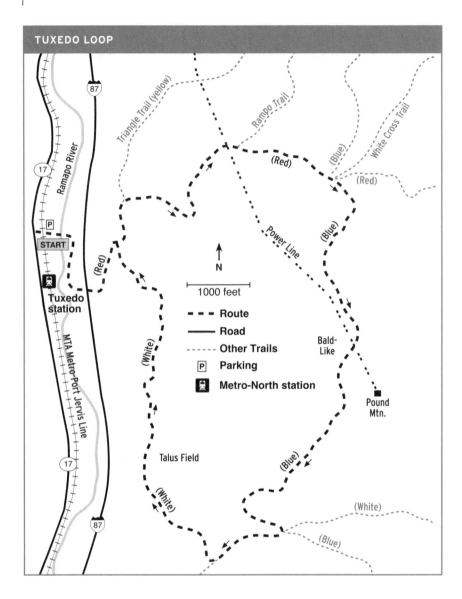

TUXEDO LOOP

This loop from Tuxedo's picturesque 1885 train station, a recently restored building listed on the National Register of Historic Places, offers you a chance to take away a full tray from Harriman's sumptuous buffet table. Everything that is unique and distinctive about hiking in Harriman, you'll find here.

Start with a road walk of 0.5 mile on the Ramapo–Dunderberg Trail (R–D), which begins with three markers (white with red dots) on a utility pole in the parking lot next to the station platform. These three markers lead along the paved path to East Village Road. Turn right across the tracks and downhill to the bridge over the Ramapo River. The trail follows East Village around a curve and under the Thruway, where the white-with-red-dot blazes direct you left onto Grove Drive, a quiet residential street. The trail enters the park on your right a short distance uphill.

A white-blazed road forks off to your right, while the R–D ascends through the grassy woods on several sections of stone steps. After 0.2 mile, the yellow-blazed Triangle Trail leaves to the left. The R–D continues its climb through and around rock outcrops for 0.5 mile to an open viewpoint of the valley below, highlighted by Tuxedo and a long stretch of the Thruway. To the west are the high hills of Sterling Forest.

The trail descends to an old road in a mature section of forest and crosses the open right-of-way of a gas pipeline, which is a frequent Harriman occurrence. Back in the woods, follow the Tuxedo–Mount Ivy Trail (T–MI), blazed in white squares with a red dash in the middle, as it goes to the right.

At first the T–MI climbs steeply, but then it gently rolls through to a grassy forest of maple and oak, which are typical at Harriman. Cross a small swamp to the base of a large rocky area known as Claudius Smith's Den. The trail ascends to a junction with two other trails.

From these rocks, the reputed hideout of a Revolutionary-era bandit leader, you can see the hills to the west, plus a section of the Shawangunk Ridge, the northern extension of New Jersey's Kittatinny Mountains. The open green spaces of the park reveal themselves to the south and southeast.

The serious climbing is behind you, but some route-finding challenges lie ahead. On the rocks and nearby trees, you'll see the blue-dot-on-white markers of the Blue Disc Trail. Be careful not to follow the white crosses of the White Cross Trail. The Blue Disc Trail will take you along the backstretch of this loop. To continue, backtrack down the way you came up the rock. Look for the Blue Disc Trail's markers that fork off downhill to the left, through an area where the treadway isn't always easy to see. You may have to search a bit for the next blazes in some stretches (sometimes needing to look backward). The trail picks up an old road in a less grassy area and becomes easier to follow. It turns to the south in an area of dense birches that predominate along a small swamp.

After the swamp, you will find yourself in another grassy area next to a creek in a small ravine. The trail first runs along the top of the ravine, then descends into it. It may seem like you are lost, but the trail eventually leads into a narrow crevice known as Elbow Brush. Be careful to keep your elbows and your knees from being scraped.

The trail leads to the edge of the gas pipeline, 0.7 mile from Smith's Den. It follows alongside the pipeline into the woods and eventually crosses it at the ridge crest (near the county line). On the other side is a long, grassy area with a few trees atop Pound Mountain. This marvelous stretch of open area feels a bit like a bald, similar to the open, grassy areas on the high peaks of North Carolina or Tennessee. You may see deer grazing, almost oblivious to your presence.

After 0.25 mile, the trail abruptly descends into a ravine with a mature, tall canopy, but gently climbs out and back into another less dense forest. Eventually it will reach the last of the three viewpoints along this hike at the summit of Dater Mountain. You can see down into the valley along Seven Lakes Drive below, with North and South hills towering behind, and might catch a glimpse of hawks gliding on the mountain breeze.

The descent from this rock leads down into a chute named Almost Perpendicular by the trail builders. Follow the switchbacks to a stream crossing. An unmarked trail forks off to the right, which may cause some confusion. Be sure to stay on the Blue Disc Trail and follow it down a rocky old road.

Turn right onto the white-blazed Kakiat Trail at the base of the slope. It continues its gentle descent, turning back to the north along an old road. It may be muddy and wet in some spots. Continue to follow the trail until it meets with an abandoned telephone-line route past boulders. The trail reaches the trailhead for the R–D at 1.25 miles from the Blue Disc junction.

MORE INFORMATION

Restrooms are located at the railroad station. Harriman State Park, Palisades Interstate Park Commission, Bear Mountain, NY 10911; 845-786-2701; nysparks.state.ny.us/parks/145/details.aspx.

TRIP 9
BELLVALE MOUNTAIN

Location: Bellvale, NY
Rating: Moderate
Distance: 3.6 miles
Elevation Gain: 440 feet
Estimated Time: 2.0 hours
Maps: USGS Greenwood Lake, Warwick; New York–New Jersey Trail Conference Sterling Forest Trails, Map #100; New York–New Jersey Appalachian Trail Map #3

Take a gentle walk on the Appalachian Trail to two incredible views.

DIRECTIONS
Follow the directions to Greenwood Lake, NY, as given for Trip 12, Bearfort Mountain.

From Greenwood Lake, continue on Route 17A to the intersection with Continental Road. There is parking there for fifteen to twenty vehicles in the dirt section between the two roads. *GPS coordinates:* 41° 14.659′ N, 74° 17.229′ W.

The NJ Transit 196/197 bus stops on request at Kain Road, 0.2 mile west of the trailhead on Route 17A.

TRAIL DESCRIPTION
The long ridge known as Bearfort Mountain in New Jersey is Bellvale Mountain at its northern end in New York, after a small settlement in the town of Warwick. No glacial tarns are found in this section, but there is some very good hiking that doesn't require too much effort.

Route 17A crosses the ridge 5.5 miles north of the state line, and the Appalachian Trail (AT) crosses at that ridge top. From there it's a nice stroll north to two of the truly spectacular places on the AT in New York east of Harriman State Park: Eastern Pinnacles and Cat Rocks.

From your vehicle, follow the shoulder of Route 17A east, back downhill. Look for an entrance into the woods across the road. This is not the Appalachian Trail itself, but one of its many unheralded blue-blazed spur trails, which become useful on this hike.

Once in the woods, you'll see another spur, to the Mount Peter hawkwatching platform, which goes off to the left. The blue trail itself goes a short

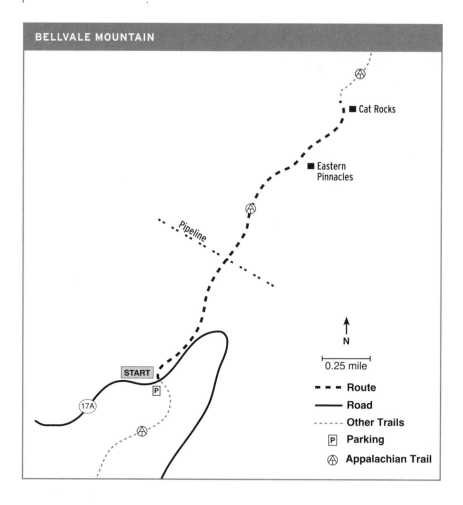

BELLVALE MOUNTAIN

Cat Rocks

Eastern Pinnacles

Pipeline

N

0.25 mile

- - - Route
—— Road
------ Other Trails
P Parking
Ⓐ Appalachian Trail

START

P

17A

distance and then turns left, traversing the roadside. You'll see that the blue blazes have been painted over white ones. If you have any doubts that you have chosen the right trail, they will be allayed in 0.1 mile when the AT comes in from its road crossing to the right.

From here, the trail continues to follow a wide dirt path, gently yet continuously ascending as it traverses the side of the ridge. Below, the highway parallels the trail at first, descending gently, and then turns away toward Greenwood Lake. About 0.4 mile along, the trail passes a campsite to the right and levels out.

The forest here is a typical Highlands montane forest of maple and scrubby chestnut oak. You can start to see open areas on the ridge top to the left. Eventually you reach an area where the trail bends to the west slightly and then widens a bit as it enters an area with tall hemlocks, where a rock outcrop to

A young hiker looks north from Eastern Pinnacles.

the right, off the trail, offers some limited views. This ends at the crossing of a gas pipeline right-of-way, where you can see down on the right toward the Greenwood Lake area (but not the lake itself).

Back in the woods on the other side of the pipeline, the trail remains wide, beginning to ascend gently through more scrubby montane woods just below the ridge top to a rise that marks the highest elevation along this hike, 1,294 feet above sea level. Coming down from it, you'll have to skirt some old blowdown where someone has carved a happy face into the wood where it was cut to allow a detour of the trail to pass through.

The descent gets a little steeper as the woods get a bit more mixed, and the trail reaches some rocky areas with natural steps. At the bottom, you will hit a rut and then climb slightly to where a blue-blazed side trail forks off to the left as you see a clearing and rock outcrop rise ahead.

You have reached Eastern Pinnacles, 1.3 miles from the trailhead. The AT's white blazes lead straight up alongside the rock (again, there is another shorter blue-blazed trail around this section, as dogs and small children may find the rock a little treacherous) to the top, the best view from this overlook.

Here you can see down into the valley that carries Lakes Road north from Greenwood Lake to Monroe. Off to the north, beyond the rest of Bellvale, is an unusual southerly view of Schunemunk Mountain, with the Hudson Highlands in the distance beyond. To the immediate west, across the Lakes Road valley, are the mountains of Sterling Forest State Park and its Doris Duke Wildlife Sanctuary, the only portion of the park closed to hunting.

You can see a small rock outcrop a little farther down the ridge. This is Cat Rocks, your next stop and the turnaround point for this hike. When you are ready to continue, follow the AT down the rocks. This takes you onto some lesser outcrops where a little hopping and skipping is necessary, but after 0.1 mile the trail finally re-enters the woods. A short distance afterward, the longer blue trail rejoins it from the left.

The AT continues to descend a rocky, moderately pitched section, finally leveling off and then crossing two brooks, one wider than the other. Here birch joins the forest. At another wide, muddy area, the trail turns left and heads slightly uphill. Soon another blue trail splits off to the left for those continuing hikers who wish to detour around Cat Rocks, the large, narrow ledge that the trail has now reached.

The AT climbs steeply over ragged, broken rocks in several stages to get to the top of this rock outcrop. Even on top, it is necessary to closely mind the crevasses between rocks—it is not a solid surface like Eastern Pinnacles, until the high spot at the north end. For that reason, dogs and children may find this scary and want to stay off.

The view from Cat Rocks is limited to the immediate vicinity and none of the surrounding landscape, but it's still impressive. You feel like you're at the bottom of a large bowl of woods. The puddingstone here shows the effects of the glaciers on the landscape, and the sheer western face has been a favorite of local rock climbers willing to make the hike out here and test their bouldering skills. You can see, if you look closely, some places where the white and red pebbles in the puddingstone were smeared flat by the passing ice.

After carefully making your way back down the way you came up, take the AT back.

MORE INFORMATION

No restrooms are available at the trailhead. National Park Service Appalachian National Scenic Trail corridor maintained by the New York–New Jersey Trail Conference, 156 Ramapo Valley Road, Mahwah, NJ 07430; 201-512-9348, www.nynjtc.org.

Location: Garrison, NY
Rating: Moderate
Distance: 3.2 miles
Elevation Gain: 530 feet
Estimated Time: 3.0 hours
Maps: USGS West Point; New York–New Jersey Trail Conference Map # 101, in the *East Hudson Trails* set

This short, yet scenic minor peak of the Hudson Highlands near a major regional landmark offers views of West Point and a changing forest.

DIRECTIONS

Take the Palisades Interstate Parkway North to the Bear Mountain Bridge. After crossing the bridge, continue north on Route 9D for approximately 4 miles. Turn right off Route 9D at the sign for Castle Rock Unique Area. You may also see a street sign for Wing and Wing Road. You have gone too far if you reach the junction of Route 403. Follow signs for the parking lot, bearing first left, and then right. The parking area is under a large tree on a small rise with space available for five to ten vehicles. *GPS coordinates*: 41° 22.216′ N, 73° 56.700′ W.

By train, take the Metro-North Hudson Line to the Garrison station. At the south end of the parking lot, take the old road with white blazes through Arden Point State Park. Follow the red-blazed trail in Glenclyffe. This is the former estate of congressman Hamilton Fish, which later became a monastery and is now part of the Garrison Institute. It is open to the public for hiking. Follow the trail east 0.3 miles uphill to 9D. Turn right, and then follow the directions from Wing and Wing Road above.

TRAIL DESCRIPTION

Sugarloaf Hill, sometimes called Sugarloaf South to distinguish it from the other Sugarloaf (north of Breakneck Ridge) in the eastern Hudson Highlands, is the pointy peak seen when looking upriver from the Bear Mountain Bridge. Like other similarly named mountains, its name derives from the loaves sugar was sold in before granulation was possible. Hiking this mountain is a sweet

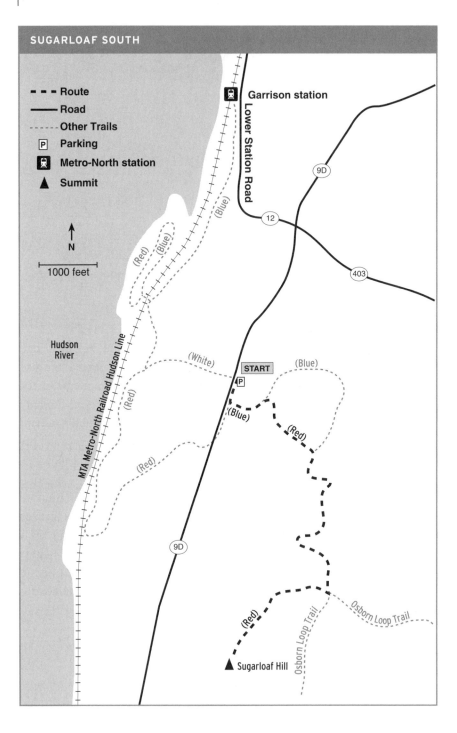

SUGARLOAF SOUTH

- - - Route
—— Road
------- Other Trails
P Parking
Metro-North station
▲ Summit

↑ N

|—————| 1000 feet

Garrison station

Lower Station Road

9D

12

403

Hudson River

MTA Metro-North Railroad Hudson Line

(Blue)
(Red)
(Blue)
(Red)
(White)
START
P
(Blue)
(Blue)
(Red)
(Red)
9D

Osborn Loop Trail

(Red)

▲ Sugarloaf Hill

experience, and the views are similar to those found on higher peaks, but without the rock scrambles.

North of Sugarloaf is Castle Rock, a turreted castle on a mountain of the same name, featuring one of the most recognizable buildings in Garrison. William Osborn, former president of the Illinois Central Railroad, first visited the Highlands in 1855, and was taken by the fresh air and natural beauty of the region. He decided to make the area his weekend home and bought the mountain and surrounding lands. The mansion was built on its summit in 1881. Eventually he made it his full-time home. Today, the whole area is listed on the National Register of Historic Places.

The mansion's turreted towers appear on the hilltop when you start this hike. That is as close as you will be able to get to the building, since it is the property of Osborn's descendants and off-limits to hikers. However, over the years the family has been active in local land conservation efforts, and donated most of the original property to the state. This hike begins in the Castle Rock Unique Area, a section owned by the state Department of Environmental Conservation (DEC), and later joins the Hudson Highlands State Park.

From the parking lot, the Osborn Loop trail is marked by blue plastic blazes. Follow the road you came up, and then turn right just before the gate. That turn takes you onto a grassy lane, which reaches another gate where the trail goes to the left into the grassy areas uphill. At an unsigned fork in the grass, head right to the unpainted gazebo, which offers a sweeping view to the north. On a clear day, you can see the buildings of West Point against Storm King and Spy Rock, with the river flowing through the narrow gap behind and Newburgh Bay in the distance.

After the gazebo, the trail is marked by red blazes. It turns right, follows a woods road to the south along the edge of the field, and descends slightly. The trail abruptly reaches a fence and property line where it turns sharply left, uphill, following the brook on the left. Then, it ascends steadily, and begins to turn away from the creek bed.

You'll notice that while the oaks and hickory trees in this typical Hudson Highlands forest are tall and mature, the forest floor is bare. When the trail switches back to ascend a steepening slope, you will soon understand why. The bases of the trees are blackened and charred deadfall lies all over the ground. When the breeze blows the right way, you can smell the charcoal.

Fires that swept the Highlands during the dry summer of 1999 damaged this area. Many popular trails were closed for months and even years, in the

The United States Military Academy at West Point can be seen from Sugarloaf South.

case of Storm King State Park (due to unexploded ordnance discovered in the woods during fire suppression efforts). The cause of the fires is unknown, but today hikers passing through the burned-over areas can see how the forest regenerates itself. A decade later, the charred wood is slowly decaying into the soil, adding nutrients to it. Small green shoots are already sprouting on the bare patches. One day, perhaps, they will be trees as tall as the ones that currently shade them.

The trail turns right at another woods road and levels off. A stone wall ahead on the right marks not only the border of previously farmed land, but also the line between the Castle Rock Unique Area and Hudson Highlands State Park. Just ahead at the fork the trail leads left and slightly uphill. An unmaintained woods road that circles the base of the mountain leads right, and can be followed back to Route 9D, near a historical marker for the site of Beverly Robinson house. Robinson was a local landowner turned Loyalist during the Revolution, and Benedict Arnold stayed there after his espionage was exposed.

The trail continues to rise gently and then switches back into the saddle between Sugarloaf Hill and an unnamed summit just to the north of it. The mountain itself rises steeply to the south.

The trail continues on level ground past a small pond on the left. You will enter a mature oak–hickory forest, with the distinctively textured bark of the chestnut oak most prominent.

At a K-shaped junction, the red-blazed trail makes a sharp right turn uphill, while the blue-blazed Osborn Loop comes in from the southeast and takes over the woods road. After the junction, follow the red blazes that lead uphill, steeply in some places. Another gazebo is visible a short distance ahead, and is a good spot to rest before tackling the steeper final section of Sugarloaf.

Light and sky are visible through the trees. When the ground levels out you have reached the top of Sugarloaf. Here the forest has scrubbier oaks and some pitch pine, typical of Hudson Highlands summits. At the far southern end of the narrow ridge is a rocky viewpoint over the Garrison area and this section of the Hudson. You can see everything you saw before and more. It's a great place to sit down, take pictures, and eat lunch before you retrace your steps and head back to the station or parking lot.

MORE INFORMATION

There are no restrooms. Trails are open year-round from sunrise to sunset. There is no fee, and only hiking and snowshoeing are allowed. Dogs, on leashes no longer than 10 feet, are permitted on trails. Castle Rock Unique Area: 845-831-8780 ext. 309; www.dec.ny.gov/lands/34747.html. Hudson Highlands State Park, Route 9D, Beacon, NY 10512; 845-225-7207; nysparks.state.ny.us/parks/9/details.aspx.

TRIP 11
HARRIMAN STATE PARK–
LONG MOUNTAIN

Location: Fort Montgomery, NY
Rating: Moderate
Distance: 1.6 miles
Elevation Gain: 320 feet
Estimated Time: 1.0 hour
Maps: USGS Popolopen Lake; New York–New Jersey Trail Conference Northern Harriman–Bear Mountain Trails, #119

Pay tribute to one of the legends of New York–area hiking at this spectacular, yet accessible, viewpoint on the Long Path in northern Harriman State Park.

DIRECTIONS
Harriman State Park is located 30 miles north of New York City. The trailhead parking lot, with room for 30 vehicles, is at the sign for the Long Path/Torrey Memorial on the north side of US Route 6, roughly midway between Thruway Exit 16 and the Palisades Parkway at Long Mountain Circle. *GPS coordinates:* 41° 18.971′ N, 74° 03.017′ W.

TRAIL DESCRIPTION
In stark contrast to the rest of the Harriman–Bear Mountain State Park, the areas north of Route 6 have relatively few trails. Much of this land abuts the West Point military reservation. Most of the Palisades Interstate Park Commission's (PIPC) holdings in this area were traded to the Army for most of the Bear Mountain land during the 1930s. At that time, trail development had not really begun. The remaining parcels, largely trailless, buffer the park and the military reservation, where cadets train for three of their four summers.

The only significant length of trail here is an isolated section of the Long Path, which leads hikers to the memorial for Raymond Torrey atop Long Mountain. The memorial, the scenic views of the surrounding mountains, and the summit's relative proximity to the Long Mountain Parkway section of Route 6 have made this a favorite with day-hikers all over the tri-state area.

From the trailhead, follow the aqua blazes north into the woods from the information kiosk. The beginning of the hike is on level ground through mature

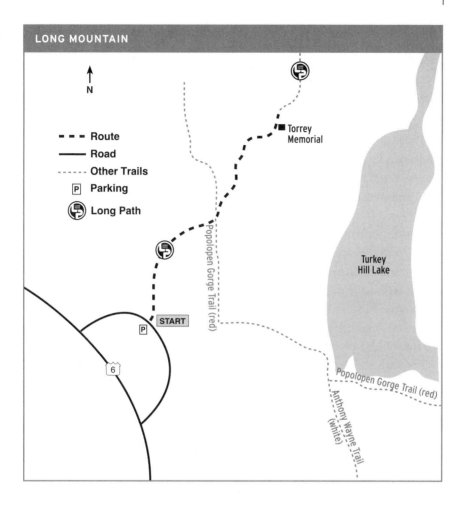

woods of maple and oak with a lush floor. The wide trail eventually meanders down into a small valley, 0.4 mile from the parking lot. The Popolopen Gorge Trail (white blaze with a red dot) comes in from the right (an unmarked woods road continues to the left). As you follow this trail, you will notice the forest getting a little scrubbier as you start to climb. At first it just goes straight uphill, but then it encounters rock steps and starts to switch back around and between them. In a few places you may need to use your hands, and a good sense of balance is necessary. Keep an eye out for the blazes on the open rock portions. The re-entry to the woods is not always identifiable.

After more climbing, the bulk of the vertical ascent on this hike, the woods open up and the ground starts to level out. At a large open area, Long Mountain's 1,157-foot summit, you will see the memorial to Torrey carved into the rock. It reads "In Memory of Raymond H. Torrey, A Great Disciple of 'The

Long Brown Path', 1880–1938." Born to a Massachusetts sea captain, Torrey worked his way through several newspaper reporting jobs to New York via the Berkshires. In 1918, he began covering the burgeoning regional hiking scene for the *New York Evening Post*.

During the Roaring Twenties, many of today's established hiking organizations got their start. Their founders were city residents who got up early on Saturday mornings and caught the ferry to Hoboken and the trains up the Hudson or into the Ramapo Valley. They spent the weekend exploring or clearing trails, and camping out. On Sunday they would catch the late train home.

Torrey was one of those hikers. He began writing a weekly column, *The Long Brown Path*, to relate the weekend's developments and discoveries in the woods and mountains north of the city and agitated for the creation of more parks. Widely read, his column helped those pioneering outdoor recreationists coordinate their activities, much as an Internet forum might do today. He helped found the organization that became the New York–New Jersey Trail Conference. Torrey also championed Benton MacKaye's proposed Appalachian Trail, and helped spur the construction of the trail's first 24 miles across Harriman State Park in 1924.

For a while, Torrey was secretary of the newly created State Parks Council. He left the job after a clash with Robert Moses—the president of the State Parks Council at the time—after the "master builder" threw an ashtray at Torrey following the newsman's use of an ethnic slur, for which he apologized.

In the 1920s, Torrey had proposed a long-distance trail from what was then the ferry landing in Englewood, NJ, to Mount Ivy in Rockland County. PIPC director William Welch had a similar idea for a trail from Fort Lee to Bear Mountain. Not much headway was made until 1932, when Vince Schaefer of Schenectady proposed a "Long Path" from Bear Mountain to Lake Placid in the Adirondacks. Unlike other hiking trails, it was not meant to be a blazed route. Instead, it was a list of points of interest for hikers to find their own way to reach.

Torrey promoted this idea heavily, describing imaginary hikes on the Long Path in his column. Other volunteers eventually blazed and cut a route north over Schunemunk to the Shawangunks and the high peaks of the Catskills beyond. In the early 1960s, after years of neglect, the Long Path was extended north to the Albany area. Today it is as much a backbone of Hudson Valley hiking as the Appalachian Trail, and efforts continue to extend its 330 miles into the Adirondacks as originally intended, and possibly even to Montreal.

In 1922, Torrey scouted the trail to the summit of Long Mountain. It became his favorite spot among the many lands he hiked. It's not hard to see why.

The summit of Long Mountain offers a view of Turkey Hill Lake.

The Popolopen Valley falls below. Turkey Hill Lake fills the valley below, with Popolopen Torne rising above. Bear Mountain rises in the distance, with the Perkins observatory tower visible on the top. Palisades Parkway can be seen wending its way to the bridge beyond. To the north, the equally impressive terrain of the military reservation stands out. To the south, the rest of Harriman State Park, with almost no evidence of civilization, spills away into the distance.

When Torrey died in 1938, his friends took his ashes here to scatter them, as he had wished. From the memorial, you can turn around and start down to the parking lot. Torrey's memorial may be on the mountaintop, but his legacy is beneath your feet and all around you.

MORE INFORMATION

There are no restrooms. Dogs are permitted, but must be muzzled and on a leash of not more than 6 feet. Harriman State Park, Palisades Interstate Park Commission, Bear Mountain, NY 10911; 845-786-2701; nysparks.state.ny.us/parks/145/details.aspx.

THE HUDSON HIGHLANDS AND THE AMERICAN REVOLUTION

Today, the lower Hudson Highlands is a peaceful, green mountain range that draws many visitors from the city to hike and picnic amid the dramatic scenery. But, had you come through during the years of the American Revolution, you would have been passing through a heavily militarized strategic choke point. Control of it was absolutely crucial to the victory of the Continental Army.

After Washington's victories in New Jersey, at Trenton and Princeton, had revitalized the Patriot's cause in 1777, the British began to realize this insurrection was not going to be put down easily and they needed to come up with a plan.

"Gentleman Johnny" Burgoyne's troops in Montreal were to push south and meet up with other British forces coming up the Hudson at Albany, N.Y. This would have cut the colonies, and the Patriots' communications and supply lines, in half. The first half of the plan was foiled by American Gens. Benedict Arnold and Horatio Gates, who held off the British over the winter of 1776–1777 from Fort Ticonderoga. Then, they defeated Burgoyne decisively at Saratoga, N.Y., in October 1777, a success that was widely regarded as the turning point of the war.

But later in 1777, British General Henry Clinton was nevertheless able to take troops up the river, and drove the Americans out of their bases at Fort Clinton (named after an unrelated American general) and Fort Montgomery. He gained access to the mouth of Popolopen Creek. While doing so, he dismantled the chain that had been stretched across the river to prevent British ships from sailing up it (some of the links are on display at West Point), but his delays cost the British at Saratoga.

Nevertheless, for the remainder of the war, the possibility remained that the British could retake the river. West Point remained manned, and lookouts were perched on mountaintops and passes throughout the region. Arnold infamously defected to the British, who were able to retake Stony Point after Anthony Wayne pushed them out in 1779.

Vestiges of the war remain on the hiking trails in the region. The 1777 and 1779 trails in Bear Mountain State Park follow the routes used by the British and Continental armies, respectively, in those years. Hessian Lake was where many of the American casualties of the 1777 battle were disposed of. Fort Montgomery is a National Historic Landmark, and the site of Fort Clinton is now partly the Trailside Zoo, also the lowest point on the Appalachian Trail.

TRIP 12
BEAR MOUNTAIN

Location: Bear Mountain, NY
Rating: Difficult
Distance: 4.5 miles
Elevation Gain: 1,130 feet
Estimated Time: 4.0 hours
Maps: USGS Peekskill, Popolopen Lake; New York–New Jersey Trail Conference Northern Harriman–Bear Mountain Trails, Map #119; New York–New Jersey Appalachian Trail Map #3

If the climb doesn't take your breath away, the views will on this heavily traveled loop with deep roots in hiking history.

DIRECTIONS
Take Route 9W to the entrance to Bear Mountain State Park, just south of Bear Mountain Bridge. Turn onto Seven Lakes Drive, and then into the entrance on the right and park in the lot next to Bear Mountain Inn ($7 fee during season) with room for 300 vehicles. *GPS coordinates*: 41° 18.766′ N, 73° 59.394′ W.

From the New York State Thruway, get off at Exit 16 and take US 6 east to Palisades Parkway and then to Bear Mountain Circle. Follow Route 9W south a quarter-mile to the park entrance on the left.

From the Taconic State Parkway, take Bear Mountain Parkway east to the junction with Routes 6, 9, and 202. Turn right across the Jan Peeck Bridge to Annsville Circle and follow Routes 6 and 202 west to the bridge via the scenic Bear Mountain Bridge Road.

Coach USA's Short Line buses from New York City stop at the inn on weekends.

TRAIL DESCRIPTION
So many things are named after Bear Mountain—a bridge, a state park, an inn, a traffic circle, and even two roads in Westchester County leading to it— that it's easy to forget that the mountain itself came first. And when you have climbed it, you'll understand why it's named "bear."

The mountain and its trails are not only steep; they are steeped in history— the history of modern hiking as well as that of the United States. In 1777 the battle of Forts Montgomery and Clinton was fought near its base, the only

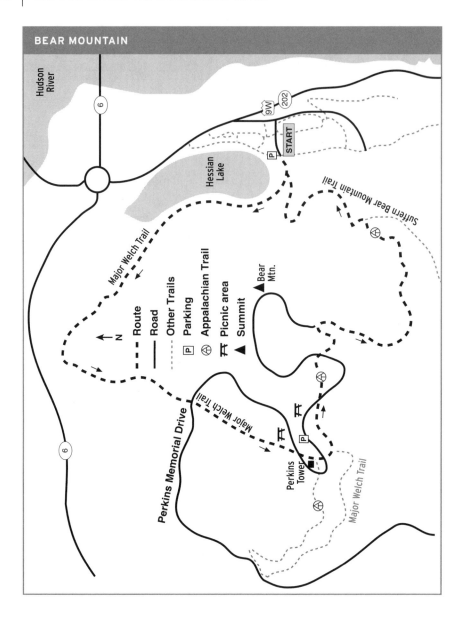

British victory in the Hudson River campaign that could have ended the Revolution. A century and a half later, one of the original stretches of the Appalachian Trail (AT) was blazed up its slopes.

You'll follow that route, now the Major Welch Trail, up the mountain. Walk behind the Bear Mountain Inn, an impressive rustic lodge listed on the National Register of Historic Places. You'll see the AT's white blazes lead down to the paved path around Hessian Lake, where the British disposed of the Continental Army's casualties. You'll also see the yellow blazes of the Suffern-Bear Mountain Trail and the red dot on white of the Major Welch Trail, all on the same lampposts.

The yellow and red blazes lead up to the southwest corner of the lake and then turn right to follow another paved path above its western shore and below some impressive rock outcrops. Eventually the pavement ends as the ascent remains gentle. Near the north end of the lake, 0.5 mile into the hike, the blazes turn left onto a narrower footpath that, after a slight ascent, leads to another long traverse that eventually crosses the outlet brook of the water tank that feeds the lake. This is a delightful place to stop for a rest, and you may feel like prolonging your visit here before continuing with the climb.

The traverse continues out onto the mountain's north slope for another 0.4 mile before turning sharply left up a long, steep rocky chute. At the top, there is a brief leveling off, then more of the same cycle. You will be using your hands and feet to work your way up long, smooth patches of pre-Cambrian bedrock, either along the edges or through their crevices, for the next 0.3 mile to your reward for all this: a section with wide-open views of Canada Hill, the Hudson, and Popolopen Torne to the north and east. Farther up, after some longer flat stretches, these vistas begin to include the bridge as well, and, in some areas, Long Mountain at the head of the gorge to the northwest.

After one brief stretch of woods, rough stone steps lead up to the summit access road. Cross it, and there's more climbing and occasional views. Finally, the brutal ascent ends on the level summit, graced with scrubby chestnut oak and maple, open areas, and large glacial erratics. You pass the mountain's 1,284-foot height of land in one open area about at the middle of the plateau, but at this point, just off the heels of climbing 900 feet in about a mile, the peakbagging experience of hitting the exact summit may no longer seem so urgent.

You will cross a gravel road and start to hear and see traffic bound for the summit. It isn't much farther. The red dots cross the road just shy of the restrooms, with the very welcome sight of a row of vending machines offering not only cold bottled water, but also sports drinks and soda. A paved path takes the trail over to the observatory complex at the west end of the summit plateau, with a sweeping view over Harriman to the west and the full length of Dunderberg, with the adjacent Timp and its steep slopes, to the south.

The trail you've followed up was named for William A. Welch, first superintendent of the Palisades Interstate Park Commission in 1912. He oversaw the development of the park into what you've seen already, and later served as

Look for a view of the Bear Mountain Bridge from an overlook on the Major Welch Trail.

one of the first chairmen of the Appalachian Trail Conference. In that capacity, he developed the combined A and T that serves as the Appalachian Trail's trademarked logo today.

Look for the logo on the rock outcrops on the south of the viewpoint. The AT descends from there into the lush woods, past an old pipeline, and then up to cross the road into a shrubby, scrubby forest more like the ones you came up through. In the next 0.5 mile, the trail skips between switchbacks on the road, passing through meadows where views open up across the river to Anthony's Nose with the Bear Mountain Bridge Road rising and falling across its face, Peekskill, and Haverstraw Bay. In some of these areas, you may notice that shortcuts have been opened up between the AT's own switchbacks. They may seem tempting, but stay on the trail to avoid further damage to the environment.

Eventually the trail reaches a paved extension of the road and follows it for 0.3 mile to a cul-de-sac. A sign on a large trash container there depicts the New York–New Jersey Trail Conference's efforts to fortify this section of the AT, the oldest and one of the most heavily used.

Keep these efforts in mind as you reach the end of the road and turn back into the woods along a deeply rutted old woods road, and then into a parklike white pine grove. The next sections of trail (again with visible shortcuts that should be avoided) descend, sometimes steeply, through rocky areas with serious erosion damage. A relocation of the trail after the pine grove is expected to open on June 5, 2010, which is National Trails Day. It will lead south past a waterfall to some more viewpoints and down stone steps. It is part of a more extensive relocation of the AT planned for later in the year that will eliminate all the road walks on Bear Mountain.

Eventually the trail bottoms out, still following a wider path than the AT typically does, in an area of tall trees where it is joined from the right by the yellow-blazed Suffern-Bear Mountain Trail, near the northern end of its own 23-mile trip across the two parks. With the park's fields and other facilities visible (and sometimes audible) through the trees, the combined white and yellow blazes cross a wide brook, then follow it down to a road that forks off to the left.

The AT's blazes are signed for the higher road to the top of the old ski jump, but the trail it follows is also signed as closed and currently it is better to take the lower road to near the bottom of the ski jump, where it comes out of the woods to the parking lot across the grass. The AT and S-BM trails turn left here to reach the lake.

MORE INFORMATION

Restrooms are located at Bear Mountain Inn (when it is open) and at the summit. Dogs must be muzzled and kept on leashes 6 feet or shorter. Bear Mountain State Park, Palisades Interstate Park Commission, Bear Mountain, NY, 10911; 845-786-2701; www.nysparks.com/parks/13/details.aspx.

TRIP 13
MANITOGA/THE RUSSEL WRIGHT DESIGN CENTER

Location: Garrison, NY
Rating: Moderate
Distance: 2.2 miles
Elevation Gain: 500 feet
Estimated Time: 1.5 hours
Maps: USGS West Point; New York–New Jersey Trail Conference East Hudson Trails, Map #101; detailed local map available at trailhead kiosk and online at the Manitoga/The Russel Wright Design Center website

This hike follows trails built by a groundbreaking American industrial designer to carefully selected views and scenery on a rehabilitated quarry, as well as to one of America's earliest environmentally sustainable houses.

DIRECTIONS
From the east end of the Bear Mountain Bridge, take Route 9D north 2.5 miles to the entrance to Manitoga, signed as the Russel Wright Design Center, on the right. Parking is available for ten to fifteen vehicles. *GPS coordinates:* 41° 20.896′ N, 73° 57.155′ W.

By train, take the Metro-North Hudson Line to Manitou. Let the conductor know you're planning to get off here, since only one exit is available. Cross the tracks and follow Manitou Station Road to the wooded area. After passing the marsh on the left, take the gated road. Follow the white blazes into Outward Bound's Manitou Point Preserve. Follow that road uphill to Route 9D and turn left. The parking area is on the right, 0.6 mile ahead.

TRAIL DESCRIPTION
After becoming a successful homeware designer, Russel Wright and his wife, Mary, built a home on 79 acres of a rundown quarry south of Garrison. The granite from this quarry was mined to build the New York Public Library.

Wright and his wife wanted to heal and restore the land, which had been extensively logged. When they were done, they named it Manitoga, which means "place of the Great Spirit" in the Iroquois language.

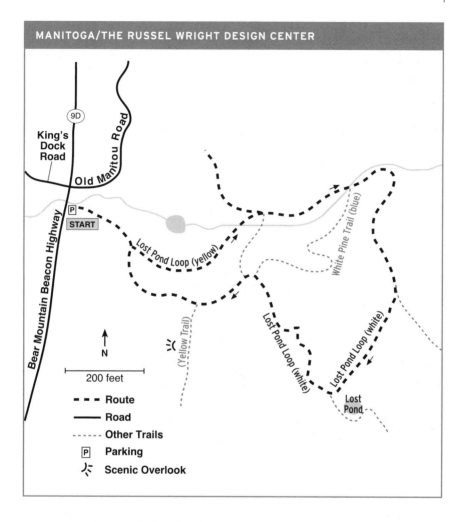

MANITOGA/THE RUSSEL WRIGHT DESIGN CENTER

In 1975, the year before his death, Wright opened the land to hikers. Today, it is a designated National Historic Landmark, the only one in Putnam County.

Follow the signs to the paths through Mary's Meadow, named after Wright's wife. Take the longest of the three trails, the white-blazed Lost Pond Loop, to nearly the top of the ridge.

Wright drew on his artistic background, particularly his early experience as a Broadway set designer, when he created the trails. Kathleen LaFrank, a local expert, has described Manitoga's woods as "especially tactile: there are things to touch, to hear, to see, and to smell, and there are places in which the volume of the space is an important part of the design."

Buried in the woods near the trailhead is Dragon Rock, the former home of Russel and Mary Wright. It was designed to blend in with the landscape.

Since Wright meant for the trails to be experienced in one direction (clockwise), begin climbing into the woods at the sign with the map. Markers with black dots in the middle indicate you are going the wrong way. From the meadow, the trail ascends through a mature forest of oak and maple, then into a brushy, rocky area high over the pond past large boulders. It comes down steadily and crosses the pond's inflow stream at a wooden bridge. Wright chose this spot for the view upstream, just after the red-blazed Deer Run Trail leaves to the right. Across the bridge is a short, yellow-blazed side trail on the left that leads to Sunset Osio. *Osio*, an Iroquois word for viewpoint, is what Wright preferred to call the vistas he created. In this case, he wanted to highlight the way the two large boulders and trees frame the sunset.

The trail continues uphill along an old woods road until it levels out. After another stream crossing, the blue-blazed White Pine Trail leaves to the right and the Lost Pond Loop continues to ascend, following an old road. It begins to level out again amid a forest of chestnut oak, maple, and hemlock. After a small clearing created by recent deadfall, it drops down to cross another stream. A sign indicates that a path along the stream goes uphill to the Osborne Loop and Appalachian Trail in Hudson Highlands State Park.

Turn left, climbing again, and follow the trail as it enters a rougher, rockier area where it is not always easy to see the next marker. By design, the trail is not maintained for the 300 yards to Lost Pond, in order to make its appearance climactic and surprising.

The pond, at the property's highest point, echoes the Dragon Rock Pond, beneath Wright's house at the trailhead, on a smaller scale, with rocky cliffs at one end topped by hemlocks. You may explore it further via the marked AT-connector trail that goes along the other side. Watch for snakes, which like to sun themselves on the rocks. There is also a narrow view up the Hudson to Wind-Gate, the bend between Storm King and Breakneck Ridge, from the woods near the trail along the pond.

The trail descends more steeply than it rose, meandering through different forest types, until it reaches the Four Corners. At Four Corners, the red and blue trails rejoin the loop in a wide grassy area framed by tall oak trees. This area reminded Wright of a cathedral, so he put some benches here.

The combined trails again descend. Another yellow-blazed side trail departs to the left. It leads up to stone steps and the Chestnut Oak Osio, where trees and branches frame a view of the Hudson toward West Point.

Continue to go down the Lost Pond Loop, past some large rocks and through muddy areas. You will return to the far end of Mary's Meadow and then the parking lot. You may or may not have visited Wright's house, but you've definitely experienced his hiking trails—works of art he created with nature as his raw material.

MORE INFORMATION

Restrooms are located at the trailhead. House tour tickets are available online at the Brown Paper Tickets website, www.brownpapertickets.org. Nonmember fees: $15 for adults, $13 for seniors, and $5 for children 12 and under. Manitoga/The Russel Wright Design Center, 584 Route 9D, Garrison, NY 10524; 845-424-3812; www.russelwrightcenter.org.

TRIP 14
BLUE MOUNTAIN RESERVATION

Location: Peekskill, NY
Rating: Moderate
Distance: 4.0 miles
Elevation Gain: 630 feet
Estimated Time: 3.0 hours
Maps: USGS Peekskill; trail map available online or at entrance kiosk

Explore a striking post-glacial landscape just south of the Hudson Highlands.

DIRECTIONS

Exit Route 9 at Welcher Avenue. Turn right and drive uphill to the reservation entrance just east of Washington Street. If there is an attendant in the booth, pay the parking fee ($8 for non-Westchester residents, $4 for residents), and follow the road ahead uphill and around the lake past the lodge to the parking lot with room for 100 vehicles. *GPS coordinates*: 41° 16.196′ N, 73° 55.301′ W.

Bee-Line Bus Routes 14 and 17 stop at Washington and Welcher, and the Croton-Harmon Metro-North station on the Hudson Line.

TRAIL DESCRIPTION

Located at the opposite corner of Westchester County, Blue Mountain Reservation, the county's second largest park, presents an interesting contrast to Ward Pound Ridge Reservation, its largest.

Pound Ridge is in the middle of a largely rural area of horse country. Blue Mountain is just outside a small city. The roads into Pound Ridge are well paved and smooth. Blue Mountain's access road is heavily potholed.

So, it might be no surprise that another major difference is that while Pound Ridge is well known to hikers in the Tri-State area, Blue Mountain isn't. Its primary user community has been mountain bikers, especially those from New York City who enjoy its ease of access via train and bus, and Westchester county distributes a map that area mountain bikers' organizations have compiled. But there is no reason hikers shouldn't come here for its interesting post-glacial landscape and the views available from Blue Mountain itself, at the east end of the property.

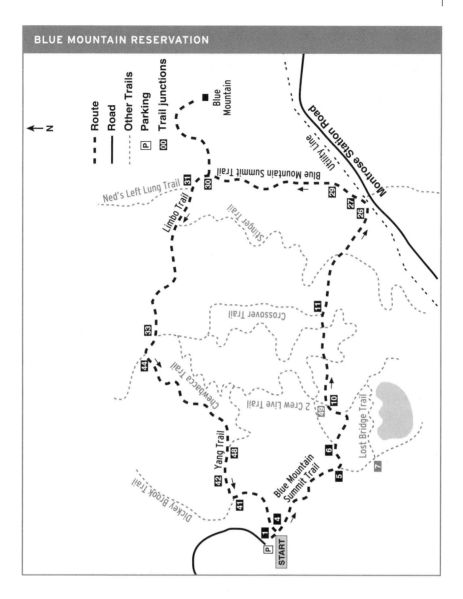

BLUE MOUNTAIN RESERVATION

From the parking lot, begin at Junction 1. You will be going uphill slowly, and almost as soon as you start you will pass a wide yellow-blazed route on the left at Junction 4.

Like Pound Ridge, Blue Mountain's trail map is dependent on numbered intersections. Unlike Pound Ridge, those numbers are not always present at junctions, and there are many more junctions than shown on the mountain biker-compiled map, especially with a lot of short bike trails, so there is some uncertainty as you hike along. Blazes are used but they are not always consistent. This route follows what is signed on the trails to make a loop to Blue Mountain and back.

As you follow the old road labeled as the Blue Mountain Summit Trail through the tall trees of this section of lowland woods, blazed with blue and green, you'll see the extent to which the reservation is marked by past glacier activity. Turn left at junction 5 (the blue and green blazes turn here as well) and, as you wind through the woods here, you'll pass a combination of small hillocks and kettle holes, the depressions in the ground created by chunks of melting glacier. In wet seasons they often become very large puddles (breeding places for mosquitoes in late summer), and are usually at least a little muddy.

You should have no problem spotting junction 11, with the Crossover Trail, and continuing ahead. The landscape is never dull. You wind on and on past large rock outcrops and kettle holes until you reach a swampy area, and then reach the gas pipeline easement shown on the map.

Here the green blazes, part of the Briarcliff-Peekskill Trailway, break with the blue ones and depart for Teatown Lake and points south. The blue continues along the middle of the easement for 0.1 mile until it re-enters the woods at another wide road, an intersection that corresponds to junction 27 on the map.

This route stays level, but the woods to the right gradually begin to slope up, indicating the nearby presence of Blue Mountain itself. At a bend in the trail just past a small pond, a large gold-on-brown arrow points right to the foot trail up the mountain.

Occasional white blazes mark the path. Here you will pass between large glacial erratics on either side before you start to climb steeply about 200 feet up to an area of more typical Highlands mountain forest of scrub oak and maple. After another small pond on the right, the trail levels slightly and another arrow points left.

The location of the viewing ledge is self-evident from here. A gap in the trees gives you a nice view west and northwest to Dunderberg, Bear, and Anthony's Nose. You really can't see out over the city of Peekskill itself, but the sections of Peekskill Bay just off it are visible.

This isn't the top of the mountain. The white blazes continue to lead up through a cleft in the rock opposite the viewing ledge to an area with an old stone shelter, campsite, and a small pond. There the path sort of peters out, near some rock outcrops that mark the mountain's summit.

Returning down to the main trail again, turn right and proceed through a muddy area to the road to the left, roughly corresponding to the Limbo Trail

Blue Mountain provides an unobstructed view of Bear Mountain, which lies on the other side of the Hudson River.

and junction 31. It strings its way between dramatic outcrops and kettle holes, and there are enough turns and junctions that it's hard to tell whether you've reached the other end of the Crossover Trail. If you stick with the numbered markers, you'll reach junction 44, where a mountain bike trail called Yang goes downhill to the left.

This takes you between some truly impressive rocks, twists, and turns past other bits of scenery. There are faint aqua blazes, and if you follow them right, you'll descend steadily to an area where another trail parallels across an old stone wall, then joins Yang where the two pass through a gap. After further twisting and turning past more rocky areas, the trail eventually parallels a larger stream and finally comes out at junction 41, the yellow-blazed Dickey Brook Trail, amid a forest of primeval tall trees.

Turn left here. The trail takes a very wide curve about 0.2 mile uphill and back to junction 4, where it's a right turn and a hundred feet to the parking lot.

MORE INFORMATION
Restrooms are located near the entrance booth (turn right and the pavilion is amid picnic grounds on left). Blue Mountain Reservation, Welcher Avenue, Peekskill, NY 10566; 914-862-5275; www.westchestergov.com/parks.

THE WILD TURKEY

The wild turkey shares the same scientific name, *Meleagris gallopavo*, as its domestic counterpart. But that's one of the few things they have in common.

For one thing, the wild turkey can fly quite well. When provoked or frightened, it takes off at speeds of up to 50 MPH, flying very close to the ground and thus making it difficult to see, much less shoot. You may observe this for yourself if you get too close to a gaggle of turkeys waddling about in the woods or strutting across a road. They will also likely make their gobbling sound extremely loud, audible for nearly a mile.

A popular bit of historical folklore holds that Benjamin Franklin promoted the turkey as a more preferable national bird to symbolize the United States than the bald eagle. The truth is that in a letter to his daughter he criticized Congress for choosing the eagle, which he considered a "rank coward" since it stole fish that other birds had hunted and was easily chased away by sparrows. But his letter was written while he was U.S. ambassador to France, spending most of his time in Paris and unable to lobby. His larger intent was to criticize the Society of the Cincinnati, an association of officers from the French and American forces chaired by George Washington, which had also adopted the eagle as its symbol.

Franklin accurately described the turkey as a "true original native of America." He considered it more exemplary of what he considered to be American virtues, in particular the courage to "attack a grenadier of the British Guards who should presume to invade his farmyard."

The wild turkey has established itself extensively across the woodlands of the Eastern United States because of its adaptability to many different habitats. You are as likely to see one or more in swampy lowlands near Long Island Sound as on rocky ridges in the Kittatinies. Often thought of as unthreatening herbivores because they are seen eating grasses and acorns, they are in fact omnivores who eat insects and sometimes small snakes and amphibians.

Unrestricted hunting and loss of habitat took such a toll on wild turkeys that by the turn of the twentieth century, there were no more than 30,000 of them in the entire country, according to estimates by contemporary game managers. Many states barred hunting of the birds in order to protect them from extinction.

Today, wild turkey may be hunted legally, in season, in every state except Alaska. It is now estimated that there are 7 million wild turkeys in the United States.

TRIP 15
TEATOWN LAKE RESERVATION

Location: Ossining, NY
Rating: Moderate
Distance: 1.7 miles
Elevation Gain: 220 feet
Estimated Time: 1.0 hour
Maps: USGS Ossining; trail map available at nature center

Get up close and personal with wildlife at this delightful little nature preserve.

DIRECTIONS
From the Taconic State Parkway, get off at Route 134 and go east. Make the sharp right onto Spring Valley Road 0.2 mile east of the parkway. Follow it around for roughly a mile to the nature center and parking lot with space for approximately 40 vehicles *GPS coordinates*: 41° 12.671′ N, 73° 49.635′ W.

From Route 9 in downtown Ossining, turn right on Croton Avenue (Route 133). A half-mile down the road, Route 134 forks left as Dale Avenue, later becoming Hawkes Avenue. At Route 9A it turns right to briefly join that road, and then turns left at the next intersection as Croton Dam Road. A left turn at Allapartus Road a mile farther on will take you to Spring Valley Road, where a right turn leads to the nature center and parking lot.

TRAIL DESCRIPTION
Tucked into the hills east of Ossining, Teatown Lake Reservation offers something uncommon among hiking destinations: the chance to preview your hike in 3-D (without having to put on those bothersome glasses).

Inside the impressive Tudor-style house next to the parking lot that serves as its visitor center and headquarters, there's a gift shop where you can get a free black-and-white trail map or buy a color version for $2. Across from the counter, in a plastic display case, is a wooden relief model of the map showing *everything*. You can see where you'll be going, and how much climbing you'll be doing, on this loop around the lake and up the hill.

If you can't wait until you get there, the answer is not much climbing, but enough to be interesting. Teatown Lake packs a lot in its 834 acres, started by a

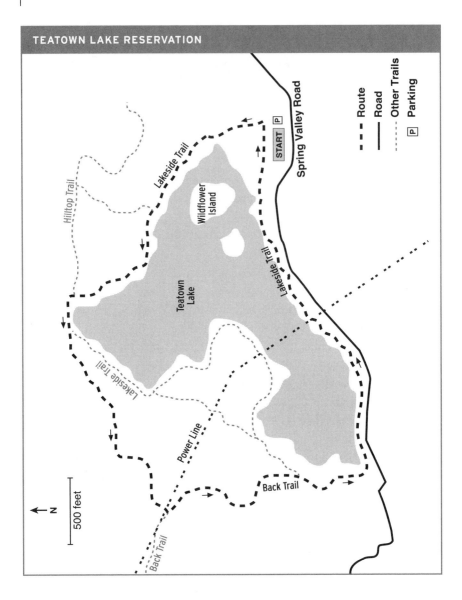

TEATOWN LAKE RESERVATION

194-acre gift from a local family in 1963. Built around the 33-acre lake it takes its name from, its extensive research and educational programs have made it a popular stop for families and school groups in east central Westchester.

Behind the nature center, follow the signs down to the blue-blazed Lakeside Trail. When you get there, you'll see Wildflower Island off to the left just offshore. Its partially covered bridge is locked, since tours are available by appointment only. If you have time, you might want to go to the visitor center and inquire about making one. It's worth it, even if you have to come back another day.

Turn left and follow the Lakeside Trail along the lake's east shore. After 0.3 mile along the lake, you'll reach the dam where Bailey Brook, a tributary of the Croton River, flows out. The orange-blazed Hilltop Trail comes in from the right. Turn left to stay with the Lakeside Trail as it crosses the brook below the dam on a small bridge. At the end, where it re-enters the woods, the Lakeside Trail turns left to follow the lake. You will continue straight ahead on the white-blazed Cliffdale–Teatown Trail, going uphill along another old road to where a black-blazed shortcut trail branches off to the left and follows a stone wall farther uphill past some stands of gray birch.

The trail levels out after 0.2 mile, crossing under one of the two power lines that cross the reservation, their wires buzzing with electricity generated at Indian Point. In the narrow woods between the two lines, the black trail ends at a yellow and green-blazed trail, the concurrent route of the Briarcliff–Peekskill and Northwest trails.

Turn left and follow the trails out of the woods and onto one of the dirt roads used to reach the power lines, and then back into the woods. The trail rounds a small, rocky knob, then descends alongside a small creek to eventually re-intersect with the Lakeside Trail.

Here the Northwest Trail and its yellow blazes end. They are replaced by the green ones of the Briarcliff–Peekskill Trailway, which passes through the reservation on its way from Briarcliff Manor in the south to Blue Mountain Reservation in the north. Turn right and follow the blue and green blazes.

Follow them down to the end of the lake, where the Briarcliff–Peekskill Trailway continues ahead while the Lakeside Trail turns left. Follow it out onto a 700-foot boardwalk (with guardrails) that floats across this end of the lake, with a viewing platform near its south end. You can best appreciate Teatown Lake from here, with the far shore, Wildflower Island, and power lines making a sweeping panorama. Herons frequently perch here in summertime waiting for sufficiently unwary fish, and you may be surprised how close you'll get before they take off.

Local lore traces the slightly unusual name for the lake and hill to a story that reads like the Boston Tea Party in reverse. It seems that a local had stashed a large hoard of contraband tea in his house at the outset of the Revolution. As the story goes, while he and his fellow freedom fighters easily made the transition to drinking coffee instead, their wives could not. The wives barricaded themselves in the house with the tea and sent word to their husbands that they

A great blue heron looks out over Teatown Lake.

would come out as long as the tea was shared. The small settlement where this happened carried the name Teatown even after it faded away into just another corner of Yorktown (where the reservation is actually located, despite its mailing address).

From the end of the boardwalk, the trail continues east along the south lakeshore. The magenta-blazed Lakeside Overlook Trail forks off about 250 feet east of the boardwalk, giving you the option of looking out over the lake from the tops of the rock ledges both trails pass. Lakeside Overlook Trail runs next to Spring Valley Road and passing traffic, however, while the Lakeside Trail remains along the shore.

Eventually you pass under the power lines again and, after 0.2 mile, reach a red trail that goes up to the right through hemlock groves to the parking lot.

MORE INFORMATION

Restrooms are located in the nature center at the trailhead. Trails are open from dawn until dusk. Dogs must be leashed. Teatown Lake Reservation, 1600 Spring Valley Road, Ossining, NY 10562; 914-762-2912; www.teatown.org.

Location: Yorktown, NY
Rating: Moderate
Distance: 1.8 miles
Elevation Gain: 400 feet
Estimated Time: 1.5 hours
Maps: USGS Mohegan Lake and Ossining

Excellent views and varied terrain make this small nature preserve in northern Westchester County an ideal short loop.

DIRECTIONS

Exit the Taconic State Parkway at Underhill Avenue. Go south 1 mile to Croton Lake Road (Route 129). Turn left and follow along the north shore of Croton Reservoir to Saw Mill River Road (Route 118). Turn left and travel 1 mile north to Locke Avenue. The preserve sign is on the left, opposite Croton Heights Road. Follow Locke Avenue uphill 0.2 mile to the trailhead lot. *GPS coordinates:* 41° 14.779′ N, 73° 47.495′ W.

Westchester's Bee-Line Bus routes 12 and 15 stop at the corner of Locke Avenue and Route 118, except on Sundays when they do not operate in that area. Route 12 also offers connecting service on the Metro-North Harlem Line from the Mount Kisco station.

TRAIL DESCRIPTION

A short hike with moderate climbs takes you to Turkey Mountain's 832-foot summit, and possibly the best views of any trail in Westchester County. The preserve is a small tract (125 acres) but within its former farmland are some diverse forest types. An open-air classroom has been built off the trail for the benefit of local school districts, which frequently take students here for field trips during the school year.

The land, sections of which have been used as ski trails, farmland, and a summer camp, was acquired by the town to protect it from development. The Yorktown Land Trust, a citizen group founded in 1986 to preserve open space in the town, handles maintenance of trails. The group publishes several

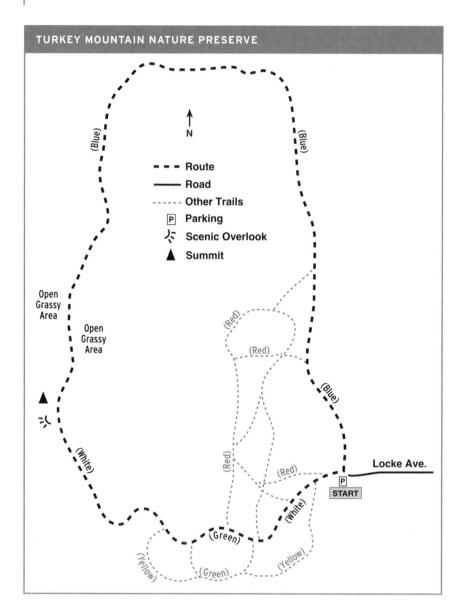

TURKEY MOUNTAIN NATURE PRESERVE

Route
Road
Other Trails
P Parking
Scenic Overlook
Summit

(Blue)

(Blue)

Open Grassy Area
Open Grassy Area

(Red)

(Red)

(Blue)

(White)

(Red)

(Red)

Locke Ave.

P

START

(White)

(Green)

(Yellow)

(Green)

(Yellow)

leaflets, including one that serves as a guidebook to Turkey Mountain and the town's other "quiet areas." (Send an email to yorktownlandtrust@gmail.com. to request a leaflet.)

The trail system consists of a network of short trails, which are ideal for very young children and educational purposes, but also a comparatively longer loop comprised of the blue- and white-blazed trails.

Start on the blue trail, which leaves from the north side of the parking lot. Well blazed and well maintained, it descends through a wet area after which the preserve's red trail comes in from the west, followed by a blue connector trail. Continuing north, the blue trail begins to slowly edge uphill through a mature forest of towering oaks and maples. Eventually, some scenic rock outcrops become visible. A neighboring power line and its right-of-way are visible through the trees.

The trail continues on a moderate climb and its well-marked blue blazes leave you no doubt about which way you are supposed to go. As the trail ascends, the forest begins to seem more like those of the Hudson Highlands to the north, and less like the local backyards.

The ridgeline becomes closer and closer too, with the sky appearing through the trees. Finally, the trail reaches a turn where it can breach the rock storey along the ridge crest and goes up the chute, turning almost 270 degrees in the process. Here it levels out and the woods become more open. The trail briefly descends slightly into a thicker patch, and then climbs back up into a more open, grassy area that hints at what views might be had but never gives them. After several more twists and turns through some shrubbier areas, it finally splits into three closely separated routes, using the bare rock for blazes more frequently than the accompanying trees. You'll want to take the middle trail, which leads you right out to the footings of the former fire tower at the mountain's summit. This is marked by a USGS benchmark set into the rock.

This is a good place to sit down, rest, eat, and drink. It's not the highest point in Westchester, an honor that goes to a viewless hill in North Salem's Mountain Lakes Camp, but you'd be forgiven for thinking it was.

To the south, the lush hills that surround Chappaqua, Mount Kisco, and Ossining seem to go on forever. Closer by, on the southeast, you can view some of Croton Reservoir, a fragment of the Taconic Parkway, and one of the bridges that carries it across the reservoir. On the west, the hills of Pound Ridge Reservation loom, and to the east are Hook Mountain and High Tor across the Hudson River. Bear Mountain, Anthony's Nose, and the other peaks of the Hudson Highlands near Peekskill are just to their north. When it's clear, you can see the ridges of the Shawangunks on the far horizon.

When you finally decide to descend, you'll be going down the white-blazed trail. At first, it goes down the steep east face of the ridge, with a relatively open canopy allowing further views in that direction. Upon an abrupt turn to the right and down a short chute, it suddenly enters a mature, open forest in an area bounded by a stone wall on the south side, a sign that this section

From the summit of Turkey Mountain, visitors can get an expansive view of the Palisades.

once was farmland. There are hemlocks here and even a few cedars, as the trail continues to lose elevation in a wide curve.

Once the trail reaches level ground, several junctions with shorter trails are close by. The yellow trail comes in from the right and then, 0.1 mile later, the short green trail comes in on the same side. Since it's a circular route, the yellow and green trails join the white-blazed trail at a low, wet area as they go over two sections of puncheons, or split-log walkways.

After returning to dry land, the trail begins climbing slightly. The green loop departs into the woods again, and then 0.1 mile later a short side trail leads to the classroom with rustic benches in a small natural amphitheater. The red trail leads left after another 0.1 mile The white trail turns to the north again, bending east where the yellow trail comes back in from the right through a wide, grassy area. Head straight another 0.1 mile and you're back in the parking lot.

MORE INFORMATION

There are no restrooms. Turkey Mountain Nature Preserve does not have a website. Information is available at the Yorktown Land Trust website, www .townlink.com/community_web/yorktown/landtrust/. The trust can be reached via email at yorktownlandtrust@gmail.com.

Location: Pawling, NY
Rating: Difficult
Distance: 5.9 miles
Elevation Gain: 858 feet
Estimated Time: 5.0 hours
Maps: USGS Pawling; trail map available at entrance kiosk

Follow a section of the Appalachian Trail through fields with beautiful views of the Harlem Valley and a very diverse nature reserve.

DIRECTIONS

From the northern terminus of I-684, continue on Route 22 north past Route 55. Turn right onto Route 68/North Quaker Hill Road. Stay on Route 68 and turn left onto Quaker Lake Road. Continue 1.2 miles and the parking lot will be on your left. Parking is available at the pullout spots on Route 22/55 just north of the trail crossing, 2 miles north of Pawling. There is room for twenty vehicles in the parking areas on either side of the highway just to the north. Another five spots are near the train station lot on the west side of the highway just south of the nursery. *GPS coordinates: 41° 35.564′ N, 73° 35.265′ W.*

By train, take the Metro-North Harlem Line to the Appalachian Trail request station. On weekends, or weekdays when it is not rush hour, it is necessary to change trains at the Southeast station, where electrification ends. Remember to purchase your ticket before boarding to avoid a surcharge. The trail itself crosses the tracks at the station and can be followed from there.

TRAIL DESCRIPTION

Approximately 65 miles north of the city, but nonetheless accessible via commuter rail, is the Pawling Nature Reserve. This 1,060-acre Nature Conservancy property sits on a ridge top in bucolic southeastern Dutchess County. A section of the Appalachian Trail runs through it, providing a backbone for a small local trail system and a nice loop route that approaches the reserve from the south and the train station.

The reserve has been protected since the late 1950s, when a local citizens' group, the Akin Hall Association, acquired the land and donated it to the

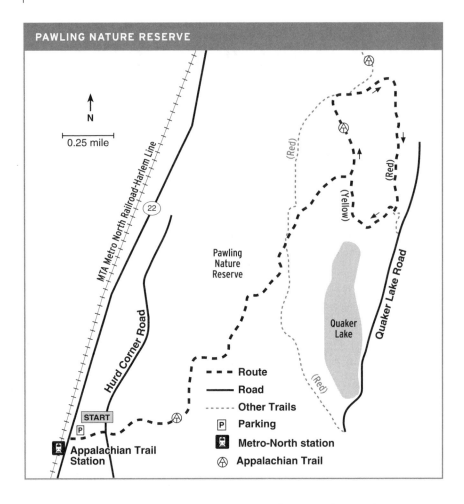

PAWLING NATURE RESERVE

conservancy. Its woodlands harbor a number of plant and animal species considered threatened in New York State.

From the train station or parking area, pick up the Appalachian Trail (AT), marked by the same white blazes used for its entire length. The AT extends 2,175 miles from Springer Mountain in Georgia to Mount Katahdin in Maine. From the informational kiosk on the east side of the highway, the trail gently climbs the side of the field ahead with blazes painted on regular wooden posts. There may be livestock grazing in the fields. If you are hiking with a dog, you may wish to leash it while in this area.

The trail reaches Hurd Corner Road 0.25 mile uphill. A stile bridges the electric fence on one side and a stone wall on the other. Ahead is a solitary water tower, which is no longer in use but is maintained as a trail landmark. Through the field you follow the trail's tread and the posted blazes up and then down to another stile that takes you to a shrubby area where you cross a stream on a small wooden bridge. After another stile, you are in a muddy corner of the next field, with some puncheons (split-log walkways) taking the trail over the wettest spots.

If you like these sections of the AT through the fields on the way up and down, thank the farmers and the National Park Service (NPS). For years, the AT either followed roads or went through forests. Despite much shorter routes through fields between trailheads, farmers often refused to allow the trail to cross their land due to concerns about liability and the effect on crops and livestock. The AT had to go up the highway and back down Hurd Corner Road to what is now the blue trail that joins it at the entrance to the reserve.

The NPS worked out leasing arrangements that alleviated farmers' concerns. Trail workers built stiles over fences so humans (and dogs) could cross freely while farm animals remain confined. Today, the trail frequently stays off the roads, and hikers appreciate the change of pace the fields offer from the many "green tunnel" sections of unbroken woods.

The trail continues to edge up the side of the field. The scenery to the south is delightfully pastoral; most of the year it's difficult not to stop and take pictures, especially if there are some cows nearby.

After climbing another stile over an electric fence, the trail continues uphill. The woods on the north side end, opening to spectacular views over the Harlem Valley. In the middle of this field, the ground starts to level off as the trail turns left and crosses the edge of the woods ahead, and then turns uphill again to almost the back corner.

At 0.8 mile, another kiosk welcomes you to the Pawling Nature Reserve. Sometimes there are maps in the box; if not, consider taking a digital photograph of the detailed map on the kiosk so you can review it later if the display on your camera is large enough. A blue-blazed side trail comes in from the left as the AT crosses a stream and then climbs through grassy areas, which were formerly farmland. A mature hardwood forest with some beech trees appears as the trail begins to traverse the side of Hammersly Ridge.

At a stone wall, the trail begins to follow some switchbacks up steeper terrain to the top of the ridge. The woods here are a bit scrubbier, more like the Hudson Highlands. The viewless summit of Hammersly, 1.5 miles from the trailhead, is just off the trail.

Continuing on, 0.25 mile to the north the reserve's Red Trail intersects. Stay on the AT. You will pass both the Yellow Trail and a swampy area with red maple. Almost a mile from its first junction, the Red Trail joins the AT again and takes a long curve to smooth out the 0.7-mile descent to the trailhead near

The Harlem River Valley can be seen from the fields along the Appalachian Trail.

Quaker Lake, where it intersects the Yellow Trail. Turn right and follow the Yellow Trail uphill for your last climb of the hike.

It will be worth it. The trail goes into a steep, hemlock-shaded gorge carved by Duell Hollow Brook, which drains the swampy areas you passed through on the ridge top. Here, plants that are rare in New York State, such as devil's bit or soapwort gentian, and animal communities including six salamander species, thrive among the mossy rocks and pleasant cascades. Hobblebush, not found often in the Hudson Valley outside the higher-elevation Catskills, is also present.

After 0.6 mile, the Yellow Trail ends where you first passed it on the AT. Turn left to make the minimal climb back to the summit of the ridge, and then the rest of the 2.2-mile stretch is all downhill, through those same fields and pastures you passed on the way up.

MORE INFORMATION

There are no restrooms. Open year-round, no fee. Pawling Nature Preserve, Quaker Lake Road, Pawling, NY 12564; 914-244-3271; www.nature.org/newyork.

THE CHESTNUT OAK

It's hard to miss the chestnut oak (*Quercus prinus*, also called "rock oak") as you hike in the woods of the New York–New Jersey Highlands. Its leaves, which gave the tree its name, strongly resemble the tooth-edged leaves of American chestnuts. Even without looking at its leaves, you can distinguish it by its unique bark. It is gray and less finely detailed than the skins of other species of oak.

Chestnut oak bark is the thickest of any oak species in eastern North America. The tree tends to need this extra protection, because while its range is from Maine to Mississippi, it is generally found on mountains and ridges, where inclement weather is common. The thick texture of the bark helps protect it from these severe conditions. The name "rock oak" comes from its tendency to sometimes grow in extremely rocky areas, like those found in some sections of the Highlands and farther north in a few locations of the Catskills.

A close relative, the swamp chestnut oak (*Quercus michauxii*) grows in wetlands (and is sometimes grown as an ornamental). However, it lacks the distinctive bark of the chestnut oak. Despite this and other differences, the two are frequently confused and some botanists have argued that the trees are actually the same species.

The preference of the chestnut oak and swamp chestnut to grow in distressed habitats like mountains and swamps also tend to limits their height. Most grow little more than 70 feet tall, although some specimens have reached twice that. Only the taller specimens are considered desirable for use as timber, often sold as "mixed white oak." Like its bark, the chestnut oak's 1–1.5-inch acorns are also distinctive as the largest of any American oak.

An interesting controversy has developed over the chestnut oak's scientific name. Karolus Linnaeus, the father of modern taxonomy who developed the system of identifying all known life forms by a pair of Latin words for their genus and species, gave one of those names to the chestnut oak. But his sample included leaves from several trees; therefore, some botanists consider the *prinus* species designation to be a result of confusion. Several alternative names have been proposed, but none has caught on yet.

TRIP 18
WARD POUND
RIDGE RESERVATION

$ 👟 🐕 🚌 ⛷ 🔖

Location: Cross River, NY
Rating: Moderate
Distance: 3.1 miles
Elevation Gain: 680 feet
Estimated Time: 2.0 hours
Maps: USGS Peach Lake, Pound Ridge; trail map available at trailhead and online

Explore the varied terrain of one of the metropolitan area's largest county parks.

DIRECTIONS

Get off Interstate 684 at Exit 5. Take Route 35 east approximately 3 miles to the junction with Route 121 at the east end of Cross River Reservoir. Turn right and then turn left into the park entrance just over the small bridge over the Cross River. Follow the entrance road to the Trailside Nature Museum and pay the $8 parking fee ($4 for Westchester residents with a Park Pass). Turn right after the booth on the road up Pell Hill. Follow to the south end of the parking lot at the top, next to the playground, with room for twenty vehicles. *GPS coordinates*: 41° 15.295′ N, 73° 35.057′ W.

The Housatonic Area Regional Transit (HART) Katonah-Ridgefield shuttle bus can also be taken from the Metro-North Harlem Line Katonah station to the hamlet of Cross River just west of the 35-121 junction.

TRAIL DESCRIPTION

Tucked into Westchester County's western corner, Ward Pound Ridge Reservation is a popular destination for picnickers and hikers alike. The former have some lovely areas in the center of the park just off the entrance road; the latter have more than 35 miles of trails, some shared with horses.

At 4,315 acres, Pound Ridge Reservation (as it's usually called, since it's mostly in that town; William Ward was the county official who spearheaded the acquisition of the land) is not only the largest park in Westchester; it's the largest county park in the New York metropolitan area. The northern third of

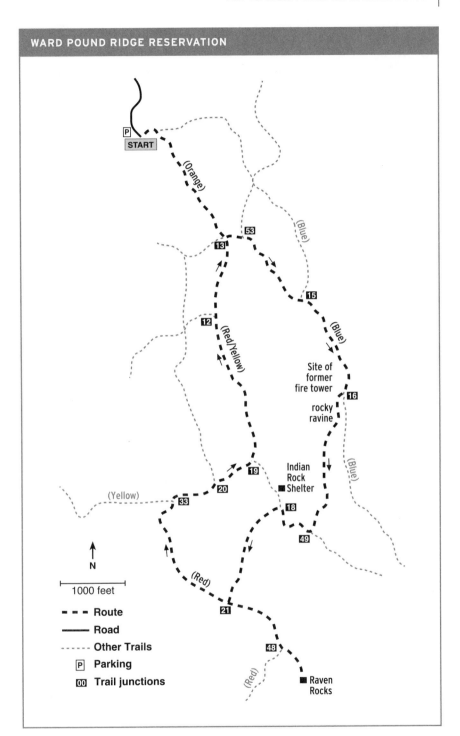

WARD POUND RIDGE RESERVATION

the park is more heavily hiked; the southern two-thirds, which still retain a wilderness feel in parts, are where this hike will take you.

The trail system uses numbered junctions (not always signed) to aid navigation. Some longer trails have colored blazes or markers; shorter trails use white blazes, when marked.

From the parking lot, follow the orange blazes that curve left, alongside the meadow, toward the small clearing with several shelters. Keep bearing left past Shelter 27 and you'll reach a wide white-blazed trail going uphill, to the left. Follow it past the rock outcrops and mountain laurel to junction 15. Turn right on the blue-blazed trail, following an old road.

You'll get into scrubbier higher-elevation forest in the 0.3 mile it takes you to reach the clearing with the water pump and former fire tower footings. At 860 feet above sea level, this is the highest point in both the reservation and the town of Pound Ridge.

Just beyond, at trail junction 16, another white-blazed connector trail leaves to the right. Follow it downhill past a rock cleft and into a small ravine. It continues descending, sometimes on stone steps, into a dense, shrubby area, leveling out at a muddy, picturesque glen filled with fern and skunk cabbage, where you cross a small brook. Ascending again, you reach junction 49. Turn right and continue ascending. In 0.1 mile, you are at junction 18, marked by a small pond on one side and the huge overhang of Indian Rock Shelter on the other.

The shelter is worth stopping to look at. Archeological investigations here have revealed that American Indians did, in fact, use this as a shelter during hunting expeditions as long as 4,000 years ago. In fact, the name Pound Ridge comes from the "pound," where the Indians kept game confined, in the area that is the reservation today.

Settlers later took over the area and farmed some of it. In 1924, Ward, a Port Chester businessman who had served in Congress for a few terms and was the county's Republican chairman for many years, saw the increasing development in southern Westchester and urged the county to acquire and preserve the mostly vacant land. In 1938 his name was added to it in memory of his efforts.

During the Depression it was home to a Civilian Conservation Corps (CCC) camp, which built many of the improvements along the entrance road, like the red pine plantation and museum as well as the shelters, often using the leftover fieldstone from the houses and stone walls the farmers left behind. Today the reservation is home to more than 1,000 different species and helps

These hikers are climbing out of a ravine along a white-blazed side trail in Ward Pound Ridge Reservation.

protect the reservoir's watershed. It has been designated a biodiversity preserve and an Audubon Society Important Bird Area.

After you're done with the shelter, take the white-blazed trail to the left. It climbs gently into a wide sort of terrace next to a rock ledge, which it parallels for 0.3 mile to junction 21. Turn left onto the red trail that follows a wide dirt road.

The trail drops to cross a creek, then climbs back up to meander alongside a small bump until junction 48, where two white trails come in from the left.

You want to take the one that leads through the grassy area to the ledge ahead, about 0.1 mile. This is Raven Rock, with a view over the Stone Hill River below. The Stone Hill flows east and then north around the edge of the reservation to merge with the Waccabuc River and form the Cross River that gives the reservoir and nearby settlement their names. On the other side of the narrow valley are some secluded Pound Ridge backyards and, in the distance, Stamford.

Return to the red trail, and follow it past junction 21, again up and over a gentle bump. This takes you 0.4 mile to junction 33, where another dirt road with yellow markers comes in from the left. You turn right here, drop downhill slightly, and see Shelter 6 in the clearing on your right. The dirt road continues uphill slightly, between two broad bumps, past junction 20, and then descends to junction 19, where the trail from the Indian Rock Shelter comes in.

Turn left, staying with the yellow and red trail, as you descend on the side of a slope with a large swamp visible through the trees to the right. The swamp feeds the stream you crossed on the way down from the former fire tower site. Past the swamp, some impressive stone bluffs appear on the right. After the red and yellow trail turns left at junction 12, continue straight ahead, through a less mature forest that indicates previous use of the land for farming. After 0.2 mile and a few stream crossings, you'll reach shelter 29 and junction 13, and you can return to your vehicle along the path you came in on.

On your drive (or walk) out, stop and check out the fenced-off area in the red pine plantation along the entrance road, another legacy of the CCC presence. This is an area where trees were downed in a 2006 storm; the fence is to keep deer out while an experimental reforestation takes place. Details and progress are noted on a nearby bulletin board.

MORE INFORMATION

Restrooms are located at the trailhead. Dogs must be leashed. Ward Pound Ridge Reservation, Route 35 & 121 South, Cross River, NY 10518; 914-864-7317; www.westchestergov.com/parks.

TRIP 19
NIMHAM MOUNTAIN
STATE FOREST

Location: Kent Lakes, NY
Rating: Moderate
Distance: 1.5 miles
Elevation Gain: 520 feet
Estimated Time: 1.0 hour
Maps: USGS Lake Carmel; at trailhead kiosk

A relatively short trip to Nimham's summit allows you take in the sweeping views of the eastern mid-Hudson from the recently restored fire tower, one of the tallest in the state.

DIRECTIONS
Take Exit 19 from I-84 at Route 312. Travel 1.0 mile south to where it ends at US 6. Turn right and proceed 2.0 miles west to Carmel. At the library and Lake Gleneida, turn right (west) on Route 52. At the very next light, opposite the county courthouse, turn left onto Route 301. Continue west across West Branch Reservoir to Gipsy Trail Road (CR 41). Turn right and go 2.3 miles north to the beginning of the fire tower road on the left, marked by a wooden New York State Department of Environmental Conservation (DEC) shingle. The trailhead lot, with room for ten to fifteen vehicles, is 0.4 mile uphill, where the road is gated. If that lot is full, more parking is available on the right side of Gipsy Trail near the entrance. *GPS coordinates*: 41° 27.244′ N, 73° 43.309′ W.

TRAIL DESCRIPTION
Is it Nimham or Ninham? Both spellings have been used for this mountain in the hinterlands of Putnam County, since both were used for the name of the Munsee chief who once owned the land and fought in court, unsuccessfully, to get it back. After using "Ninham" for many years, New York's Department of Environmental Conservation (DEC) now calls it Nimham Mountain State Forest, per a consensus among local historians that that is the more correct spelling.

The mountain is a fine tribute to the chief's memory. Rising high above its neighbors, its summit is a short climb from the parking area. You will find a 90-foot tall fire tower that offers wide views of the region.

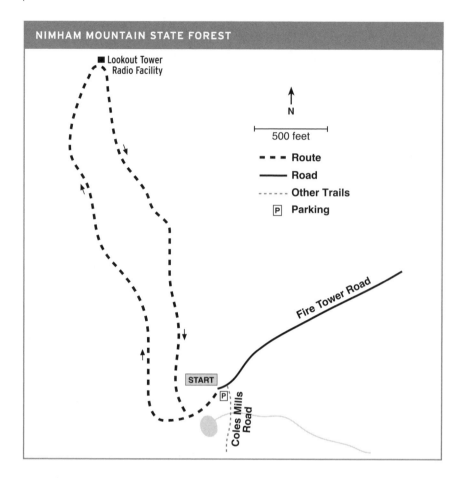

From the trailhead, at the end of the narrow road that used to serve the tower, you continue past the gate and up the road as it curves to the north. The trail ascends slowly but steadily. You can see some of the unofficial trails going off into the woods to your left. Stay on the road as it continues to wind along the slope, regularly crossing paths with the power and phone lines that serve the active telecommunications relays at the summit.

The adjacent woods are mostly hardwoods, dominated by oak and maple. They are original cover to the area, which was never seriously farmed or harvested. Along the lower stretches, some small campsites are visible.

In the middle of the ascent, the road levels off for a short distance, allowing you to relax, before you begin what will be its final ascent. You can see more sky through the trees on your left, indicating that you are getting close to a ridge. The trees grow spindlier and scrubbier, following the example of

Climb the fire tower atop the 1,340-foot Nimham Mountain to get a view of Pine Pond.

high montane forests in this region. As you get closer to the top, you can see property-line markers on the trees at the edge.

Finally, the last section of road opens and you can see the radio and fire tower complex at the summit. The road curves around to end at the small maintenance facility for the radio towers.

In the woods behind the fire tower, a small rock outcrop marks the mountain's height of land at 1,340 feet above sea level. After you celebrate gaining this summit, you may want to climb the fire tower.

Like many of the other fire towers that provided expansive views of New York from the Finger Lakes to the Adirondacks, Nimham's is a story of decline and rebirth. Built in the 1930s by the Civilian Conservation Corps, it was used until a combination of aerial overflights and improved fire prevention made it unnecessary in the years after the Vietnam War. It fell into decay and was considered to be unsafe in the early 1990s.

Area residents banded together to restore the fire tower, which was formally reopened in 2005. Every step features the name of a local donor. The tower stands 90 feet high above the mountain, the tallest fire tower in New York State.

Nimham Mountain offers excellent views due to its relative prominence within the region. Nowhere else in Putnam County can you see so much, all at once.

To the east, Pine Pond looks close enough to wet your feet. The large body of water to the southeast is a section of East Branch Reservoir. A good portion of that view is in Connecticut, and you can pick out some locations in and around Danbury if you know the area well enough. The shopping center near the Route 312 exit on I-84, where you got off the interstate, is also visible.

Looking north you'll see more of the hilly areas of southern Dutchess County within New York City's east-of-Hudson watershed. Patterson's Cranberry Mountain is visible to the northeast. To the south, the lower hills of southern Putnam and northern Westchester unfold.

The most dramatic landscape is to the west. The peaks of the Hudson Highlands on the east side of the river stand out—Sour, the Beacons, Breakneck, and Bull Hill. Scofield Ridge, Putnam County's highest peak, sits in front. It is possible to see the peaks to their west—Storm King, Black Rock, and Schunemunk. On clear days, the Shawangunks can be seen to the northwest, along with Slide Mountain and the other Catskill High Peaks.

After you come down from the fire tower, don't go back down the road. Instead, follow it to the maintenance shed and continue on the trail into the woods.

This is unmarked, but the trail is mostly obvious. There are a few forks in these early stretches. At the first fork you should take the right path; later ones bear left.

Eventually the path develops into a mountain-bike trail, complete with banked turns and jump ramps (but also good corduroy over wet spots). This trail will take you down from the scrubbier forest on the ridge top to taller hardwoods near the saddle between Nimham's main summit and its lesser 1,134-foot one. Past this point it leads into a large, unofficial campsite and then down a set of log steps underneath the utility line back to the road. Turn left, and within 200 feet you are back at the parking lot.

MORE INFORMATION

There are no restrooms. Nimham Mountain State Forest, NYSDEC Region 3 Headquarters, 21 South Putt Corners, New Paltz, NY 12561; 845-831-8780 ext. 309; www.dec.ny.gov/lands/34773.html.

TRIP 20
CLARENCE FAHNESTOCK STATE PARK–
CANOPUS LAKE

Location: Carmel, NY
Rating: Moderate
Distance: 4.6 miles
Elevation Gain: 420 feet
Estimated Time: 3.5 hours
Maps: USGS Oscawana Lake; New York–New Jersey Trail Conference
East Hudson Trails, Map #103; Appalachian Trail New York–New
Jersey #2. Trail map also available online at the Clarence Fahnestock
State Park website

**Hike an isolated section of the Appalachian Trail to a popular view-
point over Clarence Fahnestock State Park.**

DIRECTIONS
Exit the northbound Taconic State Parkway at Route 301. Turn left and follow it
east 1.5 miles to the AT crossing just past the lake. Look for an area to park near
the trailhead on the right side of the road, where you will find room for five to
ten vehicles. If that area is full there is space off-road closer to the lake and on
the other side of the road. *GPS coordinates:* 41° 27.170′ N, 73° 50.250′ W.

TRAIL DESCRIPTION
When Benton MacKaye first began developing the idea for the Appalachian
Trail (AT), he hoped the trail would be the backbone of a series of protected
areas. He envisioned a spine trail, which others could be linked to in order to
make short loops. While the trail has since become known as much for the
thru-hikers who go all the way from Georgia to Maine each year, it still works
just as well as a local route for day-hikers who like to sleep in their own beds
each night.

This trip will give you a sample of the long-distance AT experience as you
hike to the overlook at the north end of Canopus Lake and back. You may have
this section of trail to yourself, but if you are hiking between late June and
mid-July, you might encounter thru-hikers.

The AT's white blazes go north into the woods right next to the lake. At
first it descends slightly, but instead of going down to the nearby water, it turns

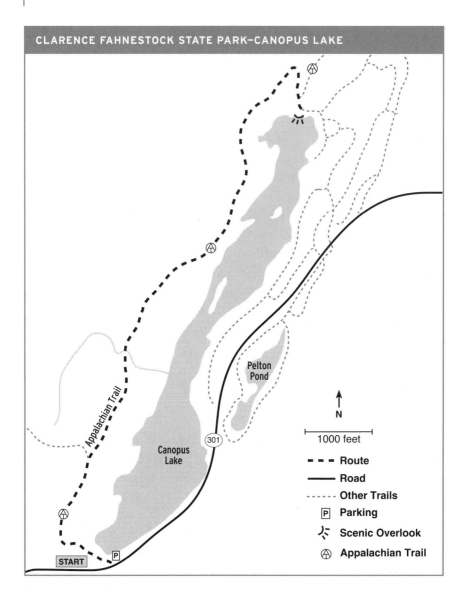

CLARENCE FAHNESTOCK STATE PARK–CANOPUS LAKE

Pelton Pond

N

1000 feet

- - - Route
—— Road
----- Other Trails
P Parking
Scenic Overlook
Appalachian Trail

Canopus Lake

301

Appalachian Trail

START

left to climb back up via a set of stone steps underneath a large rock ledge. It then turns back on the generally northeastward course it follows through the park.

It levels out, and soon the trail register appears on a tree, about 0.15 mile from Route 301. It's a good idea to sign the register even though you are just taking a day hike. Not only will it help people know where you are if they need to look for you, the usage data will help park administration and trail maintainers with their planning.

The AT continues through a section of heavy mountain laurel making green (or, in late spring and early summer, floral) walls on both sides. This growth is similar to that of the "green tunnels" (long stretches through dense shrubbery that often hangs over the trail, creating a sort of ceiling) that characterize the AT in the southern states.

After another 0.15 mile, the trail descends slightly and the laurel ends. Shortly after the woods open up, a triad of blue blazes on a tree on the left marks the eastern end of the Fahnestock Trail, which connects the Canopus Lake area with the trails around Hubbard Lodge just off Route 9.

The trail climbs a small berm. From here, you get your first sight of a scarp, a rocky cliff at the edge of a plateau, which will be a nearly constant presence off the trail for the next mile or so. The AT continues on in a trough between it and the high ground to the other side, until that high ground levels off. From the mature maple and oak forest, you can see the lake again at the bottom of the slope.

Canopus Lake was where Fahnestock State Park began. At the beginning of the twentieth century, Major Clarence Fahnestock, a New York City doctor, began purchasing abandoned local iron mines and farms in the area. His aim was to create a hunting preserve for himself and other wealthy men of the era. In 1915, when he bought a large tract from the Pennsylvania and Reading Coal and Iron Company, he had at last acquired enough land to realize his goal.

However, he was not able to enjoy it for long. He went to France with the Expeditionary Force when the United States entered World War I, and he was killed in 1918. His brother, Ernest, inherited the property and donated the 2,400 acres around this section of Canopus Creek to the state for use as a park in 1929. It has been expanded many times since then.

In the mature forest, the AT remains level. From the small berm, the trail moves farther uphill and becomes higher and sheerer. Still, you can see past it to view the abrupt change beyond the rock. There, near some of the highest ground in the park, the forest is scrubbier and the summit is more open, which is typical for ridge-top forests found in the higher elevations of the region.

The trail passes a large pool (or muddy area, depending on how much rain has fallen) and then crosses a stream. Amid so many rocks you may not be aware that there is an outlet from a swamp higher up.

The trail continues its ascent, getting closer to the ridge again. The forest around the trail changes accordingly. The lake, still visible, seems far below. Eventually the AT reaches 1,120 feet above sea level, its highest elevation on this stretch.

This is the view of Canopus Lake you'll see at the end of your hike.

The descent begins somewhat abruptly, often traversing the steep slope on narrow, rocky ledges. It levels off again and passes through a former overlook, now overgrown. Afterward, a tricky turn at a small creek leads you back onto another berm-like rise.

The AT seems to move away from the lake, and you may think you've passed your destination. Keep hiking. The trail enters another mature section of forest, and then crosses a small pool with its waters often amber-colored from tannin, the substance that gives most tree bark its color. A short distance beyond, the lake reappears to the east and one of the snowshoe trails comes up from the winter park section of Fahnestock.

The AT itself continues to climb and then traverses to a stand of birch trees, which are unusual for the region and elevation. The trail almost turns around but then climbs up steps through a steep, rocky section. Hemlocks rise high above and eye-pleasing moss covers the soil off the trail. The trees give way to shrubs and the white blazes start to appear on the rocks. At 2.3 miles from where you started, you will come to the perfect lunch spot, a rocky area overlooking Canopus Lake from the north.

From here you can see almost the entire distance you have traveled. The 105-acre lake was created in the park's earliest days by damming Canopus Brook, named for a local Iroquois chief. A view of the beach, lifeguard chairs, and cabins is to your right, 150 feet below. Westchester and Anthony's Nose can be seen to the south.

When you are done savoring this panorama, return the way you came. If you bump into any thru-hikers headed the other way, consider being a "trail angel" and offering them some water or leftover supplies you have.

MORE INFORMATION

No restrooms are located at the trailhead, but they are available at park headquarters, off Route 301. Clarence Fahnestock State Park, 1498 Route 301 Carmel, NY 10512; 845-225-7207; nysparks.state.ny.us/parks/133/details.aspx

TRIP 21
HUDSON HIGHLANDS STATE PARK–
BREAKNECK RIDGE AND BULL HILL

Location: Cold Spring, NY
Rating: Difficult
Distance: 5.9 miles
Elevation Gain: 1,250 feet
Estimated Time: 7.0 hours
Maps: USGS West Point; New York–New Jersey Trail Conference East Hudson Trails, Map #102

This trip from one train station to another travels over the Hudson Highlands' two most challenging peaks, which offer sweeping viewpoints of the river, mountains, and other sights. Summits are optional.

DIRECTIONS

The larger of the trailhead parking lots, with room for more than 30 vehicles including spaces available on the opposite side of the road, is along the west side of Route 9D between Cold Spring and Beacon, just north of the Dutchess-Putnam county line. *GPS coordinates*: 41° 26.732′ N, 73° 58.750′ W.

The smaller trailhead lot, with room for five vehicles, is just past the vehicle tunnel's north portal, 2.0 miles north of Cold Spring. *GPS coordinates*: 41° 26.601′ N, 73° 58.682′ W.

Take the Metro-North Hudson Line to the stop at Breakneck Ridge (only two trains stop here on weekend mornings). Be sure to let the conductor know you will be getting off there, as you must be in the car where the exit door will open. Purchase your ticket before boarding to avoid a surcharge.

TRAIL DESCRIPTION

On weekdays, there are two stations between Peekskill and Beacon along Metro-North Railroad's Hudson Line. The Breakneck Ridge and Manitou request stops come into use on the weekends, giving hikers from New York City and Westchester numerous options to avoid driving and reduce their carbon footprints as they savor the great outdoors.

This route is designed for hikers who would like to go from station to station through Hudson Highlands State Park. The hike is challenging, but also

HUDSON HIGHLANDS STATE PARK–BREAKNECK RIDGE AND BULL HILL

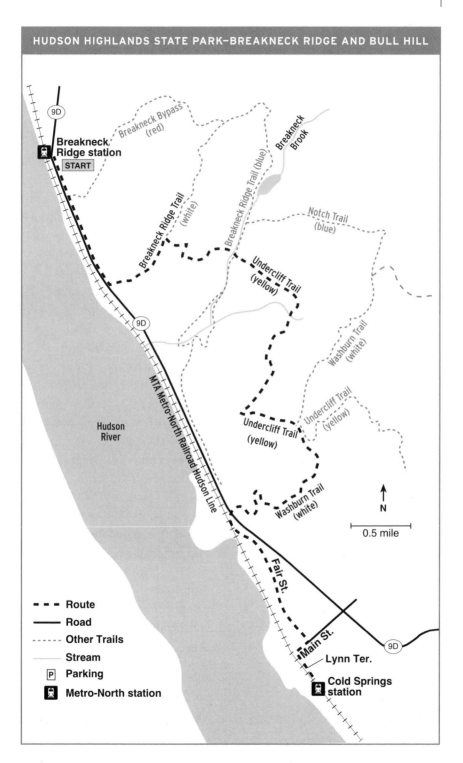

9D

Breakneck Bypass
(red)

Breakneck
Ridge station

START

Breakneck
Brook

Breakneck Ridge Trail (blue)

Breakneck Ridge Trail
(white)

Notch Trail
(blue)

Undercliff Trail
(yellow)

9D

Washburn Trail
(white)

MTA Metro-North Railroad Hudson Line

Undercliff Trail
(yellow)

Hudson
River

Undercliff Trail
(yellow)

N

0.5 mile

Washburn Trail
(white)

Fair St.

- - - Route
—— Road
----- Other Trails
—— Stream
P Parking
🚆 Metro-North station

Main St.

9D

Lynn Ter.

Cold Springs
station

rewarding when you see the stunning scenery. It is strenuous enough that you will appreciate sitting back in your seat on the way home without having to worry about driving.

After disembarking from the train on the wooden platform, cross the overhead bridge to a short path to Route 9D. The views are beautiful here, but they are just a preview of what unfolds from above. Turn right and follow Route 9D south for 0.5 mile to get to the parking lot. Walk down the west side of the busy road, then cross to the portion behind the guardrail on the east side to reach the trailhead.

Three visible white dots on a tree next to the start of the trail mark the start of the Breakneck Ridge Trail and the entrance to Hudson Highlands State Park. The mountain's name supposedly comes from a runaway ox, which local farmers pursued to one of the mountain's cliffs, where it fell to its death.

The trail begins benevolently enough by switching gently up slopes to the ground above, the neighboring road, and rail tunnels. However, it soon starts to get more difficult. A series of steep, rocky scrambles offer better views over the shoulder as a reward, but never seem to end (detour routes are available past some of the most difficult terrain). Finally, the trail levels off into some tricky traverses that at least leave the hiker standing up most of the time, until it comes out to a promontory with a sweeping view up and down the Hudson River.

In its first 0.4 mile, the trail has climbed 700 feet. This trail is popular, and you can count on not being alone if it is a nice weekend. Trails.com rated Breakneck Ridge as one of the top ten day hikes in the country.

Many hikers elect to stop and take in the scenery here. Bull Hill (supposedly named for the same animal whose death gave Breakneck its name) is visible to the south, with the buildings of the United States Military Academy just across the river. North of West Point is Crow's Nest, a key lookout for the Continental Army during the American Revolution. A wide valley separates it and Storm King Mountain just across the river, where the narrow shelf of the Storm King Highway (Route 218) can be seen.

Next to Storm King is Cornwall-on-Hudson, as the river widens into Newburgh Bay. That city is at the west side of the upper limit of the view, where the Newburgh-Beacon Bridge connects to Beacon, behind Sugarloaf Mountain to the north. Rail fans in particular may like this spot, since long sections of both the CSX freight line across the river and the Metro-North/Amtrak passenger operations on this side are visible.

Steep chutes continue ahead, but begin to alternate with flat, open overlooks, improving with height. After another third of a mile, the yellow-blazed Undercliff Trail drops off the ridge to the right, 1.5 mile short of Breakneck's summit, if you decide you'd like to go there. If not, take the Undercliff Trail

The Breakneck Ridge Trail is steep and quite rocky.

down a series of steep switchbacks. The dramatic landscape includes cliff edges, a large group of boulders called Rock Jumble, and then after a short ascent, a view south from the base of a cliff, the feature that gives the trail its name.

At the bottom of the valley, the trail crosses Breakneck Brook on a wooden bridge. It turns left when it reaches a woods road and the red-blazed Brook Trail (which can be used to shorten your hike by going right 0.7 mile to Route 9D). Almost immediately after that junction, Underwood Trail turns right again and heads through old farmland.

The trail heads west, ascending gradually to follow an old woods road with stone fortification. The road makes a series of switchbacks and eventually reaches another viewpoint where you can marvel at the steep face of Breakneck. The trail turns south and works its way across the west side of Bull Hill, Breakneck's higher southern neighbor. Viewpoints frequently open up in the rocky breaks in a forest dominated by scrub oak and occasional pitch pine.

This stretch ends at a junction with another white-blazed trail, the Washburn Trail. Turning left, that trail continues for a half-mile past plenty of views to Bull Hill's wooded summit, turning right as it leads back down.

The Washburn Trail first descends through rocky terrain with views similar to that on the Undercliff Trail. At the base of the rocky stretches it levels off, eventually winding around them to the west side of Bull Hill's southern ridge. A mix of trees that include oaks and maples grow tall again. After a short climb, the trail ascends slightly and then begins to descend through the scrubbier woods on the other side of the ridge.

This section switches back frequently on a wide road that serviced the now-abandoned quarry to the north. There are some viewpoints just off the trail, and they are worth taking a detour to explore and see an even larger old quarry visible from the village of Cold Spring to the south. The view takes in Nelsonville to the east, and Constitution Island, West Point, and the mountains near Garrison in the distance where the river bends toward Bear Mountain.

Beautiful and dramatic as they are, the quarries along the north faces of both peaks are a reminder of how ruthlessly the Highlands were exploited in the past. In the 1960s, Consolidated Edison proposed a complex power plant that would have required flooding Black Rock Forest and carving a huge chunk from the base of Storm King. The resulting litigation led to a landmark ruling that regulators could consider the aesthetic impact of development as well as its possible environmental effects. After 17 years in court, the project was dropped and the land was protected.

Rusted pipes and other remnants of the quarrying are visible in the surrounding woods as the trail descends to the quarry's edge and then down to more level ground near the west edge of the quarry, where you can take in its rugged cliffs and slowly re-vegetating woods.

The last phase of the trail is a short, descending switchback through a mature forest of chestnut oak and maple. It ends at an unpaved parking area on 9D opposite the entrance to Little Stony Point State Park, just above where Fair Street (CR 17) forks off the highway to the west. You will want to follow the road another mile into Cold Spring's quaint, historic downtown. When you reach Main Street, turn right and follow it downhill to the station, just off to the left where the road reaches the tracks.

Take the walkway on the left at the tracks.

MORE INFORMATION

There are no restrooms. Open all year, no fee, hiking or snowshoeing only. Hudson Highlands State Park, Route 9D, Beacon, NY 10512; 845-225-7207; www.nysparks.com/parks/9/details.aspx.

SAVING STORM KING

Viewed across the river from the steep slopes of Breakneck Ridge and Bull Hill, Storm King Mountain has always been the same brooding giant. But it took a legendary legal battle to keep it that way.

In 1962, Consolidated Edison (Con Ed), the electric utility for New York City and most of Westchester County, announced its plans for what would have been the world's largest pumped-storage facility, a hydroelectric power plant where water is pumped up to a storage reservoir and then allowed to flow down through a generator, at Storm King. Among its publicity materials was an artist's rendering showing a chunk of the mountain carved out for the power house.

This image galvanized the opposition, and the following year the Scenic Hudson Preservation Coalition was formed. Not long afterward, it brought a lawsuit alleging that the Federal Power Commission should not have granted the license because the project's visible impact on the Hudson Highlands was not in the public interest. The river's commercial anglers also joined in, citing the effect on their fisheries.

The aesthetic case would be tough to make, since the law only required that the government consider whether Con Ed could build and operate the plant. The judge could have dismissed that claim entirely.

But, at the end of 1965, a federal appellate judge handed down a ground-breaking decision reversing the license grant: *"The Commission's renewed proceedings must include as a basic concern the preservation of natural beauty and national historic sites, keeping in mind that in our affluent society, the cost of a project is only one of several factors to be considered."* This ruling has been described as the birth of American environmental law, giving an activist group standing to sue on the public's behalf.

While that put an end to Con Ed's original, drastic proposal (which would have also flooded most of Black Rock Forest for the storage reservoir), the project was not dead. The utility put forth various plans, amended in size and scope. A plan to put the whole facility underground was blocked by New York City due to the threat to the Catskill Aqueduct, which runs deep in the bedrock under the mountains and river. Flaws in a fisheries study killed another proposal. Finally, in 1980, Scenic Hudson and Con Ed reached an agreement to end the Storm King project for good.

TRIP 22
BLACK ROCK FOREST

Location: Cornwall, NY
Rating: Difficult
Distance: 4.3 miles
Elevation Gain: 868 feet
Estimated Time: 5.0 hours
Maps: USGS Cornwall-on-Hudson; New York–New Jersey Trail Conference West Hudson Trails, Map #113; trail map available at trailhead kiosk or online at Black Rock Forest Consortium website

Take in great views and green buildings on this loop through a diverse Hudson Highlands preserve used for teaching and research.

DIRECTIONS
Take Route 9W north from the Bear Mountain Bridge and West Point to the trailhead lot on the southbound lanes just past the Museum of the Hudson Highlands. There is a break in the concrete barrier at this point. If you miss it, go to the Angola Road overpass and turn around. There is parking available for ten to fifteen vehicles. *GPS coordinates: 41° 25.216′ N, 74° 01.666′ W.*

TRAIL DESCRIPTION
Black Rock Forest's history is intertwined with that of Storm King, its better-known neighbor to the east. Both were preserved by the actions of Dr. Ernest Stillman, who began buying land in the area during the 1920s to develop better forestry techniques. Both were threatened by the proposed Consolidated Edison power plant proposal in the 1960s, which led to a landmark ruling that aesthetics could be considered as part of a project's environmental impact. And fortunately, both are open to the public for hiking and other types of low-impact recreation today.

However, there are differences between them. Storm King is at the heart of an eponymous state park, and a private consortium owns Black Rock Forest's 3,830 acres. Stillman left the property to Harvard University when he died. Harvard decided it didn't need to maintain another large forested tract besides the one the university has owned near Petersham, Massachusetts for more than a century. Harvard turned the property over to a new organization, the Black Rock Forest Consortium, comprised of other colleges, universities

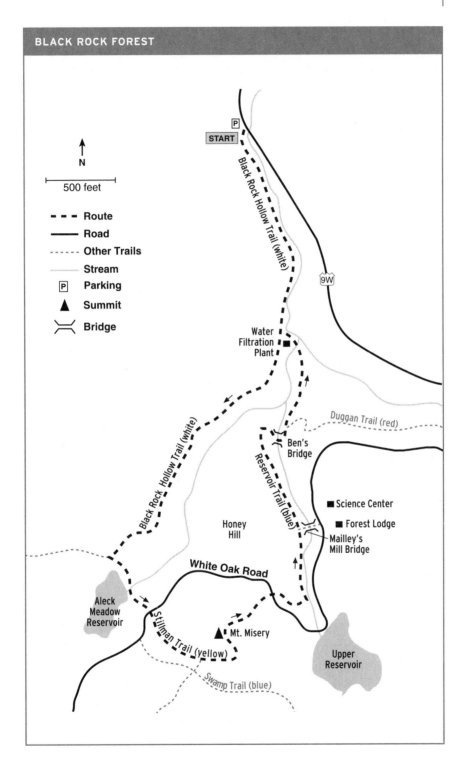

BLACK ROCK FOREST

N

500 feet

- - - Route
——— Road
.... Other Trails
——— Stream
P Parking
▲ Summit
⨝ Bridge

P
START

Black Rock Hollow Trail (white)

9W

Water
Filtration
Plant

Black Rock Hollow Trail (white)

Duggan Trail (red)

Ben's
Bridge

Reservoir Trail (blue)

■ Science Center
■ Forest Lodge
Mailley's
Mill Bridge

Honey
Hill

White Oak Road

Aleck
Meadow
Reservoir

Stillman Trail (yellow)

▲ Mt. Misery

Upper
Reservoir

Swamp Trail (blue)

and public and independent schools (K–12). While Storm King is a state park with hiking trails and sweeping views, Black Rock is a center for teaching and research with a main complex that features cutting-edge, low-environmental-impact buildings.

This hike starts with a walk along Black Rock Hollow Brook, the main stream that drains the forest. The white blazes of the Black Rock Hollow Trail begin along Peck's Road, leaving from the gate just south of the parking lot and going southwest along a dirt road. Mountain bikers use it, as you might expect, but so do employees of the village of Cornwall-on-Hudson's water department and forest staff on official business. A kiosk with a donation box is located in a clearing on the right, 0.1 mile from the trailhead. The forest features tall, mature oaks with some maples and beeches.

The brook gradually moves away and downhill from Route 9W. The *whooshing* of passing vehicles is slowly replaced by the sounds of the brook, which begins to make some picturesque cascades. You pass a small dam and reach a large filtration plant on the left 1 mile from the trailhead. Black Rock Hollow Trail then abruptly turns off the dirt road to the right and picks up an old woods road. The trail begins to climb a bit more. Red oak remains dominant, but some chestnut oak start to appear, and there are some hemlocks showing signs of damage from adelgids, the aphids that have killed many hemlocks in the Hudson Valley by sucking their sap dry.

The trail traverses up the side of the increasingly steep hollow carved by the brook until it ends at a junction with the yellow-blazed Stillman Trail, 0.9 mile from the pumping station. Turn left and follow it along the base of the dam that impounds the creek into Aleck Meadow Reservoir, one of six within Black Rock Forest.

The Stillman Trail is also part of the 150-mile Highlands Trail, which crosses the Highlands region, blazed with a light blue diamond in most protected areas. Currently it stretches from the Delaware River at Riegelsville, Pennsylvania, to Storm King. Future plans call for it to be extended in both directions, allowing it to connect southern Pennsylvania with Connecticut.

After crossing the dam, the trail begins a stiff ascent of Mount Misery, where steep, rocky stretches justify the name. In the middle of a large field of talus boulders, another white-blazed trail, the Scenic, leaves to the right. Stay on Stillman Trail, which continues its steep ascent. It reaches the peak's rocky 1,268-foot summit at 0.8 mile from the Black Rock Hollow Trail junction, amid the usual Highlands mountain forest of scrub oak and pitch pine. Views are available to the north and west, with the dam and part of the reservoir standing out.

A portion of this hike follows the Black Rock Hollow Brook.

From the summit, the Stillman Trail descends steeply, crossing one of the forest's dirt roads 0.1 mile down. At 0.2 mile, the trail comes to a junction with the blue-blazed Reservoir Trail, which branches off to the left just before another one of the reservoirs. The Reservoir Trail descends along the west side of the reservoir's outlet brook.

Soon the buildings of the forest's administrative complex become apparent through the trees to the right. You can check them out by following an unmarked, but obvious, side path that leads over the short, covered Mailley's Mill Bridge to the parking area.

The buildings are usually open, and if the staff isn't busy they'll gladly show you around a little. They can tell you about how the wood used to construct the buildings was all harvested in the forest, so resources would not be used up transporting it. They will explain how the windows are designed to use as much natural light as possible, without heating up the buildings too much. You will also learn how effective the composting toilets have been. You may find it interesting to see the meter that shows how much electricity the solar cells are generating and selling back to the local utility.

The facility contains overnight accommodations, conference rooms, and research laboratories. Guests have ranged from primary grade students from the local school districts that are consortium members to professors and graduate students from Columbia and NYU (also members). Research in the forest has led to hundreds of published papers, and a great diversity of species identified within.

Going back over the bridge, the Reservoir Trail continues its descent down the outlet brook's gorge. The red-blazed Duggan Trail comes in on the right just before crossing Black Hollow Brook again at Ben's Bridge. A short distance later, it ends at the same pumping station where the Black Rock Hollow Trail turned into the woods on the way in. That trail can then be followed for a mile back to the parking lot.

MORE INFORMATION

Restrooms are available at the forest headquarters complex. Black Rock Forest is closed during New York State firearm big-game season, from the third Saturday in November to the fourth Tuesday in December. Black Rock Forest Consortium, 129 Continental Road, Cornwall, NY 12518; 845-534-4517; www.blackrockforest.org.

TRIP 23
STEWART STATE FOREST

Location: New Windsor, NY
Rating: Moderate
Distance: 4.2 miles
Elevation Gain: 380 feet
Estimated Time: 2.5 hours
Maps: USGS Maybrook; NYSDEC map available at trailhead and online at Stewart State Forest website

Hike through fields, woods, swamps, and mud to sweeping vistas in this recent addition to the New York state forest system.

DIRECTIONS
From I-84's Exit 5A, take Route 747 south 2 miles to where it ends at Route 207. Turn right onto Route 207 west. Continue 2 miles to the Weed Road trailhead with DEC shingle. The parking lot has room for twenty vehicles. *GPS coordinates*: 41° 28.198′ N, 74° 09.853′ W.

TRAIL DESCRIPTION
For many years, the lands west of Stewart International Airport have been a popular spot for the people of Orange County to hunt, fish, snowmobile, and hike. No one knew for certain how long that would continue, since the "Stewart Buffer Lands" had been condemned to expand the airport and many local politicians and businesses sought to make them available for development.

That all ended in 2006, after the British company that had leased the airport sold its lease to the Port Authority of New York and New Jersey, effectively ending the seven-year experimental privatization of the airport. As part of the assumption of the lease by the Port Authority, all the land west of Route 747, and some east of it, was added to the existing Stewart State Forest (created when the airport had first been privatized).

The 6,700-acre Stewart State Forest is mostly low elevation; almost half of it is wetlands. While other outdoor enthusiasts continue to practice their hobbies in this area, hikers in the New York tri-state area have not turned much attention to it. The 22 miles of trails, including a hike to Buchanan Hill, the gem of the park with its wide-open views, are not to be missed.

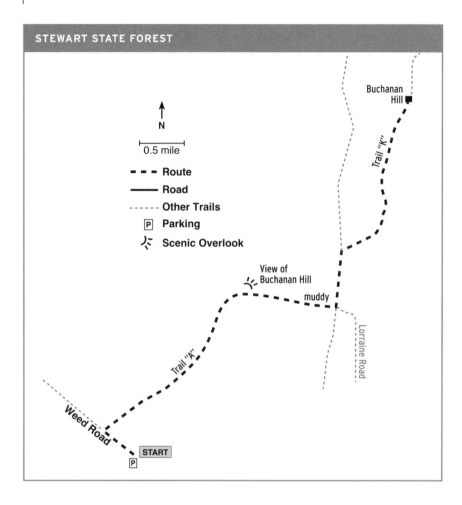

STEWART STATE FOREST

N

0.5 mile

- - - Route
—— Road
----- Other Trails
P Parking
Scenic Overlook

Buchanan Hill

Trail "K"

View of Buchanan Hill

muddy

Lorraine Road

Trail "A"

Weed Road

START

P

Begin at the Weed Road trailhead, the center of the Department of Environmental Conservation's (DEC) cooperative hunting program when the state Department of Transportation still owned the land. DEC produced a trail map (available at the kiosk) and blazed a trail system throughout the many old farms and woodlots that make up the forest.

Follow the paved road past the gate and slightly downhill. After 0.2 mile, with the gate still in sight, you will see large, orange DEC plastic snowmobile trail markers and smaller blue ones on the right. Almost as soon as you start down the blue-blazed trail, which follows a dirt road, it bends past a large white pine on the left and continues along some muddy areas. This is a harbinger of what is to come in much greater quantities later on. As befits a wetland area, Stewart State Forest features some of the muddiest hiking in New York outside of the Adirondacks. In all but the driest weather, hiking boots

Breakneck Ridge (left) and Storm King can be seen from Buchanan Hill in Stewart State Forest.

are a must here, and in the winter you should wear gaiters to cover your legs as well.

The trail winds around into a field, crossing on a slight trace past the blue-marked post in the middle. There is no such marker in the middle of the next field you enter across the hedgerow, but there are enough tracks to follow. In these fields, the grass grows high in summertime, so remember to check yourself for deer ticks and shower or bathe thoroughly after your hike.

At the end of the second field, the trail passes the dirt road on the right and follows a muddy one uphill in the woods. It then turns right along the edge of another field. All these fields were part of 337 farms that were condemned in the early 1970s for a development plan to build the region's fourth major jetport, with a long runway for supersonic transports. The plan was later abandoned when the 1973 fuel crisis made it unlikely that the expanded airport would be successful.

The trail reenters the woods, crosses a roadbed, and enters an area of maple and cherry trees with a grassy floor. The trail comes out into a field with a sweeping view of Buchanan Hill, your ultimate destination. Follow the posts downhill and to the right. At the bottom corner, the trail passes through a marshy, muddy area and then comes out into another small field. In the short stretch of woods between this field and the next, the trail fords a small stream.

Be aware of some extremely deep mud wallows before and after the stream. You may see small frogs enjoying this spot too.

When you're done slogging across, you will follow the edge of another field. Turn left and follow a stone wall on much drier ground, then cross it about 200 feet later at a break in the wall into another field edge. The trail picks up a larger stream on the left, and then comes out to Maple Avenue, a disused paved road. Here, a DEC mileage sign says you have walked 1.6 miles from the trailhead.

Turn left, and you will see hickory trees planted by the farmers to shade the road. Opposite a large Norway spruce 0.3 mile down on the left, the trail marked "Buchanan Hill Loop" begins. This is an old road, blazed only with blue DEC markers as a footpath. It crosses some swamps and then slowly begins its gentle ascent of the hill, turning slightly past more old fields until reaching the first of the meadows atop the hill.

You can see just about everything there is to see to the west of here, mostly the rolling hills of central Orange County, but also the Shawangunks and sometimes the Catskills to the northwest. Continue up the gently sloping road past the posts and the hedgerow to the next meadow, where the view is even more expansive. At the end of the path through this meadow, the ground finally levels out. Crossing the next hedgerow brings you to a meadow facing south and east, where the scenic highlights of the Newburgh area sprawl before you.

Prominent to the south is Schunemunk Mountain, the county's highest at 1,664 feet, with Woodcock Hill in front. To its east are Storm King, Breakneck, Sugarloaf North, and the Beacon Mountain-Fishkill Ridge chain at the northern end of the Hudson Highlands. To the east are some of the outer areas of Newburgh and Snake Hill.

The trail turns into a section that becomes extremely overgrown in summer near the hill's height of land. Here you will want to return the way you came rather than completing the loop back to Maple Avenue via Whalenburgh Pond.

MORE INFORMATION

One portable toilet is located at the trailhead. Stewart State Forest is closed to non-hunters during firearm fall hunting season, from the third Saturday in November to the fourth Tuesday in December. Stewart State Forest, DEC Region 3, 21 South Putt Corners Road, New Paltz, NY 12561; 845-256-3076; www.dec.ny.gov/lands/50095.html.

TRIP 24
SHAWANGUNK GRASSLANDS
NATIONAL WILDLIFE REFUGE

Location: Wallkill, NY
Rating: Easy
Distance: 3.1 miles
Elevation Gain: Level
Estimated Time: 2.0 hours
Maps: USGS Gardiner

This former military airfield has become one of New York's most crucial habitats for grassland-dependent bird species. For humans, it boasts stunning views of the nearby Shawangunk Ridge and surrounding countryside.

DIRECTIONS

From Route 208 at the hamlet of Wallkill, turn left on Wallkill Avenue into the small downtown. A block farther, turn left again and cross the Wallkill River on Bruyn Turnpike (CR 18) at the post office. Follow this straight road west for 2 miles to a rise topped by a four-way intersection with Hoagerburgh Road. Turn right. Follow Hoagerburgh past the farms about 1.75 miles to the sign and parking lot, which has room for approximately ten vehicles, on the right. *GPS coordinates:* 41° 38.207′ N, 74° 13.150′ W.

TRAIL DESCRIPTION

Shawangunk Grasslands was just another wooded patch of land in southern Ulster County until 1942, when the U.S. Army needed facilities to train as many new pilots as possible. Stewart Field, outside Newburgh, was already at full capacity. The 565-acre plot near the former hamlet of Galeville was cleared and surfaced to create four 3,500-foot runways.

It remained in active military use until the post-Vietnam War drawdown of the 1970s. Thereafter, federal marshals and FBI agents trained on the site until 1994, when the Department of Defense decided it no longer needed the site. The Town of Shawangunk was hoping to convert the entire airfield into a park, but the Fish and Wildlife Service prevailed, pointing to evidence that the grassy areas between the runways had become valuable nesting areas

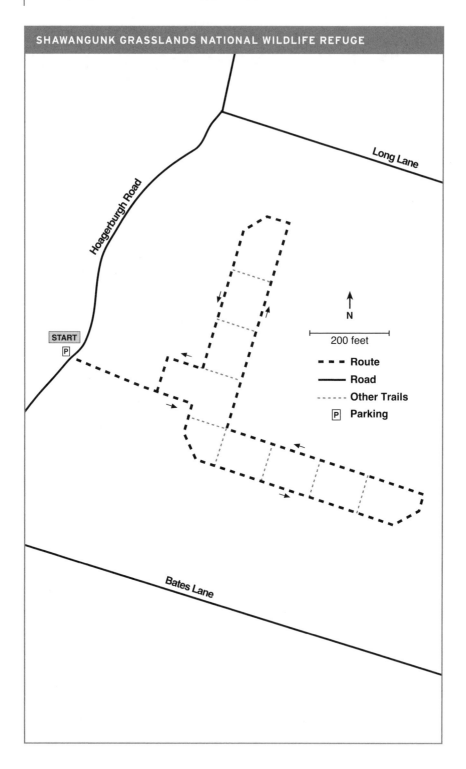

SHAWANGUNK GRASSLANDS NATIONAL WILDLIFE REFUGE

Long Lane

Hoagerburgh Road

START

P

N

200 feet

- - - Route
— Road
- - - Other Trails
P Parking

Bates Lane

for grassland-dependent migratory bird species. It was designated a national wildlife refuge and opened in 1999 under the management of Wallkill River National Wildlife Refuge to the south.

Today, it seems almost impossible to imagine planes taking off and landing here. Nature has begun to reclaim the area, making it look like a patch of African savanna in the mid-Hudson Valley.

This hike is an excellent outing for a day when you would like a long walk, but not a climb. You will be in a large open area with no shade or shelter, so apply sunscreen and be prepared to leave if a thunderstorm appears to be in the offing, as can happen in the ridge's rain shadow, where the combination of moist valley air meeting cooler prevailing winds often causes localized precipitation. It is very easy to shorten this loop if you follow the taxiways between the abandoned runways.

Visitors to the refuge must stay on the roads at all times, due not only to the refuge's stated purpose, but also because some possible hazardous materials may remain from the time the Army used the land. As a result, there are no conventional paths or trails, just old roads and runways that haven't felt landing gear in almost 40 years.

Beyond the gate at the end of the parking lot, a paved road leads east through a grassy area with woods on either side. Follow it roughly 0.3 mile east to where it descends slightly past a small pond, the only significant body of water on the property. Here the open area of the former airfield, the 400-acre grasslands, is visible in its entirety.

At this point the paved road forks to the left, with a less-used dirt road continuing straight ahead. Follow the dirt road onward. It leads in a few hundred feet to one of the main runways, with a conveniently located bench.

Turn right at the bench. At the junctions with the other main runways are large yellow Xs, an indicator to pilots that the airfield is closed. However, illegal touch-and-goes have continued. If you see any aircraft landing or taking off, please write down the plane's registration number, take photos or video if you have the appropriate equipment, and let the Federal Aviation Administration know.

You should soon reach the southwest corner of the runway system. Bear left and follow the southern runway eastward. Grass has already begun to break through the tarmac, and the Fish and Wildlife Service (FWS) plans to remove all of the pavement and leave paths behind in order to create 30 acres of additional grassland in the core area.

Look north and you will see miles of the spectacular Shawangunk Ridge. The rock faces of Millbrook Mountain, Gertrude's Nose, and the summit of the

The Shawangunk Ridge can be seen off in the distance from Shawangunk Grasslands National Wildlife Refuge.

ridge near Cragsmoor are visible to the immediate west. The Skytop tower at Mohonk Mountain House can also be seen in the distance.

At the end of the southern runway, turn left on the short taxiway to the other east–west runway, where you will only be able to turn left again to continue. The view to the east from here, where you can see neighboring houses and backyards, takes in the undulating landscape to the east, where glacial ridges separate the Wallkill Valley from the Hudson River.

Within the refuge, the view offers large expanses of thick, high Kentucky bluegrass broken by the occasional tree, usually white ash, cedar, or pin oak. In a good breeze they make waves like a green lake.

The vegetation neatly conceals the runways themselves—if there are other walkers about, as there often are in good weather, they will seem from a distance to be striding through the hip-deep grasses. The FWS mows the grass regularly to keep the area from returning to forest similar to that which buffers it.

Return almost to the place where you first reached the runways. Here you will see another large yellow X on the pavement at the junction with the easterly of the two north–south runways. Bear right.

That takes you north and into the sight of the town of Shawangunk's Galeville Park and its wooden gazebos. This 55-acre area can be entered from Long Lane north of the refuge and offers the best views of the grasslands without actually going into it. The FWS plans to develop an interpretive trail that can be routed into the refuge from the park.

At the end of the runway, turn left onto a taxiway and then left again onto the last of the four runways, where at this point the pavement has given way to gravel and loose rock. Occasionally, you may see some of the bird species the refuge protects—bobolinks, eastern meadowlarks, horned larks, and the upland sandpiper, among others—flying about or even walking around on the tarmac. Mostly, they remain in their nests in the grassy thickets, which is why neither dogs nor joggers are allowed in the refuge.

Birders come to Shawangunk Grasslands to see the short-eared owl. This is one of the few owl species known to hunt in daylight.

Once the pavement resumes, a dirt road branches off to the right after 0.4 mile. Take the dirt road and it will turn to the left after a couple of hundred feet, passing the side of the small pond. It becomes paved again and brings you back to the first fork, which completes your loop. You can then go back up the road to the parking lot.

MORE INFORMATION

Open year-round; no fee; dogs are not allowed; hiking or snowshoeing only. Shawangunks Grasslands National Wildlife Refuge, Hoagerburgh Road, Shawangunk, NY 12589; 973-702-7666; www.fws.gov/northeast/shawangunk/index.htm.

THE SHORT-EARED OWL

The common name of *Asio flammeus*, the short-eared owl, comes from the small tufts of feathers on its head that resemble mammal ears. The tufts are usually seen only when the animal is threatened; otherwise they lie flat against the other head feathers.

Like most owls, the short-eared owl prefers to be nocturnal. It will generally engage in most of its activities, including hunting, between sunset and sunrise. Unlike other owls, it has no objection to hunting in daylight, although it prefers the later times of day when the sun is lower to the horizon. This has made it a favorite attraction for birders.

Research in Britain has suggested the short-eared owl's comfort with low light may be because it hunts when the vole, its preferred prey, is most active. (It also has been known, when hunting, to fly to areas where voles are abundant.) If it cannot find voles, it will eat other rodents, and sometimes even smaller birds.

The short-eared owl hunts by flying low over the ground with its feet extended. It flits around more like a bat or moth than a bird. Then it descends, feet first, and seizes its prey. This hunting style limits its ideal habitat to predominantly grassy areas, since this flight pattern is impossible in the woods.

Short-eared owls breed between March and June, with April their peak month. After the males court the females by making great spectacles of themselves in flight and belting out a scratchy, bark-like call, the females who choose them lay 4-7 eggs, which hatch after 3-5 weeks. Short-eared owls have been known to feign injured wings to lure predators away from the nest. The chicks fledge and leave the nest after four weeks.

Although the short-eared owl has ten subspecies and is found on almost every continent, New York is at the southern end of its breeding range in North America. Its population has been declining in New York in recent years and it is listed as an endangered species by the state Department of Environmental Conservation (DEC).

These small birds of prey do seem to like airports, however. In addition to being spotted at Shawangunk Grasslands National Wildlife Refuge (a former airport), they have been found at Calverton Executive Airpark, the largest remaining grassland in Long Island. This has led to a reconsideration of plans to greatly expand the airport, formerly a facility of the Grumman aircraft manufacturing company.

TRIP 25
HIGHLAND LAKES STATE PARK

Location: Scotchtown, NY
Rating: Easy
Distance: 3.5 miles
Elevation Gain: 90 feet
Estimated Time: 2.5 hours
Maps: USGS Goshen

Once used as farmland and for a pair of summer camps, this currently undeveloped tract offers a nice woodland walk.

DIRECTIONS

Exit Route 17 at Route 211, just west of I-84. Follow for approximately 5 miles east to Camp Orange Road on the left. Turn to go uphill 0.75 mile and park at the bend in the road. Space is limited, but there is room for approximately five vehicles.

If coming from an eastern or northern direction, take I-84 to Route 208. Go north 2 miles to Route 17K at Scotts Corners and turn left. After 3 miles, you will reach the village of Montgomery and the east end of Route 211. Turn left and look for Camp Orange Road on the right, roughly 3 miles from Montgomery. *GPS coordinates:* 41° 29.242′ N, 74° 18.887′ W.

TRAIL DESCRIPTION

When you think of hiking in a state park, you may think of large parking lots with nice kiosks leading to a sophisticated trail system. Highland Lakes is not that kind of state park.

In 1964, the Palisades Interstate Park Commission (PIPC) bought 800 acres of farmland and summer camps along the ridges to the north of the Town of Wallkill, considering this southern section of the Comfort Hills a valuable natural and recreational resource for future generations.

Over the next ten years, PIPC continued to buy property and sometimes used eminent domain to acquire the land. When it was done, 3,115 acres in Wallkill and neighboring Crawford and Montgomery were under its purview. It was named Highland Lakes State Park after the two small glacial lakes between the ridges in the northern portion of the park.

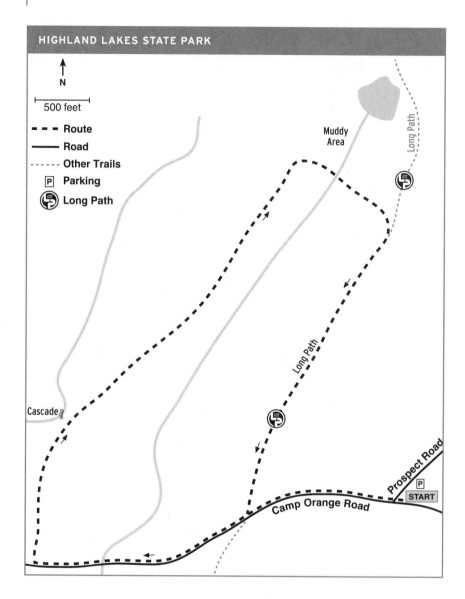

A section of the 330-mile Long Path, the long-distance trail which starts at the George Washington Bridge and goes to the Schenectady area, has been routed through here, and it is the only marked hiking trail in the entire park, comprised mostly of old roads. The Long Path makes an excellent backbone for this loop route, which follows roads marked as horse trails. There are no sweeping views on this hike, but the woods and occasional fields along the route are in various stages of forest development, making for an interesting and varied hike.

A small stream runs alongside this old road in Highland Lakes State Park.

From the trailhead, follow the continuation of Camp Orange Road, which once led to the former Newburgh YMCA camp of the same name, into the woods. The forest is a combination of mature trees, an immature maple grove, and some remaining quaking aspen from its pioneer phase.

The dirt road continues ahead, going slightly uphill and curving south into some of the clearings of a farmstead, now overgrown. At a junction marked by stone walls, 0.4 mile from the parking area, the Long Path's aqua blazes become visible. Turn right and follow the blazes along another road through tall woods into a less mature forest in a slightly elevated area.

You reach a junction where a once-magnificent oak tree has been snapped at the trunk. Although the aqua blazes go to the right, you will bear left. Follow a wide unmarked path down into a muddy, grassy stretch between some wet areas. When it rises again, a marked horse trail comes in obliquely from the left. Turn here and traverse alongside the rise you just started climbing, passing another horse trail that goes into the woods to the right a short distance from the junction. Eventually, this road reaches a plateau among mature forest with some pretty scenery. The trail turns northward again.

Increasing wet areas presage a small stream drawing alongside the old road briefly before going farther downhill in a series of cascades.

The trail reaches a three-way junction with another marked horse trail that comes in from a high hill to the right. Turn left here and follow the trail along the woods road through another area with wet spots. Small streams cross here, with swampy areas on either side.

Development of the park has remained a low priority. The land has gradually been reclaimed by nature, and the area has become a *de facto* preserve, used primarily by local equestrians and hikers. The lack of a management plan has led to some illegal use, such as that by all-terrain vehicles. Despite the size and visibility of the park (you can see the ridges when traveling east on I-84), it has not received much attention from the greater New York hiking community.

You may find this primitive hiking experience interesting. You can imagine yourself as a traveler on pre-industrial roads. In an era when even a horse was something of a luxury, many trips between towns in the region took place on roads much like these: step, by muddy step.

Eventually the trail begins to rise gently into drier terrain, starts to curve again, and Long Path comes in from the right to merge with the road. A few hundred feet ahead, you will find you are back at the junction where you started this loop. Long Path turns left, but keep going straight to get back to your vehicle. Perhaps one day, if a trail system is more firmly established, you can tell people you hiked it when it was still a primitive experience.

MORE INFORMATION

There are no restrooms. Dogs must be muzzled and leashed at all times. Leashes cannot be longer than 6 feet. Highlands Lake State, c/o Palisades Interstate Park Commission—Admin. Bldg., Bear Mountain, NY 10911; 845-786-2701; nysparks.state.ny.us/parks/5/details.aspx.

2

NORTHERN NEW JERSEY

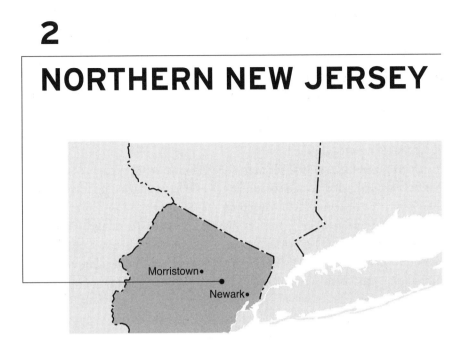

Northern New Jersey comes in two halves: the suburban sprawl of the northeast, and the mountains and lakes of the northwest. Those who think the whole state looks like the former are setting themselves up to be pleasantly surprised by the latter.

This duality began to evolve millions of years ago. As the landmass of Pangaea split up into the beginnings of today's continents, one of the rifts that didn't succeed in becoming an ocean filled in with sediment and became the Newark Basin, a lowland area that stretches from the Palisades through Trenton all the way to Gettysburg, Pennsylvania. Today this area is referred to by geologists as the Piedmont Province, and is one of the state's most developed areas. It is broken only by the Watchung Mountains, where areas such as the Watchung and South Mountain reservations have been set aside.

To its west, the Highlands Province was once a coastal area, sometimes under shallow inland seas. Around 400 million years ago, during the Ordovician era, the motion of the underlying plates changed, and orogeny, or mountain formation, began. This took almost 250 million years, pushing the Appalachians higher than today's Himalayas, until the continents began to break up and the mountains rose no more.

As a result, the Highlands contain some of New Jersey's oldest rock, pre-Cambrian gneisses and granites formed up to a billion years ago. These are especially resistant to erosion, resulting in the steep slopes found on Pyramid Mountain and Bearfort Ridge.

In the extreme northwest, the Highlands yield to the Great Valley of the Appalachians and the Ridge and Valley Province. Here, as you can see at Rattlesnake Swamp and High Point, the slopes are smoother and the valleys wider, more like Pennsylvania and Virginia.

During the Ice Age, the glaciers covered most of these areas. They left behind tarns like Terrace Pond and larger bodies of water like Lake Passaic, which eventually dwindled into today's Great Swamp.

When European settlers, first the Dutch and later the English, began arriving in what became known as New Jersey in the seventeenth century, these divisions shaped their settlement patterns. Instead of today's informal division of the state into North, Central and South Jersey, they thought in terms of East and West Jersey.

East Jersey was the coastal and Piedmont areas, where settlers found fertile soils to their liking and cleared land for their farms. West Jersey was the hillier Highlands, with little prospect for farming but with hills rich in iron ore. The settlers' descendants would find that material very useful when they rose up against the British crown in the 1770s. Traces of the Revolutionary War-era iron industry can still be seen some places in the woods, most notably in the stone smelters off Clinton Road on the way to the Terrace Pond trailhead.

After our country's independence was won, the divided geography would continue to shape the state's development. The Passaic River powered industrialization in its lower valley, from the Alexander Hamilton-planned city of Paterson to the river's mouth at Newark. The suburbs swelled with workers from these factories as well as the more affluent, who began living year-round in what had once been summer resort towns and commuting to their jobs in New York City by train.

With all these people came the need for open space. Industrialists themselves protected land at High Point and what is now Ringwood State Park. New York and New Jersey joined together to establish Palisades Interstate Park. Essex County created the first county parks department in the country in order to protect South Mountain. The struggle for open space continues today, with Pyramid Mountain and the Great Swamp among the newer areas protected.

TRIP 26
HIGH POINT

Location: Montague, NJ

Rating: Moderate

Distance: 2.8 miles

Elevation Gain: 380 feet

Estimated Time: 1.5 hours

Maps: USGS Port Jervis South; Appalachian Trail New York–New Jersey Map #5; New York–New Jersey Trail Conference Kittatinny Trails, Map #123

Walk the Appalachian Trail to New Jersey's highest point and its panoramic views.

DIRECTIONS

Take Interstate 84 west to Exit 1. Take Route 6 to the traffic light. Turn left and go under the interstate and across the state line. Follow Route 23 south approximately 4 miles uphill to the park entrance. Look for an entrance to a dirt parking lot on the right just past where the Appalachian Trail crosses the road. Parking is available for approximately 25 vehicles. *GPS coordinates*: 41° 18.192′ N, 74° 40.048′ W.

TRAIL DESCRIPTION

There is no subtlety in the naming of New Jersey's highest mountain. Why, it must have been decided, use the name of a former governor or president, an American Indian name, or even the nearest community, when you can just call it what it is: "High Point." Nothing more, nothing less. It's even more appropriate when you consider the mountain's location within the state—almost in the northernmost corner, so it is at the high point of the map of the state as well.

From its summit obelisk, High Point justifies its name quite well. There are 360 degrees of views available of three states.

The Appalachian Trail (AT), while not going over the summit of High Point itself, comes near enough to offer an excellent approach for hikers. From the parking lot, follow the short path through trees at the west end to the AT. Turn right and follow the white blazes along the edge of the stand and then across Route 23. (Be careful to look both ways; it's a busy state highway and southbound traffic has a limited view.)

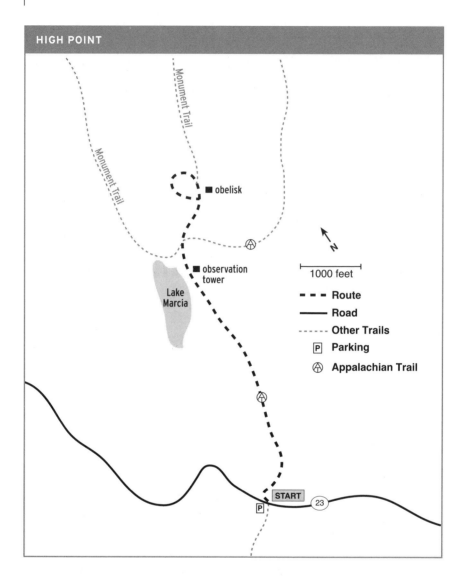

On the other side of the highway, continue across the grass to where the trail re-enters the woods. Once you do, it's fairly easy to follow for the first 0.2 mile through relatively open, mature, tall trees. Shortly thereafter, the trail starts to ascend gently, soon reaching the areas of shrubby undergrowth, spindly trees like chestnut oak and pitch pine with open woods, and rock outcrops that typify Highlands forests.

Close to the top of a small plateau you can see more open areas near the ridgeline. As you hike along, there are also open areas on your left, the remnants of old landslides or fires, where you can see out into the upper Wallkill River Valley to the east.

Visitors at the summit of High Point look north to the Catskills.

The trail is well within the state park now and fairly close to its facilities, although you'd never know it. Almost a mile from the start, it reaches the end of this plateau at a drop where a view opens up to the north, with the High Point obelisk front and center. No sign marks it, but this point, about 1,680 feet above sea level, is the highest point on the AT in New Jersey. You don't need to block the trail for long here. Descend, and you will reach a small wooden platform you can climb for nearly the same view.

The obelisk isn't far away now. Continue descending on the AT, as the trees get taller and denser again. In the low ground between the knob you have just descended and the High Point summit, 0.2 mile from the observation platform, the Monument Trail, blazed with a half-red, half-green rectangle, leaves to the left. Take it up, across the road, and then up the last steep slope to a 220-foot granite monument.

Take a look around. On a clear enough day, you'll be amazed at the view. Looking south, you can see back down the Kittatinny Ridge to Sunrise Mountain, New Jersey's second-highest peak, and farther down the broad upper Wallkill Valley to the southeast. Off to the east, over Wallkill River National Wildlife Refuge, is Pochuck Mountain, the beginning of the geological Highlands, and the long ridge of Wawayanda Mountain beyond, after which the ridges become hard to distinguish. It is said that the New York City skyline is even visible on the clearest days.

Continuing northeast into the portions of New York that are usually visible, the checkerboard-like patterns of brown and green north of Pochuck indicate the Black Dirt Region of Orange County, the bed of a former glacial lake known for the rich soil that gives the region its name. Beyond it is Schunemunk Mountain, Orange County's highest, and the Hudson Highlands beyond.

The first thing you'll notice looking northeast is the continuation of the Kittatinnies into New York, where they become the Shawangunks. You can see how they drop to low heights immediately to the north of High Point, going below 1,000 feet in elevation as they cross Sullivan County, then rise above 2,000 feet to form the white cliffs at Mohonk Mountain House west of New Paltz. From this angle, you also can easily appreciate the way the range splits at its northern end, southwest of Kingston.

Now look due north. The Catskill Plateau rises in that direction, and it should be no surprise that you can see some of the High Peaks in that range. Slide Mountain, the range's highest at 4,180 feet, is easily distinguishable by its whale-shaped summit ridge, and nearby a knowledgeable viewer can pick out Peekamoose, Table, and some other peaks in that vicinity. Between those peaks and the upper Shawangunks, the clearest skies will reveal Twin and Indian Head mountains on the Devil's Path in southern Greene County—more than 70 miles away. Because they rise twice as high as High Point, they can be seen over the curvature of the Earth from here.

Much closer, the twin communities of Matamoras, Pennsylvania, and Port Jervis, New York, nestle alongside the Delaware River below to the west. Many buildings and structures, such as the Mid-Delaware Bridge connecting the two cities and Port Jervis's red-roofed Queen Anne-style former train station, are readily apparent. Beyond Matamoras to the west are the many low peaks of Pennsylvania's Poconos.

The opportunity to take in these views was made possible by the Kuser family, which once owned the land that became High Point State Park. A display in the obelisk tells the story of how Colonel Anthony Kuser bought the land around High Point early in the twentieth century as a summer retreat for his family. He was interested in conservation, and collected and bred bird species, as well as helping to found the New Jersey chapter of the Audubon Society. In 1923, the family donated the summit lands to the state, and it became New Jersey's first state park.

To return to your car, hike back the way you came.

MORE INFORMATION

Restrooms are available at the park office near the trailhead and at the summit. High Point State Park, 1480 Route 23, Sussex, NJ 07461; 973-875-4800; www .state.nj.us/dep/parksandforests/parks/highpoint.html.

TRIP 27
RATTLESNAKE SWAMP LOOP

Location: Blairstown, NJ
Rating: Moderate
Distance: 4.6 miles
Elevation Gain: 400 feet
Estimated Time: 3.5 hours
Maps: USGS Flatbrookville; New York–New Jersey Trail Conference
Kittatinny Ridge Trails, Map #121; Appalachian Trail New York–
New Jersey Map #6

**Take in the spectacular Delaware Valley on this loop near the AMC
Mohican Outdoor Center.**

DIRECTIONS

Take Interstate 80 west across New Jersey to Exit 12. Turn right and follow
County Road 521 north 5 miles to Blairstown and the junction with Route 94.
Follow it south 1.0 mile to Mohican Road and turn right. After approximately
1.3 miles, bear left onto Cobblewood. Turn right on 4 Corners Road after 0.1
mile. At Gaisler Road, 1.5 miles from Cobblewood, it becomes Camp Road.
Continue past power lines and end of pavement to Delaware Water Gap National Recreation Boundary and Appalachian Trail crossing. The Mohican
Outdoor Center is roughly 1.2 miles from Gaisler Road. A large parking area
is located 0.1 mile into the camp on your left with room for 40 vehicles. *GPS
coordinates*: 41° 03.575′ N, 75° 00.005′ W.

TRAIL DESCRIPTION

The Hudson isn't the only major river within the New York City metropolitan area. Far out at its western fringe is the Delaware, which also carves out
spectacular scenery where it encounters the main ridges of the Appalachian
Mountains. Some outdoor enthusiasts prefer this region to the Hudson despite
its distance from the city, as it is considerably wilder.

At New Jersey's western edge, the pristine nature of the Delaware Valley is
the unintended result of a plan that would have made it the complete opposite.
After the defeat of the Tocks Island Dam project in the late 1970s, the federal
government found itself with 70,000 acres of land in both New Jersey and
Pennsylvania that it had expected to flood. The land was instead transferred

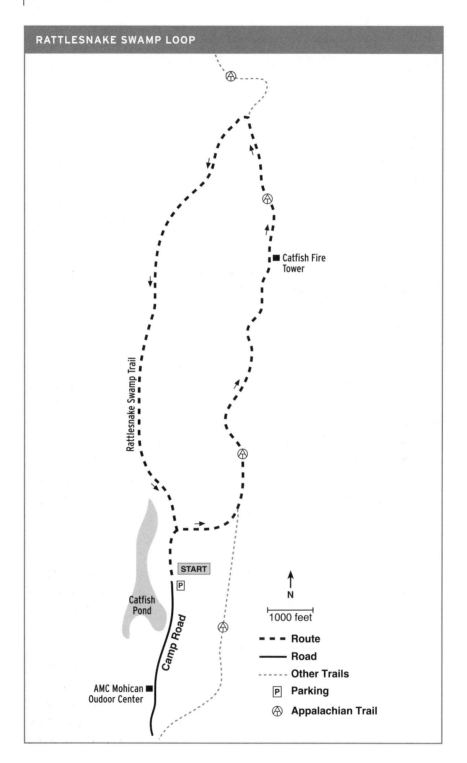

RATTLESNAKE SWAMP LOOP

Catfish Fire Tower

Rattlesnake Swamp Trail

START

Catfish Pond

AMC Mohican Oudoor Center

Camp Road

N

1000 feet

- - - Route
—— Road
····· Other Trails
P Parking
Ⓐ Appalachian Trail

Look for a view of Lower Yards Creek Reservoir from the Appalachian Trail at its junction with Rattlesnake Swamp Trail.

to the National Park Service, which developed it into the Delaware Water Gap National Recreation Area.

The remoteness of the Water Gap area makes hiking it mostly suitable for overnight backpacking. However, an excellent loop is available from the Appalachian Mountain Club's Mohican Outdoor Center north of Blairstown, a destination for families and vacationers and a stopping point for thru-hikers using the same section of the Appalachian Trail you'll follow.

From the parking lot, continue along the road past Catfish Pond, another of New Jersey's glacial tarns similar to Sunset Pond to the south and Terrace Pond in Passaic County. A wooden wellhouse on the right is ideal for filling up with fresh, cold water from the lake's aquifer.

About 0.2 mile from the parking lot, the road will end at a clearing with some of the buildings from the former Boy Scout camp. A sign will indicate that the trail starts to your right, and at the back of a small clearing behind a shelter you'll see the orange blazes of the Rattlesnake Swamp Trail. Follow it another 0.2 mile, over some sections on wooden logs, until you reach the point where the trail divides.

Turn right and begin climbing moderately and steadily around switchbacks past shelters and campsites. In 0.3 mile, you will reach the ridgeline, where the forest changes to the more open, grassy summit forests typical of the Highlands Region. After working your way across the ridgeline, you will pass a more open area on the right where there is evidence of a past fire that the forest is recovering from. This leads you right to what seems to be the edge of the cliff, where the trail ends at the Appalachian Trail (AT), and there is a sweeping overlook to the east. Directly below in the valley are the roads you came up from Blairstown on. The Kittatinny Ridge, New Jersey's "endless mountain," goes on in both directions, but is more visible to the south. There you can see the highest area of Warren County, around Upper Yards Creek Reservoir.

To the north the trail rises again, and that's where you're going to go. Turn left and follow the white blazes. They will lead you through the open, shrubby ridge forest, with views similar to the one from the junction reoccurring, for a mile of gentle, winding ascent to the Catfish Fire Tower, painted red and white for the benefit of low-flying aircraft.

The tower is officially closed, but the views are still good without climbing it. The same eastern view presents itself, and now you can see to the west over the river and into Pennsylvania. Had the dam been built, you would have been looking at the silvery surface of its lake.

A picnic table near the tower is a good place to lunch or snack. When you're done, continue north along the AT. The trail follows the gravel road to the fire tower for 0.3 mile, and then turns left through a brushy area for 0.1 mile, after which it returns to the road and turns left.

The trail descends for about 300 feet, and then turns left into the woods again. The descent becomes steady and rocky as the forest becomes taller and denser with the drop off the ridge line. Eventually the trail reaches the cleared right-of-way for the old telephone line to the tower, and follows it for a hundred feet through thick mountain laurel. Once the trail turns off, it descends sharply into a wooded area where the laurel gives way to rhododendron, and then reaches the gravel road again.

The AT's white blazes indicate a right turn, but you'll go left. First you pass Rattlesnake Spring, an excellent water source, then you reach the northern end of the Rattlesnake Swamp Trail.

This is the beginning of a 2-mile-long section that will complete the loop, paralleling the ground you covered on the ridge. Here you'll get to see the swamp side, following the unnamed stream that eventually feeds Catfish Pond.

At first, a stream undulates gently through forest similar to that found along the fire tower road. After a while birches on the side herald one of the swampy areas, worth looking out on from a few spots along the trail that offer a view. The swamp ends and the hardwood forest returns, unbroken except for the trail.

There is some variety when the swamp's outflow stream widens and hemlocks begin to shade the trail, which bends slightly to the left to stay on the slope. The woods begin to get shrubbier, creating a sort of "green tunnel," interrupted only by small stream crossings. Slowly, the trail climbs a little into more open woods.

The swampy north end of Catfish Pond comes into view for a while, but then the trail swings away from it back into the woods to a more open area of forest with a large depression to the left. Finally, it reaches the junction near the camp buildings where you began this loop. Return to the parking lot the way you came.

MORE INFORMATION

Restrooms are located at the Mohican Outdoor Center Blueberry Hill Lodge. Dogs must be kept on a leash of six feet or shorter at all times and are not allowed inside buildings at Mohican Outdoor Center. Delaware Water Gap National Recreational Area, 570-426-2452; www.nps.gov/dewa/index.htm. AMC Mohican Outdoor Center, 50 Camp Road, Blairstown, NJ 07825; 908-362-5670; www.outdoors.org/lodging.

TOCKS ISLAND DAM

Tocks Island, 6 miles upriver from the Water Gap in the Delaware, isn't much to look at. But its name evokes a political and legal struggle that has shaped the modern Delaware Valley the way the Storm King lawsuit shaped the Hudson (see essay, page 101).

In 1955, the Army Corps of Engineers decided that a 160-foot-tall earthen dam at Tocks Island would be the perfect means of flood control. By expanding Sunfish Pond on the ridge above the river, a pumped-storage power station could also be built, and a 37-mile lake would be created along the Delaware itself, expanding the area's recreational opportunities and water supply. The Delaware River Basin Commission (DRBC), formed a few years later by Delaware, New Jersey, New York, and Pennsylvania, endorsed the idea. Congress and President Lyndon Johnson gave it final approval in 1965.

That was when everything began to go wrong. First, Supreme Court Justice William O. Douglas, who in his spare time had section-hiked the Appalachian Trail, led a protest hike to Sunfish Pond that forced the cancellation of the plan to expand it. Coercive tactics used by the Corps to force homeowners to sell land at low prices aroused local resentment. The dam's engineering was questioned.

Then it went from bad to worse. The Vietnam War and eviction struggles were diverting money the Corps had expected to have available to build the dam. Some of the homeowners had been required to leave immediately, although the land would not be flooded for the dam for some time. In 1970, the Corps decided to make some money from these properties. It placed ads in New York City newspapers offering the houses as rentals.

The ads were answered primarily by hippies who wanted to live off the land. Many more came without benefit of a rental agreement and stayed in any empty house they found. While some of these communes got along with their more traditional neighbors, many didn't. It took until 1974 for federal marshals to evict the last squatters. By then, any remaining local support for the dam project had collapsed. The DRBC changed its mind about it the following year, and President Jimmy Carter recommended Congress de-authorize it in 1978. In the meantime, the National Park Service began managing the condemned land as the 70,000-acre Delaware Water Gap National Recreational Area.

In 2002, Congress finally de-authorized the Tocks Island Dam. By then, the never-built dam had left its only positive legacies: the Delaware Water Gap NRA and a region barely touched by late twentieth-century development.

TRIP 28
MAHLON DICKERSON RESERVATION

Location: Jefferson, NJ
Rating: Moderate
Distance: 4.4 miles
Elevation Gain: 300 feet
Estimated Time: 3.0 hours
Maps: USGS Franklin; available online and at main park entrance

Sample the New Jersey Highlands with a loop past Morris County's highest point and a nice variety of terrain.

DIRECTIONS
Take Interstate 80 west to Exit 34B and follow NJ 15 north 4 miles to the Weldon Road exit. Get off and turn right. Follow Weldon Road north another 4.5 miles into the reservation and its second entrance on the left, leading to a parking lot with space for 50 vehicles (not the entrance to the trailer/RV area, just before it begins to go downhill). *GPS coordinates*: 41° 00.728' N, 74° 33.883' W.

TRAIL DESCRIPTION
If any of the state's 21 counties could come close to an idealized vision of New Jersey, it would be Morris. East of Interstate 287, it consists of nice, leafy suburbs with ample commuter rail service. Morristown, the county seat, is resplendent with colonial charm and Revolutionary War history. West of 287, the land opens up to the bucolic charm of its horse country southwest and the rugged Highlands terrain in the northwest.

But what Morris lacks in that region are the large state parks and forests that its neighbors in the north and west have in great, sprawling abundance. The county itself has made up the difference, though, with its own park system rivaling what the state offers.

In its largest park, the 3,200-acre Mahlon Dickerson Reservation (partly shared with Sussex County), you'll find, in addition to the ballfields and picnic facilities close to the road, a 12-mile trail system that takes you to Morris County's highest point and past an assortment of terrain.

From the parking lot, follow the diamond teal blazes of the Highlands Trail along the paved path through the picnic tables to where the pavement ends. A

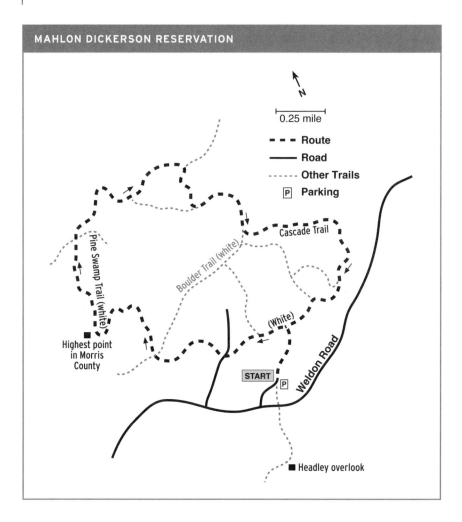

MAHLON DICKERSON RESERVATION

N

0.25 mile

- - - Route
——— Road
.... Other Trails
P Parking

Cascade Trail

Pine Swamp Trail (white)

Boulder Trail (white)

(White)

Highest point in Morris County

Weldon Road

START P

Headley overlook

mere 0.1 mile into the woods, the trail reaches the white-blazed Pine Swamp Trail that loops around the reservation.

Turn left on the Pine Swamp Trail and follow it through a mature hardwood forest to a split 0.2 mile ahead, where the white trail goes right. Bear left onto the unmarked path, a former route of the Pine Swamp Trail, which leads in another 0.1 mile to the RV area, where there are restrooms and a water fountain.

Across the road you'll see a sign for the Pine Swamp Trail, although you're not back there yet. Take the path that leads 0.1 mile past old campsites to a low area. You will merge with a trail coming in from the left blazed with yellow mountain-bike markers, and then at a junction 100 feet farther, bear left onto

Headley Overlook provides a nice view to the west.

the Pine Swamp Trail, now also carrying the yellow discs and blue horse-trail markings.

The trail drops down slightly into a damp area, then begins the most sustained climb of the hike in a series of long switchbacks into a forest of tall oaks and maples. When this levels out, it curves gently past the summit of the rise you have been climbing. A sign across from a bench indicates you have reached the highest point in Morris County at 1,395 feet above sea level (the actual height of land is 100 feet to the left in the woods). The trail reaches a junction with a blue-blazed trail and crosses Pine Swamp's inlet brook, giving you a look at this wetland near the upper end of the Wallkill River basin. You climb a small bump afterward, where tall hemlocks begin to appear in the forest. The trail traverses around the slopes leading to another depression, and a green-blazed trail descends into it to the right. Continue along the Pine Swamp Trail.

The trail climbs slightly to traverse a slope along the reservation's northern boundary, where the forest floor becomes rocky and mossy, and hemlocks become more dominant, giving it the feel of a higher-elevation forest. After 0.1 mile, the trail descends and the forest returns to a more typical mix of hardwoods as you reach the Highlands Trail junction just below where it crosses Sparta Mountain Road. On this section, turn right and follow the combined

Highlands and Pine Swamp trails down into a pleasantly grassy area drained by a small stream that the trail crosses once. At a three-way junction where the green trail from Pine Swamp returns, the two trails turn left and work their way to a shrubby area where a short bypass exists to take you around a muddy spot. From there it climbs up to a stream crossing at a small cascade.

Just past this, the unblazed Cascade Trail branches off to the left. Follow it down into the valley alongside the stream. Eventually both the stream and the trail turn right, paralleling nearby Sparta Mountain Road. Next to a picturesque spot where a path from the road comes down, a sign tells you this is the Cascade Trail.

From here, the ascent begins again, winding back and forth. Eventually it levels out and reaches one of the few vistas available from the reservation, looking over Jefferson's two secondary school buildings and the relatively undeveloped landscape of Oak Ridge and Newfoundland to the northeast; the developed area around Berkshire Valley is concealed by the hill behind the schools.

Continue on the trail to a fork 0.1 mile ahead. The Cascade Trail turns left; you'll turn left and descend along an unmarked path to another fork near a small stream. Turn left here and start climbing. It's arduous given what you've already done, but what you're losing in vertical feet by taking this short cut, you're more than making up for horizontally. The trail turns right, becomes gentler, and reaches the Pine Swamp and Highlands trails in 0.1 mile.

Turn left at this junction. You cross the creek at the floor of the ravine you've been climbing, and on the other side the ascent continues as the old road surface gets gravelly. When it gets level, you'll reach the junction where you began the loop. Turn left on the Highlands Trail and follow it back to the parking lot. A rock there has a plaque memorializing the reservation's namesake, Mahlon Dickerson, one of the most accomplished politicians in the county's history. In the early nineteenth century, he served as a state assemblyman, governor, justice of the State Supreme Court, U.S. senator, and secretary of the Navy for two presidents.

MORE INFORMATION

Restrooms are located at the trailhead and RV area. Dogs must be kept on leashes. Mahlon Dickerson Reservation, Lake Hopatcong, NJ 07849; 973-326-7631; www.morrisparks.net/aspparks/mahlonmain.asp.

TRIP 29
BEARFORT MOUNTAIN

Location: West Milford, NJ
Rating: Difficult
Distance: 4.3 miles
Elevation Gain: 780 feet
Estimated Time: 4.0 hours
Maps: USGS Greenwood Lake; New York–New Jersey Trail Conference North Jersey Trails Map #116; New York–New Jersey Appalachian Trail Map #4

Take in sweeping views and glacial tarns, and scramble up and down stony cliffs from this loop west of Greenwood Lake just south of the state line.

DIRECTIONS

Get off the New York State Thruway at Exit 15. Follow Route 17 north through Sloatsburg to Route 17A and bear right onto the onramp. Follow past Sterling Forest to Greenwood Lake. Turn left onto Route 210 in the center of town. Follow south along the lakeshore roughly 2 miles to the marina at the New York– New Jersey state line and turn right into the parking lot, which has space for ten to fifteen vehicles at the rear. *GPS coordinates*: 41° 11.126′ N, 74° 19.878′ W.

From the south, take County Route 511 along the lake from West Milford, New Jersey. The parking lot is a left turn from this direction, just around a bend with trees, so take care when approaching.

The NJ Transit 196/197 bus route to Warwick passes by the trailhead and has a request stop at Lake Shore Road just south of the state line, a short walk away.

TRIP DESCRIPTION

The glaciers that extended over New Jersey's Skylands more than 10,000 years ago during the last Ice Age created more than the mountains hikers climb. In the valleys between them, they left behind pristine ponds and lakes.

One of the region's largest, Greenwood Lake, straddles the New York state line and is 7 miles long. It may come as a surprise that it wasn't originally that large. Nature got a boost in 1837 when an existing lake named Long Pond was dammed for water power, creating today's scenic and recreational resource.

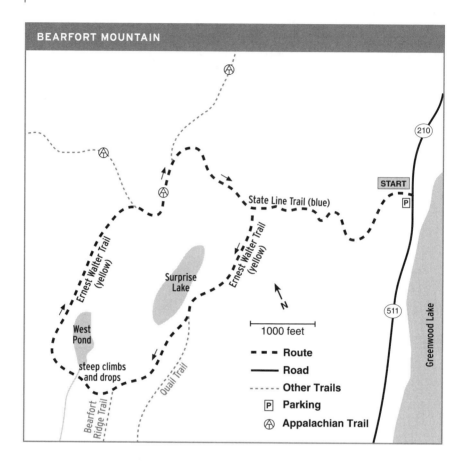

The lake can be fully appreciated from viewing spots on the long ridge to its west, known in New Jersey as Bearfort Mountain. This hike will take you up to one glacial tarn and past two similar to Terrace Pond to the south in Abram Hewitt State Forest.

To get to the ridge top, you'll start on the State Line Trail, blazed with blue dots on white markers. It doesn't actually follow the state line, remaining in New Jersey for its entire length, but it stays close, always within a few hundred feet.

Beginning just behind the kiosk, the State Line Trail climbs moderately at first past a small cascade on the left. The trail then levels out for a while before climbing again, switching back through a second-growth forest where rock outcrops become more visible. One of them, in wet enough seasons, even produces a spring next to the trail. Eventually the trail levels off briefly, long enough for you to appreciate the next, steeper section. Two routes (not on map) have evolved here, both at least partially blazed. The left one is less steep, the right one more direct. They reunite where the grade goes back down to merely being moderate.

A large rock story becomes apparent off to the left uphill. The State Line Trail continues to wind around through woods, increasingly dominated by maple and chestnut oak, until it reaches a large tree right at a break in the rock story. Here a cairn with a splash of yellow paint marks the junction with the Ernest Walter Trail, 0.8 mile from the trailhead.

After catching your breath, make the left turn uphill. The climbing doesn't stop, and the trail gets very rocky, but you'll notice after a while that there's an open rock area on the left. Eventually the trail leaves the scrubby woods and goes onto the rock itself. You'll want to take care with your footing here, as the views over the lake open up. The best place to take it all in is the highest point along the ridge, a nice flat spot sheltered by a pitch pine.

Greenwood Lake sprawls below you. The New Jersey end, in West Milford, is visible, but the New York end is not. The large island below you is entirely within New Jersey. On a good day in summer, there are likely to be plenty of boats on the water. Beyond are the other hills of the area, in Sterling Forest and other protected areas.

In the late nineteenth and early twentieth centuries, the lake and the communities around it became a popular and fashionable summer resort for New Yorkers. Babe Ruth could often be found in the clubs and speakeasies of West Milford between Yankee games. The wealthy American financier J. P. Morgan built a summer getaway, The Boulders, on the east shore.

Continue until the trail finally turns to the east and re-enters the woods. It descends slowly into some wetter areas before reaching, 0.2 mile farther, a large clearing at the side of Surprise Lake, one of the two glacial tarns along the Ernest Walter Trail. There, in addition to views over the lake, you find a junction with the orange-blazed Quail Trail, which follows an old tote road back down to Warwick Turnpike.

The two trails are close together and a little hard to distinguish at first, but then the yellow blazes bear right. The trail eventually works its way along the wet and grassy areas next to the lake's outlet brook until it reaches a grove of pure rhododendron, sometimes forming tunnels to the point that you may have to duck as you descend through them.

Eventually some mountain laurel starts to grow amid the rhododendron, and the tunnels widen and end. You will come out on rocky ledges next to the swamps, and eventually the trail turns and crosses the stream, giving you the opportunity to climb up the rocky ledges on the other side, down them, and then up another set.

Steadily plugging away at this will get you to a short, level area of woods, where you will ascend to an open area of rock. On it, you will see the three white blazes that indicate the north end of the Bearfort Ridge Trail, which also goes back to Warwick Turnpike and the trails to Terrace Pond. There are nice views here to the southeast and the rest of the extensive ridge.

Continuing, you finally reach the highest elevation of the hike, a plateau at about 1,380 feet above sea level. At its west end, the trail forks and a crude sign indicates a view a short distance to the right. Following this fork leads to a rocky outcrop with a view over the very small West Pond, the other glacial tarn on this trip. It is similar to Terrace Pond but much smaller.

Back on the trail, the drop into the valley that carries the pond's outlet brook is almost vertical in some places, and this may be difficult for dogs and small children to handle. After crossing the heavily tannic stream on some rocks, you'll get to climb more rocks and negotiate more glacial hurdles until the trail finally bends to the north for the backstretch of the loop.

It follows the tops of the rock fins for the next 0.5 mile. A drop off the fins into a birchy area with lots of mud indicates that you are coming to the junction with the Appalachian Trail (AT). When you do reach it, turn right. First, you'll go up a rock stair to a bare area, and then back down into a level, scrubby woods. The AT leads over a couple more rocky areas, then down again into the wood, and over another rock outcrop. It winds eastward, up and over another rock, and then drops down and turns north.

Shortly afterward, at another flat, rocky spot with pitch pines, the AT reaches its "last exit in New Jersey," where the paint on the rocks indicates the State Line Trail forks off to the right while the AT continues on ahead into New York.

The State Line Trail completes the loop portion of the hike. It is 0.4 mile down past more rocky fins to the other end of the Ernest Walter Trail, and then back to your vehicle.

MORE INFORMATION

No restrooms are available. Wawayanda State Park, 973-853-4462; www.state .nj.us/dep/parksandforests/parks/abram.html

AMC AND THE HIGHLANDS CONSERVATION ACT

The New York metropolitan area is so densely populated and sprawling, it is easy to forget it has a natural backyard. That would be the 3.5-million-acre Highland region, which includes the New York–New Jersey Highlands as well as parts of Pennsylvania and Connecticut. The Highlands, a region of steep and forested valleys overlying the ancient igneous and metamorphic rock of the Reading Prong, provide outdoor recreational opportunities, food, and water for millions of people in the nearby Northeast Corridor.

In the last couple of decades, local, state, and federal governments have joined conservation organizations such as the Appalachian Mountain Club (AMC) in recognizing the Highlands' importance and protecting it, as exurban development has begun to reach it. New Jersey took the lead with the Highlands Water Protection and Planning Act in 2004. Supported by AMC, the act created a 15-member council to protect water resources and biodiversity.

AMC had been active in the Highlands even before recent efforts (the first meeting to preserve Sterling Forest, on the state line, took place in a member's house). It is a member of the Highlands Coalition (www.highlandscoalition .org), an alliance of nonprofit organizations and government agencies that has worked to protect and preserve the Highlands.

The Coalition and AMC secured the passage of the federal Highlands Conservation Act in 2004, which makes matching funds of $11 million a year for ten years available to the four states for land and water conservation projects in the Highlands area. Projects funded by this have included the acquisition of additional land in the Wyanokie Range, around Assiniwikam Mountain, near Wanaque, New Jersey, to further protect the large reservoir of the same name, which provides water to many of North Jersey's largest cities.

In New York, AMC and its Coalition partners have supported efforts to acquire the remaining portions of Arrow Park, a vital area along the Appalachian Trail corridor between Sterling Forest and Harriman State Park. Farther north, they have also supported efforts to further protect the 63,000-acre Great Swamp in Dutchess and Putnam counties.

AMC also actively supports efforts to make these important natural areas accessible to hikers to appreciate. In addition to helping complete the original Highlands Trail from the Delaware River to the Hudson, AMC is working to plan and develop a network that will better connect trails through the Highlands in Pennsylvania.

To find out more, including what you can do to help, visit www.outdoors .org/hikethehighlands.

TRIP 30
ABRAHAM S. HEWITT STATE FOREST–
TERRACE POND

Location: Upper Greenwood Lake, NJ
Rating: Moderate
Distance: 3.1 miles
Elevation Gain: 260 feet
Estimated Time: 3.5 hours
Maps: USGS Wawayanda; New York–New Jersey Trail Conference
Map #116, in *North Jersey Trails* set

**This classic glacial tarn is located near Passaic County's highest
elevations, with views of the Manhattan skyline on clear days.**

DIRECTIONS
From Route 23, turn right on Clinton Road near Newfoundland. Follow 7.3
miles to the trailhead on the right, with parking for ten to fifteen vehicles on
either side of the road. If you reach a break in the woods on either side of the
road (a gas pipeline right-of-way), you have gone too far. *GPS coordinates*: 41°
08.518′ N, 74° 24.444′ W.

There is room for a few vehicles at the trailhead. More spaces are available
on the other side of the road, near the entrance to the Project U.S.E. Wildcat
Mountain Wilderness Center, an outdoor education program.

TRAIL DESCRIPTION
Sunset Pond, a National Natural Landmark along the Appalachian Trail in
Warren County, is New Jersey's best-known glacial tarn. (*Tarn*, from an Old
Norse word for pond, refers to those bodies of water left behind by melting
glaciers and usually found in isolated mountain regions.) But Terrace Pond is
more accessible and more frequently visited than Sunset Pond.

You reach this trailhead by following Clinton Road, legendary for its
rumors of strange and spooky occurrences, through City of Newark watershed land.

This hike is a rewarding loop to Terrace Pond, atop Bearfort Ridge to the
east. It is in Abram S. Hewitt State Forest, named after the nineteenth-century
industrialist, later a congressman and mayor of New York, who, among his
other interests, owned the area's iron mines.

see the pipeline's arrow-straight course for miles to the west. Keep a sharp eye for the blue blazes on the right side of the cut. The trail turns back into the woods near the crest of the ridge. The turn is not obvious, so pay close attention to avoid inadvertently drifting off and continuing uphill. If you go the wrong way, backtrack down until you are on the blue-blazed trail again.

Once off the pipeline, the trail continues up the same hill, but more steeply than it did before. Some stretches require some hand-and-foot scrambling. Soon, this effort is rewarded with a large rock outcrop on the left of the trail. The view to the west and south is more expansive than it was from the gas pipeline.

Atop Bearfort Ridge, the long fin-like rock outcrops and the troughs between them testify to the presence of the Wisconsin glacier during the last Ice Age. Geologists believe that twenty thousand years ago this glacier reached its greatest extent just south of here, then began to retreat. A portion of its ice settled into this depression on the ridge and became the pond.

This route gets a little complicated near the pond, the nexus of the local trail system. The trail descends, finally joining the white-blazed Terrace Pond Circular Trail near a short path to a viewpoint that takes in the whole body of water. As you turn left, this vista changes and gives you more opportunities to appreciate the pond's pudding stone cliffs and clear waters—a sight evoking the rocks and lakes depicted in Roger Dean's Yes album covers given the right light and even more so with fall foliage reflecting in the water

Don't dive into the waters. Signs along the trail warn that swimming is strictly prohibited due to previous accidents, some of which were fatal. A rescue is difficult in this area. What you might want to do instead is stop to have lunch or a snack. There are many spots where you can sit down overlooking the pond.

The Terrace Pond Red Trail, unsurprisingly blazed in red, leaves to the right midway down the east side of the lake. Farther down a short distance are views from a high area just off the trail to the southeast, including the Manhattan skyline on clear days.

Return to the Terrace Pond Circular Trail, which continues around the pond in a counterclockwise direction and moves away from its cliffs. You reach water level in a muddy area and cross a small brook and then pass the yellow-blazed Terrace Pond South Trail.

The white trail continues east from this junction, then turns north again. Before it returns to Terrace Pond's east side, the Yellow Dot Trail (blazed with a yellow dot bordered in white), leaves to the right, descending the east side of the ridge and eventually ending at the Terrace Pond South Trail. The white

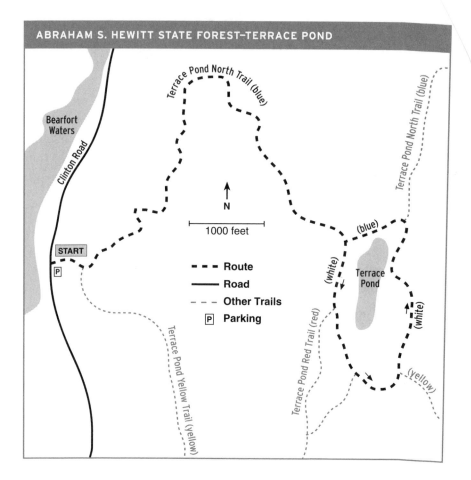

Once you pass the reservoir, the road begins to straighten out. Keep an eye out for the trailhead, since it is unsigned, on your right. A short path, blazed with blue and yellow, splits ten feet from the trailhead. Turn left onto the blue-blazed Terrace Pond North Trail. It heads north, trending eastward as it gently ascends through rocky hardwood forest broken by the occasional hemlock stand. Wet areas are bridged with either stepping stones or split-log puncheons that serve as bridges.

Open space appears in the woods ahead approximately 0.4 mile from the fork. This is the right-of-way of one of New Jersey's major natural gas pipelines. Here the trail turns right and follows the break uphill, climbing more steeply. ATV tracks are frequently present, and in times of wet weather large, deep puddles may have accumulated in the flat areas.

Views open up to the west into Sussex County. To the north, on the slopes, the Shawangunks and Catskills become visible on clear enough days. You can trail continues on, rising to the cliffs on the eastern side of the pond with pitch pine flourishing in the thin, rocky soil. To the east is the highest ground in Passaic County, with several unnamed summits.

At the northeast corner of the pond, the blue-blazed Terrace Pond North Trail veers off to the north with the gas pipeline. The combined blue and white blazed trail continues its circuit of the lake, going left. Cross another stream, then hike back up to the cliff tops, once again enjoying the views over the pond. In a quarter-mile you are back at the junction where you started the circuit and are ready to return to where you parked.

MORE INFORMATION

There are no restroom facilities. Trails are open year-round; only hiking and snowshoeing are permitted. Abram S. Hewitt State Forest, c/o Wawayanda State Forest, 885 Warwick Turnpike, Hewitt, NJ 07421; 973-853-4462; www .state.nj.us/dep/parksandforests/parks/abram.html.

THE LEGENDS OF CLINTON ROAD

If you drive down Clinton Road in daylight, you may not appreciate why it has a bad reputation. (Even outside New Jersey it is known as one of the state's most notorious back roads.) But if you drive this main route to Bearfort Mountain, Terrace Pond, and the adjacent portions of Abram S. Hewitt State Forest and Wawayanda State Park at night on the way home from a hike, you will understand why.

For 11 miles in West Milford Township (between Route 23 at Newfoundland and the small, unincorporated settlement of Upper Greenwood Lake), this two-lane blacktop winds and meanders past long stretches of woods, a large Newark reservoir, and a few houses. Until the late twentieth century, parts of it weren't even paved. It is not a county highway and, since neither end is in a highly populated region, it receives very little traffic.

So perhaps it is not surprising that legends of all sorts of dark, sometimes paranormal, happenings have arisen over the years. Around 1915, travel guidebooks cautioned those who might pass through on their way to and from the small town of Clinton (now flooded) that the road there was a notorious bandit hangout.

In the late twentieth century, *Weird NJ* magazine began to collect readers' stories about supposed gatherings of witches, devil worshippers, and the Ku Klux Klan in the nearby woods. It described the horrible fates awaiting an unlucky traveler who might stumble upon them. Strange creatures supposedly lurked within these woods, especially escapees from the now-closed Jungle Habitat, a drive-through safari park, elsewhere in the township. There were stories about cannibalistic locals who would trap drivers or mysterious black pickup trucks that would appear if a vehicle stopped in the wrong driveway and would chase it back to civilization. A ghostly Camaro reportedly appears if, while on the road, you mention the young girl who supposedly died in it.

Nothing escapes the legends, even when there's a rational explanation. Cross Castle, demolished by the city of Newark in the 1990s, was the residence of a reclusive millionaire, it is true, but there is no evidence of secret cell activities going on in the basement. Similarly, the slightly conical stone structures in the woods near the reservoir are Revolution-era iron smelters, not Druidic temples.

All the same, you may be tempted to toss a quarter over the bridge below Clinton Reservoir at midnight, to see if the ghost boy decides to throw it back.

TRIP 31
ASSINIWIKAM MOUNTAIN

Location: West Milford, NJ
Rating: Moderate
Distance: 2.2 miles
Elevation Gain: 200 feet
Estimated Time: 1.5 hours
Maps: USGS Wanaque; New York–New Jersey Trail Conference North Jersey Trails Map #115

This short loop leads to sweeping, wild North Jersey vistas from one of the state's most striking ranges.

DIRECTIONS
From the south, take Route 23 to Union Valley Road (County Road 513) at Newfoundland. Follow north about 4 miles to Gould Road and turn right. Continue along Gould to Wooley Road and turn left. At Macopin Road, turn right. Pass Bubbling Springs and turn left a mile down the road onto West Brook Road. About 2.5 miles along, turn right onto Snake Den Road West (if you pass the other Snake Den Road, with the sign for the Weis Center, you've gone too far). Follow the road uphill a mile to where it becomes dirt. At Boy Scout Lake, you will see the signs for Camp Wyanokie and the beginning of two trails, one white with yellow dots and the other white with red. If the camp isn't busy, there is room here and at the pullout with the water pump up the road for five to ten vehicles. *GPS coordinates*: 41° 04.326′ N, 74° 20.860′ W.

From the north, take Union Valley Road south from the southern end of Greenwood Lake to Macopin Road, which forks off to the left uphill at a gas station, and follow the remainder of the previous directions.

TRAIL DESCRIPTION
Since Interstate 287 was completed through Passaic and Bergen counties to the New York State Thruway in 1993, more travelers have had an opportunity to see the Wyanokies, a crown-like group of peaks just north of the rock cut north of Exit 55. The Wyanokies are in the southerly of the two units of Norvin Green State Forest's 5,000 acres. The most common destination for hikers within them is Wyanokie High Point, the top of the crown. This trip, however, will take you to the higher Assiwikinam Mountain at the northwest corner

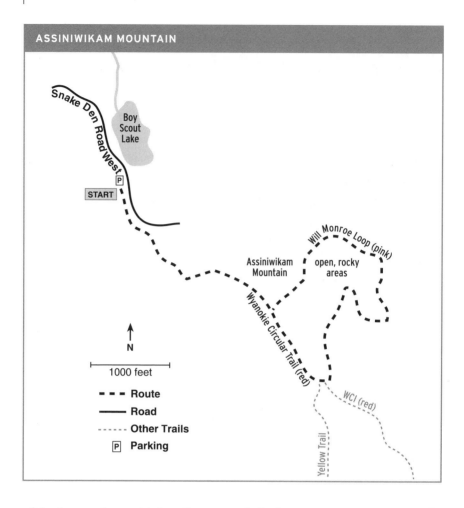

of the forest, where with less distance and climbing you can get some equally sweeping views from its open, rock-hop summit.

From Camp Wyanokie, a facility for the residents of the West Essex communities (the Caldwells, Roseland, and Fairfield), follow the road and the red-dot markers of the Wyanokie Circular Trail 0.2 mile to the end, where the trail leaves the dirt road just past the barrier at the state-land boundary. It goes over some small bumps thick with immature hardwoods before leveling out to cross the stream that feeds Boy Scout Lake. Once across, it climbs again, traversing gently into another stand of young hardwoods before the pink-blazed Will Monroe Loop comes in from the left.

William Monroe, its namesake, was a forestry professor at what is now Montclair State University. In the 1920s, Monroe first cut and blazed most of the trails in the Wyanokies with the help of local members of the Vermont-

From Assiniwikam Mountain, you can enjoy the view of the New Jersey Skylands.

based Green Mountain Club. This effort helped make lands the state had inherited from the estate of Western Union president Norvin Green (1818–1893) a viable state forest. The state continues to expand the area when land is available, such as the former location of the Jungle Habitat safari park to the north of here.

Continuing straight on the Wyanokie Circular Trail, the traverse takes you to a four-way intersection where the red dots continue ahead, a yellow trail goes off to the right, and the pink blazes of the Monroe Loop come downhill from the left. Monroe Loop is the trail you'll want to take.

Follow it uphill as it wends alternately through patches of dense, immature woods and more open, grassy woods with stunted chestnut oak and maple typical of the Highlands. The ridgeline keeps getting tantalizingly closer, but it always turns out to be either higher than it appears or the trail keeps traversing rather than going directly uphill.

Finally, at a point where the trail seems to just reach the edge of a rock that's certain to have a view but instead looks like it's heading downhill, turn right and come out on the rock. Not only will you see a pink blaze ahead, you'll see a lot more.

There is no timberline on a mountain anywhere in New Jersey, but here you could be forgiven for feeling like there was. The trail follows along the tops of rocks and short paths between them as it bends back to the south, with a few small trees cropping up from the gaps in the rocks.

Here you can see, over the tops of the trees at the edge of the clearing, the mountains to the north and west, such as Bearfort. Follow the trail as it loops across the rock tops (children and dogs may want to take this slowly). It re-enters the woods but soon comes out to some other large, rocky, viewless clearings, one of which is the mountain's 1,180-foot summit. The trail continues south through more wooded sections to the edge of the summit cap, where it begins to loop back around past some large downed trees.

After 0.1 mile you reach another area with a wider view than just mentioned, nearer the north end of the summit plateau. High Point and the other Wyanokie peaks are visible to the south. Behind them is a section of Wanaque Reservoir and the viaduct on I-287.

To the north are Saddle Mountain and some of the other nearby peaks. The many skeletal dead trees poking from the slopes, and the steep drop between the two peaks, as well as the open, rocky nature of the summit, give this vista in particular a wild feel not often found in New Jersey. In fact, it feels almost like the Adirondacks.

The trail then leads into the woods, past some large outcrops. Eventually the Monroe Loop winds back and forth down the mountainside and rejoins the Wyanokie Circular Trail. You passed this point on the way up; a right turn leads back to Camp Wyanokie, Boy Scout Lake, and your vehicle.

MORE INFORMATION

Restrooms are available at Camp Wyanokie when it is open. Dogs must be leashed. Norvin Green State Forest, 973-962-7031; www.njparksandforests.org/parks/norvin.html.

TRIP 32
RINGWOOD STATE PARK

Location: Ringwood, NJ
Rating: Moderate
Distance: 3.5 miles
Elevation Gain: 400 feet
Estimated Time: 2.5 hours
Maps: USGS Ramsey, Sloatsburg; New York–New Jersey Trail Conference North Jersey Trails Map #115

This isolated hike through a remote patch of New Jersey's Skylands region takes in the state botanical garden and a popular local swimming spot.

DIRECTIONS
From the south, follow Greenwood Lake Turnpike (County Road 511) to Sloatsburg Road on the right, just before crossing an inlet of Wanaque Reservoir. Continue north 2.0 miles to Morris Road on the right. Morris Road will lead you right into the New Jersey State Botanical Garden and parking (area A) on the left. A $5 parking fee is charged during summer weekends. *GPS coordinates*: 41° 07.633′ N, 74° 14.295′ W.

From the north, take Exit 15A from the New York State Thruway. Follow Route 17 north 1.0 mile to the Sterling Mine Road turnoff. Take that road (County Road 72) uphill several miles into Orange County. Continue past the Long Meadow Road intersection into New Jersey, where it becomes Sloatsburg Road and passes Ringwood Manor on the right. Morris Road is on the left 1.5 miles south of the state line.

TRAIL DESCRIPTION
Sussex County may have the higher hills and mountains, but it is the northern portion of Passaic County that has North Jersey's wildest lands. The large tracts that protect the watersheds, which provide drinking water to Newark and many other communities in the region, augment most of the state parks and forests in this area.

This rugged landscape of woods, mountains, and lakes has come to be called the Skylands. Francis Lynde Stetson, lawyer to legendary financier J. P. Morgan, gave his estate the same name. He purchased the land in 1891 and built the estate near the county's northeastern corner in Ringwood on a

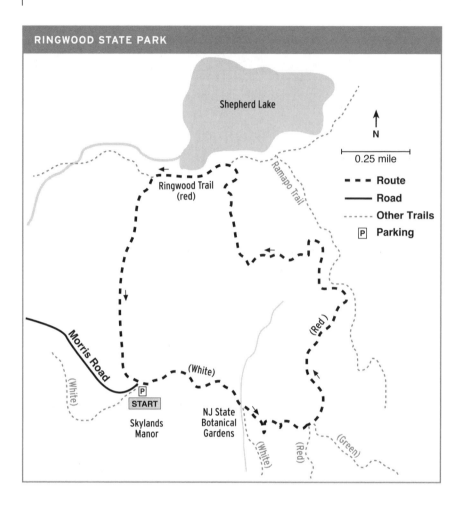

thousand acres that had been part of Ringwood Manor, home to various iron-makers dating back to pre-Revolutionary times.

After Stetson's death the property passed to Clarence MacKenzie Lewis, another Wall Street wizard, who built a forty-four room Jacobean Revival mansion and hired John Russell Pope (the architect who designed the Jefferson Memorial in Washington) to lay out and plant gardens during the 1920s. Lewis made it his summer home. The whole tract was eventually purchased by the state in 1966. By 1984 it became the New Jersey State Botanical Garden, one of several units of 4,000-acre Ringwood State Park.

This hike gives you a broad sampling of the park's offerings, from the heavily used botanical garden and Shepherd Lake areas to isolated mountaintops.

Starting from the parking lot, you will notice the white blazes of the Crossover Trail turn off the main road onto a paved path from the information

Shepherd Lake is a popular swimming spot in Ringwood State Park.

kiosk. Follow the paved path around the edge of the botanical garden past a Tudor-style outbuilding. Roughly 0.1 mile later, the blazes direct you to turn left into the woods. A dirt road carries the trail gently downhill 0.3 mile to a crossing over an unnamed stream that drains into Cupsaw Lake and, ultimately, Wanaque Reservoir.

Just past the reservoir the Halifax Trail, blazed with a green-dot-on-white marker, intersects and leaves to the left. Follow it as it slowly switches back and forth along gentle slopes, up the south face of Mount Defiance, the highest peak in the park. The forest slowly changes from mature hardwoods to the scrubbier, grassy heath of Highlands summits. Eventually, near the top of the rise, there is an overlook just off the trail to the left. It looks south, taking in a small section of Wanaque Reservoir and the lands around it.

The trail drops into the shadow of a high rock ledge, and the forest canopy becomes tall and mature again. After a short descent into a slightly wet area, the trail meets the red-dot-on-white Ringwood–Ramapo Trail. You will turn left on this less-used path, working your way over to a breach in a stone ledge and up onto Mount Defiance's summit plateau. The forest again becomes grassy and more open. The path meanders for a while to the mountain's

1,040-foot summit just off the trail on a rocky rise near the west side of the plateau. A short descent below, another viewpoint presents itself to the west. From here you can see the hills flanking the state line out to West Milford, and some of the Ringwood Manor buildings to the north. Immediately to the west is Thunder Mountain, home of a state-owned shooting range.

The trail continues to descend moderately down Defiance's north slope to a grassy gas pipeline right-of-way. Once across it, in a forest of very tall oaks and maples, you will join a wide mountain-bike trail. This trail is part of a large network made possible by a 1995 purchase that extended the park eastward into Bergen County, almost doubling its size. A short distance past that junction, stay on the mountain-bike trail as the Ramapo–Ringwood Trail forks off to the right, uphill.

The mountain-bike trail is unmarked, but easy to follow. In many areas the mountain bikers have created challenging bends and jumps that you can, of course, detour past. The trail continues uphill from here but not as high. After this traverse, it switches back, descends into a wet area with a few streams, and then eventually crosses a dirt road that leads to the shooting range.

Once across this, the trail continues through the woods into several more wet areas. It eventually reaches a large red pine plantation through which Shepherd Lake is visible. Finally, it descends to the dirt road along the lake's side, where you turn left to rejoin the Ringwood–Ramapo Trail.

Eventually, the road leads to the large, heavily developed recreational area at the lake's south shore. You may swim in the roped area when lifeguards are on duty (10 A.M. to 6 P.M. from Memorial Day through Labor Day). Boats are available for rent here should your plans include exploring the lake farther, just south of the New York state line.

When you wish to return to where you parked, follow the trail markers to the middle of the three roads that lead away from Shepherd Lake (it will be the level one). Leave the trail and follow the road 0.5 mile back to a junction with the botanical garden entry road and the Crossover Trail, just below parking area A.

Keep to the right and watch for passing traffic. The road walk saves you from ending the hike with a steep climb, if you had to continue along the Ramapo–Ringwood Trail to its junction with the Crossover Trail.

You might want to tour the botanical garden and Ringwood Manor, a short distance north of the park on Sloatsburg Road. The manor is a National Historic Landmark. Robert Erskine lived here while he worked as George

Washington's surveyor-general during the American Revolution. Free tours are given from Wednesday to Sunday year-round from 10 A.M. to 3 P.M.

MORE INFORMATION

Restroom facilities are located near the trailhead and at Shepherd Lake. Ringwood State Park is open daily at 8:15 A.M. Swimming is permitted only when lifeguards are on duty from 10 A.M. to 6 P.M. between Memorial Day and Labor Day weekends. Ringwood State Park, 1304 Sloatsburg Road, Ringwood, NJ 07456; 973-962-7031; www.state.nj.us/dep/parksandforests/parks/ringwood.html.

TRIP 33
PYRAMID MOUNTAIN
NATURAL HISTORIC AREA

Location: Montville, NJ
Rating: Moderate
Distance: 2.2 miles
Elevation Gain: 320 feet
Estimated Time: 1.5 hours
Maps: USGS Boonton; map available at trailhead and online at
Pyramid Mountain Natural Historic Area website

It doesn't take much work to get to the great views and sights in this small county park.

DIRECTIONS
Get off I-287 in Boonton. Follow Main Street across town to Boonton Avenue (County Road 511) and turn right. Follow 2.0 miles to Rockaway Valley Road, where 511 continues north at a slightly offset intersection. The parking area and visitor center are on the right 1.5 miles north of that intersection. Use the upper entrance because this is a one-way parking lot, which has room for 30 vehicles. *GPS coordinates*: 40° 56.801′ N, 74° 23.306′ W.

TRAIL DESCRIPTION
Outdoor enthusiasts in northern New Jersey have long known that Pyramid Mountain is a special place. This small 934-foot bump near Boonton's Taylor-town Reservoir boasts a diverse forest with some species that are otherwise rare in the state. The mountain is home to Tripod Rock, a large glacial erratic sitting on three smaller boulders, and also offers sweeping views to the east and west.

But Pyramid Mountain wasn't protected until 1987, when the county acquired 1,500 acres there. Since then, an extensive trail system has been cut and blazed, and the county has built some impressive facilities at the park's entrance area along Boonton Avenue in Montville. These have made Pyramid Mountain an excellent destination for hikers.

The blue-blazed Mennen Trail starts next to the kiosk at the trailhead. It leads into the woods, and then crosses a newer trail (not on map), which

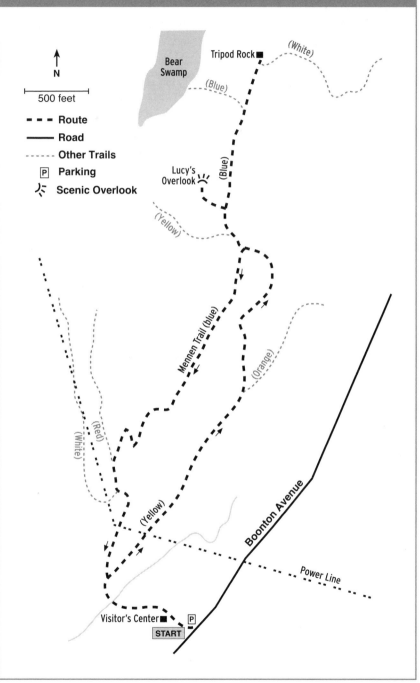

PYRAMID MOUNTAIN NATURAL HISTORIC AREA

N

500 feet

- - - Route
— Road
----- Other Trails
P Parking
Scenic Overlook

Bear Swamp

Tripod Rock

(White)

(Blue)

Lucy's Overlook

(Blue)

(Yellow)

Mennen Trail (blue)

(Orange)

(Red)

(White)

(Yellow)

Boonton Avenue

Power Line

Visitor's Center

P

START

crosses the road. Stay on the Mennen Trail, which leisurely meanders through a forest of maturing maples.

After 0.1 mile the trail leads to a wooden bridge crossing Stony Brook, impounded farther upstream to create the reservoir and Fayson Lakes. A yellow-blazed trail forks off to the right and remains low while the blue trail begins to climb.

Turn right onto the yellow trail and start your loop here. Ahead you can see the clearing in the woods made by a power line, which cuts across the Pyramid Mountain property. The trail crosses it, and enters a mixed forest of tall oaks, maples, beech, and hickory. To the left, uphill, an impressive series of rock ledges begins to rise. On the right, the picnic facilities of a Ukrainian-American retreat can be seen. (Stay off the short paths that lead there; it is clearly posted as private property.)

Approximately 0.3 mile from the power line, an orange-blazed trail continues the traverse along the hillside to the reservoir. Bear left and continue uphill on the yellow trail, as it finds a breach in the ledges and makes some rocky climbs to limited views to the east. It soon levels out again and turns first to the north then curves gradually around to the west where the Mennen Trail comes in from the left.

The two trails continue north together, blazed in both colors, for about 200 feet before the yellow trail departs to the left, toward Bear Swamp. Continue along the blue-blazed Mennen Trail north into an area where mountain laurel walls off the trail on both sides. Then pass a side trail with white-bordered blue markers and keep going.

The shrubbiness abates and the forest opens. Cross the municipal boundary from Montville into neighboring Kinnelon, where more boulders are strewn amidst the trees. One is at the center of a wide spot in the middle of the trail.

These boulders are glacial erratics, carried here in ice from their original formations and left behind at the end of the last Ice Age when the glaciers melted. Erratics are frequently found in the New York–New Jersey Highlands, and geologists have used them to determine the pace and extent of glaciations at different periods.

A slight descent brings you to a three-way junction where the Mennen Trail turns left and joins the white-blazed Kinnelon–Montville (K–M) Trail in going downhill. Continue ahead roughly 300 feet along the K–M Trail, to Tripod Rock on the left.

An obvious place to take an extended break, Tripod Rock is the biggest attraction in Pyramid Mountain Natural Historic Area and its visual icon. It is actually four rocks. Three on the bottom support a massive 1,440-cubic-foot boulder two feet above the ground. Due to the triad of nearby stones, which neatly frame the sunset on the summer solstice, some people believe that humans put these stones here. Be careful while exploring this area. If you climb neighboring stones to get a better view or photograph Tripod Rock, you should know that the top surfaces are not flat and their sides are steep.

Head back to the K–M Trail and turn around to follow it back to the Mennen Trail and the side trail you passed earlier. This time, turn right and follow the side trail about 400 feet slightly downhill to Lucy's Overlook. Views of Rockaway and Jefferson townships are visible to the west.

Stay on the Mennen Trail instead of following the yellow trail back down the way you came up. The Mennen Trail continues across the top of Pyramid Mountain, through grassier areas. Deer sometimes graze in this open, scrubby ridge-top forest. Near the 934-foot summit is an eastern viewpoint where you can see, over Turkey Mountain, the Watchung ridge to the east, and the two Claridge House high-rises in Verona. The midtown Manhattan skyline can be seen next to them.

The Mennen Trail descends and passes some dramatic ridges. Switchbacks lead to a junction with the red trail just next to the power line. Continue alongside the power line over the ridge crest to make a slight loop through some more mature forest. The trail then crosses the open cut. From here, it is another 0.1 mile back to the yellow trail, which forked off from where you started.

MORE INFORMATION

Restroom facilities are located at the visitor center, and a portable toilet is available at the trailhead. Dogs must be leashed. Pyramid Mountain Natural Historic Area, Morris County Park Commission, 53 East Hanover Avenue, P.O. Box 1295, Morristown, NJ 07962; 973-334-3130; www.morrisparks.net/asspparks/pyrmtnmain.asp.

TRIP 34
PALISADES INTERSTATE PARK

Location: Alpine, NJ
Rating: Easy
Distance: 1.5 miles
Elevation Gain: 100 feet
Estimated Time: 1.0 hour
Maps: USGS Yonkers; New York–New Jersey Trail Conference Hudson Palisades Trails #109

Sweeping views of the Hudson River from the cliff tops are highlights of this short walk through a historically significant park that straddles the New Jersey–New York border.

DIRECTIONS

Take Exit 3 off the Palisades Parkway, which leads directly to State Line Lookout. (If coming from the north, do not take Exit 3 to Route 9W as there is no way to cross the road. Instead, use the U-turn signed for this exit just to its south.) At the lookout there is space for 100 vehicles. *GPS coordinates*: 40° 59.357′ N, 73° 54.399′ W.

Coach USA's Red and Tan bus service stops on Route 9W near Alpine Boy Scout Camp. You can follow a trail across a footbridge over the parkway to the Long Path and hike up to the lookout, 0.5 mile to the north.

TRAIL DESCRIPTION

For most of its length in New Jersey, Palisades Interstate Park is a narrow strip including the parkway, the cliffs, and the land below. From its southern end near the George Washington Bridge, the Long Path runs close to the parkway. The trail passes through its rest stops and scenic overlooks. The traffic is not only audible, but also visible through the trees that buffer the road from the edges of the Palisades themselves. Only in the northeast corner of the state does the highway turn sufficiently inland to allow the trails to have a large enough portion of uninterrupted land for quiet, enjoyable hiking.

This section includes part of Route 9W, which is now closed to vehicles, and several old roads marked as cross-country ski trails. The mile-long access road runs out to the cliff edge, intersecting the Long Path and other trails,

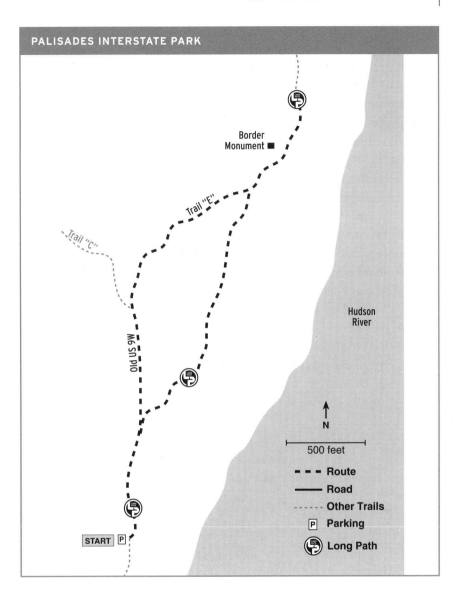

PALISADES INTERSTATE PARK

Border Monument ■

Trail "E"

Trail "C"

Old US 9W

Hudson River

↑
N

500 feet

- - - Route
—— Road
----- Other Trails
P Parking
Long Path

START P

before ending at a parking lot with a visitor center, a picnic area, and viewing platforms.

You might want to enjoy the panoramic view from this overlook, before you start hiking. Stone walls prevent you from getting too close to the sheer cliffs, which drop several hundred feet to the Hudson River. On the opposite side you can hardly miss the city of Yonkers to the south, the Riverdale section of the Bronx, the George Washington Bridge, and some of the Manhattan skyline beyond it on a clear day. You can easily see the Metro-North Hudson Line tracks along the river's east shore, and the assortment of passenger trains that use them. By following the stations upriver from Yonkers, an observer familiar with the line can tell that the small community directly across the river is Hastings-on-Hudson. Woods separate it from Dobbs Ferry to its north.

When you are ready to start your hike, follow the Long Path's aqua blazes. They are visible and signify a turn at the road just west of the visitor center. They lead to a short path through the woods before returning to the pavement, once part of Route 9W, and turning left.

Travel 0.3 mile north along the pavement, past more observation promontories and binoculars, to where the trail splits off to the right, into the woods. It leaves the road and the busy lookout area behind, gently winding through a ridge-top forest of chestnut oak and maple, gradually yielding to more mature hardwoods as the woods surround the trail. The Long Path is a wide dirt route, and it is easy to see how its name was derived from a line in a Walt Whitman poem, *"The long brown path before me leading wherever I choose."*

At 0.6 mile from the parking lot, ski trail E comes in from the left and is marked by a sign. Continue on the Long Path, which descends slightly and reaches a large stone obelisk atop a small stone outcrop. This is a boundary marker for the state line, a "witness post" in an accessible location indicating the boundary's eastern terminus in the middle of the nearby Hudson River channel.

The marker's placement and the inscriptions on it reflect the settlement of a great dispute during the colonial era between the two colonies. For almost half a century, New York insisted on a border close to the current one. However, New Jersey claimed a line that reached the Delaware River at Cochecton in Sullivan County approximately five miles north of the current border, north of its apex in Port Jervis, which would have put present-day New York communities like Unionville and Warwick in the Garden State. The dispute occasionally escalated into a shooting war, but was resolved in 1773, when it was clear the two colonies were going to have bigger things to worry about very soon.

The actual state line, just past the monument, is marked by a chain-link fence. It was put there by Columbia University's Lamont-Doherty Earth Observatory, which resides on a large stretch of land just west of the park on the New York side.

Go down the stone steps past the monument to an opening in the fence, and into the southernmost corner of Rockland County, New York. The trail continues to descend along rough steps, with a guardrail on the cliff side. Although the trail levels out, the guardrail continues.

Hikers enjoy the view of the Hudson from the Palisades just past the New York state line.

The guardrail ends as you get to some of the viewpoints along here. Continue to be careful. There are some very sheer dropoffs on the trail. About 0.2 mile north of the state line, at one of these passages, you'll see a rock outcrop ahead. This allows for another view of the Hudson River.

At this location, much more intimate than State Line Lookout, you can see some of the same things. Dobbs Ferry is clearly visible, almost directly across the river. If you follow the Hudson Line north you can easily pick out Irvington as well, and the exclusive small community of Ardsley-on-Hudson north of it. At the north end of this panorama is the eastern half of the Tappan Zee Bridge.

The story of these trails, the views they offer, and Palisades Interstate Park began in the late nineteenth century, when the cliffs were regularly being quarried to build taller and taller buildings in Lower Manhattan. Concerns began to be raised that the beautiful Palisades might be mined until nothing beautiful was left. The governors of New Jersey and New York, Foster Voorhees and Teddy Roosevelt, respectively, jointly purchased some of the land to protect it. This event occurred shortly before Roosevelt assumed the vice presidency in 1901.

It was the first time that states acquired land to protect it from exploitation, a distinction that has earned the park its designation as a National Historic

Landmark. The Palisades Interstate Park Commission has grown to manage parkland as far north as the Shawangunks, including Harriman and Bear Mountain state parks.

After you have taken in the view, return to New Jersey via the junction south of the border monument. Take ski trail E to the right. This takes you down a somewhat wilder, less-used route that ends at an old section of Route 9W, now closed to vehicles. Turn left and proceed uphill to make your way back to the parking lot.

MORE INFORMATION

Restrooms are located at State Line Lookout visitor center. Palisades Interstate Park, P.O. Box 155, Alpine, NJ 07620; 201-768-1360; www.njpalisades.org.

THE GEOLOGY OF THE PALISADES

The most visible section of the Palisades, just north of the George Washington Bridge, is the one that gave the cliffs their name, since they resemble a line of stone columns. But the cliffs are just a small part of a unique and fascinating geological feature—the Palisades Sill.

A sill is created when magma, or molten rock, forces its way between existing layers of older rock. This happened on a very large scale 200 million years ago at the end of the Triassic Period. Pangaea, the conglomeration of all the landmasses that became today's continents, was beginning to break up and drift apart.

This was not a smooth process. As you might expect, rifts formed in the land. Geologists believe that this began happening around where what is today eastern North America and northwestern Africa were joined.

Some of the rifts became the Atlantic Ocean. Others became what are called the Eastern North America Rift Basins, stretch marks on the land that run from North Carolina to Nova Scotia. They collected sediment after they had stopped expanding.

One of the largest, the Newark Basin, stretches from Rockland County, New York, into southeastern Pennsylvania. On its northeastern edge to Staten Island is the Palisades Sill (some research has suggested it re-emerges in two parts of Pennsylvania as well). Over the 100 million years since it first forced its way up from the inner layers of the earth, erosion laid the top third bare as today's cliffs.

It shows all the characteristics of a sill: Its minerals are primarily igneous, or of volcanic origin, such as diabase, pyroxene, and olivine, whereas the rock above and below the sill is much older sandstone and arkose, which have their origins as sediment collecting underwater.

Geologists are divided as to the origins of the Palisades Sill. It is always difficult to determine where igneous rock came from, but it is even more so in the Palisades. Was it one single magma flow or several separate events? One olivine-rich layer near the bottom of the sill suggests that there were at least two magma flows.

Another possibility is that the volcanic rocks of the Watchung Mountains to the west indicate that those mountains were formed by the same magma flows. But no connection has yet been found between the two ranges.

TRIP 35
GREAT SWAMP NATIONAL
WILDLIFE REFUGE

Location: Meyersville, NJ
Rating: Easy
Distance: 3.0 miles
Elevation Gain: 20 feet
Estimated Time: 1.5 hours
Maps: USGS Chatham; available at website

Venture into the only federally designated wilderness in the New York metropolitan area.

DIRECTIONS

Get off I-287 at Exit 30A (North Maple Avenue). Turn left at the end of the ramp and follow North Maple south past the Verizon complex and through downtown Basking Ridge. About 1.5 miles from the interstate it becomes South Maple Avenue. Continue for another mile to Lord Stirling Road and turn left. Follow another mile to the Passaic River, where it crosses into Morris County and becomes White Bridge Road. Continue 2.0 miles to where it crosses New Vernon Road and then becomes unpaved. It reaches a dead end 0.4 mile from New Vernon Road, with parking available for roughly fifteen vehicles. *GPS coordinates:* 40° 42.366′ N, 74° 28.085′ W.

TRAIL DESCRIPTION

Many hikes are particularly enjoyable in summer, since that is when the ideal combinations of blue skies, green woods, and golden sunshine present themselves. While there are several reasons to hike in other seasons of the year, including winter, the full splendor of nature reserves itself mostly for the warmest months of the year.

There are some exceptions, however. It's best to visit some low-lying wetland areas like New Jersey's Great Swamp National Wildlife Refuge in late spring or early autumn. While you can certainly visit in summer, be aware that while you are appreciating nature, the bugs will be appreciating you, unless you've liberally prepared yourself with the best insect repellent you can find. You also will find boots to be a good idea. While you will not hike through any areas covered with water, it is called a swamp for a reason and there are muddy sections.

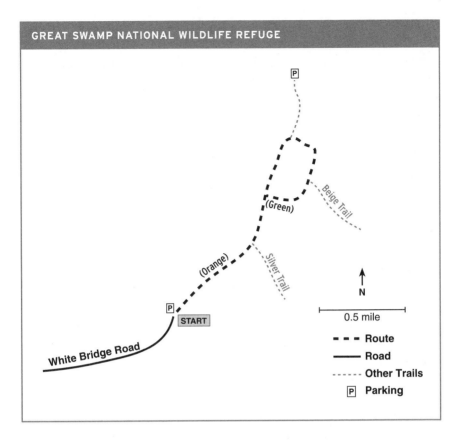

GREAT SWAMP NATIONAL WILDLIFE REFUGE

(Green)

Beige Trail

(Orange)

Silver Trail

START

N

0.5 mile

━ ━ ━ Route

───── Road

------- Other Trails

P Parking

White Bridge Road

This hike follows part of the course of the former Meyersville Road through the eastern half of the 7,700-acre refuge, the largest federally protected area in North Jersey. Cross the gate and follow the dirt path in the middle of the grassy strip that once was the road. You will pass through some lush but immature woods at first, then across the lower end of a clearing. Eventually some occasional orange plastic markers will appear on the trees, telling you this is the orange trail.

In 1968, this portion of the Great Swamp National Wildlife Refuge was designated as a federal wilderness area, giving it the maximum possible protection available for federal land. This limits it to "passive" recreation such as hiking, hunting, and birding, and bars the use of any motorized equipment on the property except for emergencies. To date, it is also the only designated wilderness in the New York City metropolitan area.

You return to the woods, where you can feel the wilderness surround you. At this point you are not even 0.5 mile from the parking lot, yet it feels very far away. Other than the trail, there is no evidence of civilization here.

The woods that surround the trail are lower than the old roadbed the trail follows. They may appear dry, even in periods of wet weather, but they too are part of the swamp ecosystem. The Great Swamp is the sole remnant today of what was originally Glacial Lake Passaic, which covered most of eastern Morris County when glaciers melted at the end of the last Ice Age. Eventually its waters found a path through the Watchung Mountains to the sea through what is today the city of Paterson, forming the Passaic River.

The subsoil in the drier areas, called floodplain forest, is often as moist and damp as the areas that are visibly flooded, and this creates a distressed environment where certain tree species flourish that would not do so otherwise in this region. Beeches and some birches, usually not a dominant species at this elevation, contend in the woods with the maples and oaks that are.

There are also other species you would expect to see, like a stand of bitternut hickory off the trail at one point. Please respect the wilderness ethic and stay on the trail so as to leave the landscape as undisturbed as possible.

Eventually the trail passes a short silver-blazed side trail, another former road, and turns north, invisibly crossing the line between Passaic and Harding townships in the process. Another bend brings you to an area where the green trail forks off to the right. Continue north another 0.3 mile through some tall stands of spruce, which thrive in this distressed area, and then past some open areas to where the green trail returns. Turn right.

You'll pass through some areas heavily carpeted in club moss, another species that does well in and around swamps. On your way to this point, you may have seen deer and some of the birds that live here. The Great Swamp is important for the region's biodiversity, providing habitat for 244 bird species, 33 mammal species, and 25 species considered threatened or endangered, mostly reptiles or amphibians like the box turtle, wood turtle, and several salamander species. In 1966, it was designated a National Natural Landmark.

This extraordinary level of federal attention is a result of how the Great Swamp National Wildlife Refuge came to be. The early settlers had recognized the value of the land when they bought it from the Delaware Indians in 1708. The settlers took timber for wagon wheels, and then grew alfalfa when the timber was exhausted. By the late nineteenth century, alfalfa could no longer be grown, and the land was abandoned.

In 1959, the Port Authority of New York and New Jersey looked at the site and decided it would make a perfect location for a new airport to replace Newark and handle large, noisy jets. Area residents were strongly opposed to this and formed a local group that, with the help of some national conservation groups, persuaded Congress to buy 2,800 acres and set it aside as a national wildlife refuge. Their efforts are continued today by the Friends of the Great Swamp National Wildlife Refuge (www.friendsofgreatswamp.org) and the Great Swamp Watershed Association (www.greatswamp.org), the latter of which works to protect the swamp's 55 square miles of watershed across Morris and Somerset counties.

You get a sense of this watershed as you follow the green trail along the far side of its loop, past the wetter areas that abut the headwaters of Black Brook, one of the tributaries of the Passaic that drain the swamp. The river has its source farther to the west, in Mendham, but it is the Great Swamp's additions to its flow that turn it from a country creek into New Jersey's longest river entirely within the state.

When you get back to the orange trail, turn left and return the way you came. If you have time and want to see a little more of the Great Swamp, turn right when you get back to New Vernon Road and go north 0.7 mile to the Wildlife Observation Center on the left. Here there are short boardwalks over the watery areas that lead out to wildlife observation blinds.

MORE INFORMATION

No restrooms are available. No dogs are allowed in this area. Great Swamp National Wildlife Refuge, 241 Pleasant Plains Road, Basking Ridge, NJ 07920; 973-425-1222; www.fws.gov/northeast/greatswamp.

TRIP 36
WATCHUNG RESERVATION

Location: Mountainside, NJ
Rating: Moderate
Distance: 3.8 miles
Elevation Gain: 150 feet
Estimated Time: 3.0 hours
Maps: USGS Chatham; trail map available at trailhead kiosk and online at the Trailside Nature and Science Center website

Historical and natural sights, such as a pine plantation, deserted village, and scenic gorge, abound in this suburban oasis, Union County's largest park.

DIRECTIONS

From I-78 westbound, exit at Route 24 westbound. Get off at the first exit for Broad Street in Summit, and follow it 0.5 mile to Orchard Street. Turn left and then right at the next light onto Morris Avenue. Approximately 1 mile later, bear left onto Glenside Avenue. Continue for 2.0 miles into the reservation, over I-78, to W. R. Tracy Drive on the left. Turn sharply, go downhill, and cross Lake Surprise. Then head back uphill to bear right into the Trailside Loop. Make the first right turn to the trailhead lot. *GPS coordinates*: 40° 41.185′ N, 74° 22.495′ W.

Coming from the west, get off I-78 at Glenside. Turn right and follow to W. R. Tracy Drive. Turn sharply and go downhill and cross Lake Surprise. Then head back uphill to bear right into the Trailside Loop. Make the first right turn to the trailhead lot.

TRAIL DESCRIPTION

Wedged between the developed suburbs of Berkeley Heights, Mountainside, Scotch Plains, Springfield, and Summit, the Watchung Reservation helps make those towns special places to live. Many a local child grew up exploring, on foot or bike, the marked and unmarked paths on the reservation's 2,045 acres.

The heavily populated adjacent areas, with many streets and backyards abutting the reservation, have led to much informal trail development over the years. Many of the trails are unmarked. The county has recently blazed a small

WATCHUNG RESERVATION

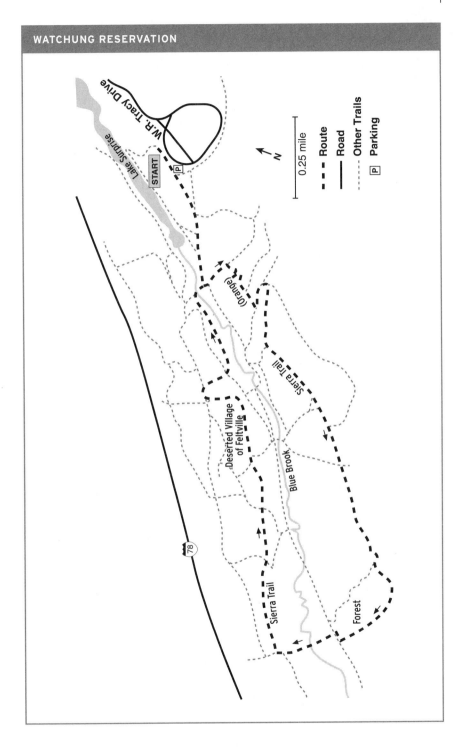

0.25 mile

N

- - - Route
——— Road
········· Other Trails
P Parking

W. R. Tracy Drive

Lake Surprise

START

P

(Orange)

Sierra Trail

Deserted Village
of Feltville

Blue Brook

Sierra Trail

Forest

78

set of trails near the Trailside Center in the middle of the reservation. The 11-mile Sierra Trail is a long loop.

This hike will follow portions of both the marked and unmarked trails as well as the many bridle paths across the reservation.

From the trailhead, follow the wide bridle path that leaves to the west, sloping gently downhill through a towering mature forest of oaks and maples. You pass a grassy area on the left used for scout camping. Cross another bridle path that leads directly downhill to Lake Surprise, which you can already see through the trees. Turn right at the next bridle path junction, 0.2 mile from the trailhead, to go down to the dam that impounds the headwaters of Blue Brook to create Lake Surprise. There are nice views to the west over the lake.

There was considerable disruption to the reservation from government activities in the twentieth century. A Nike missile base, now the site of the Watchung Stables, was built in the eastern reservation in the 1950s. It was one of many sites intended to protect New York from nuclear attack before the U.S.–Soviet Anti-Ballistic Missile treaty limited such protection to Washington and Moscow. In the 1970s the state Department of Transportation proposed to build 13 miles of I-78 across the northern edge of the reservation. The project was not completed until 1991 due to years of litigation from local residents who wanted to protect the park.

Even today, with the interstate running through its northern edge, the reservation is still a lovely patch of woods nestled in the trough between the First and Second Watchung ranges. The first rises from the lowlands east of New York City. It has both intensive use areas like the Trailside complex where the trailhead for this hike is located, and long tracts of old-growth forest. Scattered among the mature hardwoods are a number of natural and historic sights worth seeing. This hike will take you past two of them, the Pine Plantation and Deserted Village, as well as Lake Surprise and a scenic gorge.

Turn left and take the path that follows the south side of the brook. It is not marked and becomes narrow, but is still easy to follow. After another 0.25 mile, it leads to a junction with the blue trail just before a bridge crossing a tributary of Blue Brook at the end of a small, wide gorge. Turn left and follow the blue trail.

The trail leads up along the side of the creek 0.1 mile until it ends at the orange trail. Turn right on the orange trail and follow it across the bridge then up the short switchbacks on the other side to where it levels out again. Another 0.1 mile will bring you to the other end of the blue trail. You will continue straight ahead and stay on the blue trail, while the orange trail turns left.

The best views in the Pine Plantation are straight up.

A few hundred feet and the trail turns to the right as it reaches the edge of an even larger gorge. The white-blazed Sierra Trail comes in obliquely from the left. Here you turn and follow that trail up the east side of the gorge 0.1 mile until you take the unmarked path shown on the trail map down into the gorge. Cross a narrow section of brook and then head up to an unmarked, yet obvious, trail going along the other side of the gorge.

Turn right and go back down the gorge. From this side you can see just how steep, narrow, and twisted it gets in some places. Another section, with exposed bronzy rock, was once the site of an old copper mine, although this has become difficult to see over time.

Presently you reach the Sierra Trail again, just above an area with lots of pines, and turn left to follow it deep into the western reservation. Over the next 0.75 mile, the trail crosses several more tributaries and one of the major bridle paths before it eventually reaches the back of Sky Top Picnic Area, where restrooms are available.

The trail finally turns downhill, eventually entering an area with regularly spaced red pines filling out the canopy over a grassy floor. This pleasant area, the Pine Plantation, is the result of a Civilian Conservation Corps reforestation project in the 1930s. As other tree species rise to fill in the understory and challenge the pines for dominance, it has become less distinct from other areas of the reservation, but it is still different.

The trail ends at another bridle path, but follow the white blazes to make a loop through the pines back to Sky Top. Turn left almost as soon as you get on this path in order to follow the bridle path that goes across Blue Brook. It leads gently uphill to reach the Sierra Trail again in a patch of former farmland. The white blazes come in from the left; carefully follow them when they go right again, leading through 0.4 mile of a cut to the end of a paved road.

This is the beginning of the Deserted Village, once known as Feltville. Today it is listed on the National Register of Historic Places. David Felt, a Boston businessman, established the lumbering and milling community in the early nineteenth century. However, after his death, the businesses could not be sustained, and by the end of the century the village had been abandoned and many of the houses torn down.

Paved Cataract Hollow Road passes some of the remaining houses that have been restored to house park employees, the church, and a store building. Just past them, the white blazes signal a return to the woods.

The trail briefly follows a bridle path, then turns to the right and descends to the brook. A short connector trail leads to the unmarked path along the north side of the brook, where you can turn left. Follow it through the tall, almost cathedral-like trees back to the path at the Surprise Lake Dam. From there, you can easily retrace your original steps uphill, and to the left to return to the parking lot.

MORE INFORMATION

Restrooms are located near the trailhead. Parking lots close at 9 P.M. Trailside Nature and Science Center, 452 New Providence Road, Mountainside, NJ 07092; 908-789-3670; www.ucnj.org/trailside.

TRIP 37
SOUTH MOUNTAIN RESERVATION

Location: Millburn, NJ
Rating: Moderate
Distance: 5.2 miles
Elevation Gain: 350 feet
Estimated Time: 4.0 hours
Maps: USGS Roselle, Caldwell; available at Millburn library for $4

Walk in George Washington's footsteps and follow the upper Rahway River in Essex County's largest park.

DIRECTIONS
Take Interstate 78 westbound to Exit 50A. Turn right on Vauxhall Road northbound and go 0.7 mile to where it crosses into Essex County. Turn left on Millburn Avenue. Bear right onto one-way Essex Street after 0.5 mile. Continue for 0.2 mile to the light at Lackawanna Place and turn right. After crossing under the railroad tracks, turn right on Glen Avenue. A dirt road leaves to the left 250 feet from the intersection, leading to parking for ten to fifteen vehicles. Free parking is also available on weekends and holidays in the train station lot. *GPS coordinates*: 40° 43.603' N, 74° 18.309' W.

If arriving by train, take NJ Transit's Morris and Essex Line to Millburn. The road to the parking lot is just across Glen Avenue from the station—you will see the three yellow blazes that mark the beginning of the trail on a tree. The NJ Transit #70 bus also stops at the train station.

TRAIL DESCRIPTION
Today, the Hobart Gap between Summit and the part of Millburn Township that Stewart Hartshorn developed into Short Hills in the twentieth century carries the busy Route 24 freeway along the Essex–Union county line. But in the late years of the American Revolution, this break in the Watchung Mountain ridges was a strategic hot spot patrolled by nervous local militiamen.

They were nervous because the British could, at any time, push off their base on Staten Island and try to force the gap. If they succeeded, the road to Morristown and the New Jersey interior was wide open. In 1780, the British tried exactly that, getting as far as Springfield before stiff local resistance

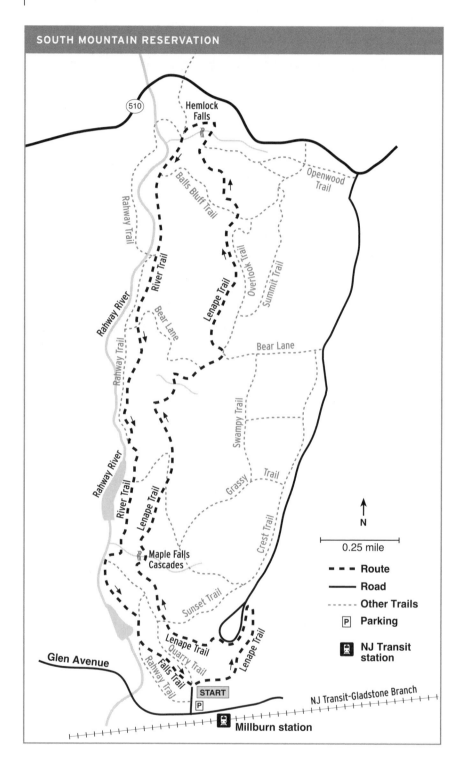

SOUTH MOUNTAIN RESERVATION

510

Hemlock
Falls

Openwood
Trail

Balls Bluff Trail

Rahway Trail

River Trail

Lenape Trail

Overlook Trail

Summit Trail

Rahway River

Rahway Trail

Bear Lane

Bear Lane

Swampy Trail

River Trail

Lenape Trail

Grassy

Trail

Rahway River

Crest Trail

N

0.25 mile

Maple Falls
Cascades

Sunset Trail

Lenape Trail

Quarry Trail

Lenape Trail

Glen Avenue

Falls Trail

Rahway Trail

START

P

NJ Transit-Gladstone Branch

Millburn station

- - - Route
—— Road
- - - Other Trails
P Parking
NJ Transit
station

Hemlock Falls is one of the most popular destinations in South Mountain Reservation.

turned them back. The battle helped put an end to any British attempts to regain a foothold in the northern colonies.

This loop through the 2,000-acre South Mountain Reservation starts with a trip to Washington Rock, supposedly the place where General Washington looked over the battlefield. From the parking lot, take the yellow-blazed Lenape Trail to the right. Pass the campsites and shelter and begin your ascent through the woods. The trail takes wide traverses, switching back and forth along grassy stretches as it passes between the backyards of houses below and some old water tanks above.

It finally levels at a grassy plateau and comes out on paved Crest Drive, no longer open to vehicles at this point. Turn left and follow the pavement to the circle at the end. Washington Rock is right there, with a limited view out over Millburn. Continue along the Lenape Trail for 0.1 mile. A better version of the view is available a short distance to the left of the trail via a short path that leads through a grassy area to a rusty chain-link fence at the edge of a sharp cliff.

From here you look first over downtown Millburn, directly in front of you. Downtown Springfield, with the recognizable tower of Springfield Presbyterian

Church, is on the other side of I-78 to the left. Beyond them, the land rises, taking the interstate up toward the Watchung Reservation. Here you can appreciate the military significance of the Hobart Gap even today.

Impressive as this is, the hike has barely begun. Continue along the Lenape Trail as it winds around the hillside. The forest remains grassy and open as you reach Maple Falls Cascades, a steep brook that lives up to its name at this elevation only after heavy rains. It continues into trees that eventually get higher and higher, creating a cathedral-like feeling in the forest. Other trails cross, but stay with the yellow blazes. You'll cross other ravines that carry streams down to the headwaters of the Rahway River's West Branch. After crossing these and turning around several times on Lilliput Knob, the trail begins to climb again.

After the climb, the trail levels out in a very open, grassy area. Near its northern end, you cross the Millburn–Maplewood township line. You pass a fenced-in paddock as you descend into mature woods similar to those you have already crossed. Going up and down several ravines, you eventually reach Hemlock Falls.

This pleasant, shaded waterfall is the northern apex of your loop. It's a nice place to rest, and you may want to take the time to explore the area a little. Follow the steps up to the far side and around to where the short Falls Overlook Trail, blazed with red dots on white, leads out to the creek's rocky path above the falls and allows views toward the ridge on the far side of the reservation. It's a surprisingly wild vista for such a heavily developed suburban area.

The Essex County Park Commission, the first county park agency in the United States, was created in 1895 and made South Mountain its first project. Acquiring a large contiguous tract of land was difficult and took several years, since there were many different owners. Even as that was being undertaken, the landscaping firm of Olmstead Brothers, founded by the sons of Frederick Law Olmstead, co-designer of Central Park, were planting in some areas and culling in others to ensure a forest as diverse as possible. Their father reviewed their work, making it one of the last American properties to show his direct influence.

In the 1930s, the Civilian Conservation Corps built most of the reservation's campsites and trails. Later facilities included the popular Turtle Back Zoo and the nearby South Mountain Arena, the main training facility for the New Jersey Devils. The Parks Commission was merged into a larger department in 1979. A private group, the South Mountain Conservancy (www .somocon.org), was established to help support the reservation.

Your return route will be the low road, so to speak. From the falls, follow the Lenape down the side of the creek to the third bridge, where it intersects a wide, old dirt road. The Lenape turns right here, while across the road the white-blazed Rahway Trail begins.

Turn left and continue down the road. It follows alongside the river it gets its name from, with the Rahway Trail occasionally joining or running close by. The tall trees return. As you get farther south, you will hear vehicles on Brookside Drive a short distance away.

Two miles down, as you pass the outlet pond below the Paper Mill Playhouse, the road climbs a bit as it starts to turn eastward. The Rahway Trail joins and rejoins several times, offering a more level route and some interesting shrubby areas next to the water. Both can be followed back to the parking lot.

MORE INFORMATION

Restrooms are available in the Millburn Library when it is open. Dogs must be leashed. South Mountain Reservation, South Orange Avenue and Cherry Lane, Millburn, NJ 07041; 973-268-3500; www.essex-countynj.org/p/index .php?section=parks/sites/so.

3

LONG ISLAND AND CONNECTICUT

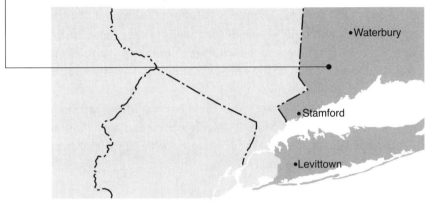

Connecticut and Long Island aren't twins. But they are siblings facing each other across Long Island Sound.

Connecticut came first. The grouping of continents into Pangaea during the Triassic period, beginning 250 million years ago, drove up the metamorphic rocks that now make up the northern Appalachians and their foothills at Pootatuck and Upper Paugussett state forests. When they pulled apart almost 100 million years later in the Jurassic period, Connecticut's defining geological feature was created: the Eastern Border Fault.

This massive break in the land extends north 130 miles from New Haven to Keene, New Hampshire, roughly bisecting the state. The land on the west tilted, eventually filling with sediment near the fault that led to the lands just west of the Connecticut River becoming some of the most fertile in the state. But that would not have happened without help eons later from the various Ice Ages. Some of the ice sheets covered the future Constitution State and scoured the soft sands of the sea to the south, leaving behind little intersecting piles of debris 50 miles offshore: Long Island.

The northerly pile, the Harbor Hill Moraine, where the Muttontown Preserve is located, became the South Fork, while the Ronkonkoma Moraine became the North Fork east of its heights at Manetto Hills and West Hills parks, the latter home to the island's highest point.

South of the moraines, the glacial outwash created the Hempstead Plains, one of the few natural prairies east of the Appalachians. South of that, nearer the shore, grew the pine barrens that are still preserved in abundance on the eastern island, but west of that, they are limited to fragments like Connetquot State Park Preserve and the Massapequa Preserve.

When English and Dutch settlers came down the sound in the seventeenth century, they found both shores to their liking. In Connecticut they found much fertile soil in the glacial till left over from the Ice Age and many good harbors, and by the end of the century established one of the most autonomous of the original colonies.

South of the sound, on the North Shore of Long Island, settlers found the lush forests of places like Nissequogue River State Park and Muttontown. In his famous rhapsody at the end of *The Great Gatsby*, F. Scott Fitzgerald imagined Long Island as it appeared to them:

> . . . a fresh, green breast of the new world. Its vanished trees . . .
> had once pandered in whispers to the last and greatest of all
> human dreams; for a transitory enchanted moment man must
> have held his breath in the presence of this continent, . . . ,
> face to face for the last time in history with something
> commensurate to his capacity for wonder.

The dreams Long Island fueled were, at first, the farms that fed New York City. At the end of the century, the titans of the Gilded Age built in its woods and fields estates that rivaled those of English nobles.

Later still, in the twentieth century, Robert Moses (see essay, page 9) hiked and boated extensively all over the western island from his home in Babylon. He saw in its undeveloped beaches the possibility for the green, open spaces the city's masses needed and the parkway system to get them there. He fought with some of these landed gentry, and compromised with others, to build it in the span of a few years. As they did in Connecticut, those roads helped make Long Island the heavily suburbanized area we know today, with a few well-preserved open spaces.

TRIP 38
MASSAPEQUA PRESERVE

Location: Massapequa, NY
Rating: Easy
Distance: 2.0 miles
Elevation Gain: Level
Estimated Time: 1.0 hour
Maps: USGS Amityville; Long Island Greenbelt, Nassau–Suffolk Greenbelt Trail

Some of the few remaining pine barrens in Nassau County flourish in this green, wetland oasis at the southern end of the Nassau— Suffolk Greenbelt Trail.

DIRECTIONS

Take Exit 44 from the Long Island Expressway. Take the Seaford–Oyster Bay Expressway (Route 135) south to the Sunrise Highway (Route 27). Follow it east one mile to the preserve area. At Lakeshore Boulevard, turn around to the other roadway and pull into the small parking area on the right. There is room for approximately fifteen to twenty vehicles. *GPS coordinates:* 40° 40.620′ N, 73° 27.787′ W.

If arriving by the Long Island Rail Road's Babylon Branch, get off at Massapequa and head toward the park at the east end of the station's parking lot. You will see the white blazes for the Nassau–Suffolk Greenbelt Trail on a tree where the paved path from the station meets the paved path along the lake. Turn right here and follow under the railroad tracks to the parking lot.

TRAIL DESCRIPTION

Until the middle of the twentieth century, western Long Island was a largely rural area, a landscape of potato farms, family estates, and woodlands occasionally interrupted by small villages. Today, more than a half century after Robert Moses, Long Island State Parks commissioner at the time, threaded his parkways and expressways to the beaches, it has become heavily developed, densely populated suburban sprawl.

Pockets of the old Long Island still remain. Many are in large private landholdings on the North Shore or Wheatley Hills. Some are open to the public, like the Massapequa Preserve on the South Shore. This stretch of 423 acres

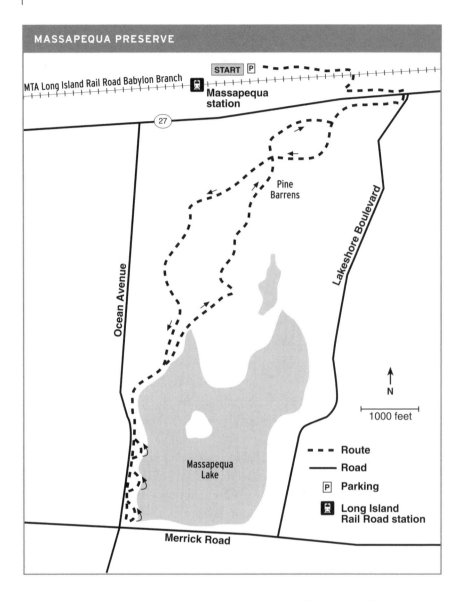

MASSAPEQUA PRESERVE

START P

MTA Long Island Rail Road Babylon Branch

Massapequa station

27

Pine Barrens

Ocean Avenue

Lakeshore Boulevard

N

1000 feet

Massapequa Lake

- - - Route

—— Road

P Parking

Long Island Rail Road station

Merrick Road

along the lower four miles of Massapequa Creek was long owned by New York City for its water supply system, a remnant of long-abandoned plans to tap Long Island's watersheds. In 1981, it was transferred to Nassau County and became the Massapequa Preserve, an undeveloped oasis in the center of one of Long Island's most bustling postwar suburbs. It also serves as the southernmost section of the Nassau–Suffolk Greenbelt Trail, a 22-mile long route which makes use of a great deal of open space between Massapequa and Cold Spring Harbor State Park on its northern end.

Massapequa Lake is popular with birds in this extensively suburbanized area.

This hike gives you a short sampling of the southern section of the preserve, just above where the creek drains into the Atlantic Ocean. You begin this hike at a small parking lot for preserve users only; it is off-limits to commuters, so space is usually available. The Greenbelt Trail follows the paved path between the tracks and the lot here. To begin, turn right.

White blazes lead you along Sunrise Highway to a light at Lakeshore Boulevard, where you cross this major arterial road. Once across, turn right, following the fenced-off, paved multiuse path along the other side of Sunrise Highway west to where it turns into the Preserve itself.

The trail turns right onto a footpath soon afterward. Stay on the multiuse path as it follows the west side of the creek, then turns away from it into the mature woodlands where the Greenbelt Trail crosses it again. Continuing to stay on the multiuse path, you see dense shrubs and tall, extremely old maples and oaks, possibly even some surviving elms, between the path and the backyards of the houses that abut the preserve. On the east side, you can catch glimpses of the pines you will see more closely later on.

Gradually, the multiuse path turns to the south and the woods between it and Ocean Avenue thin until you are in a grassy, more parklike area near Massapequa Lake (sometimes called Caroon's Lake). Continue down the multiuse path to where it ends at the corner of Ocean Avenue and Merrick Road. Next to you is the Greenbelt Trail information kiosk. The customary three blazes on an adjacent tree mark the trail's southern terminus. You will follow this trail back to the parking lot.

At first, once you turn around, you are going back the way you just came, save for three stretches where the trail follows lightly used paths on the lake shore barely 20 feet east of the multiuse path. There are views over the lake from some of them. You may see some of the 200 different bird species that have been observed stopping here during their lengthy migrations.

When you return your attention to the trail, look for the point where the pavement re-enters the woods. On your right, next to a broad view over the lake, you will see a rough dirt path descend slightly into a thicket. There are no blazes to indicate this, but this is the trail.

Up to this point you have seen the Massapequa Preserve as walkers, joggers, skaters, and bicyclists see it. Now you will see it as hikers do. At first, the trail will wind through green-tunnel thickets along the lakeshore until the paved path is no longer visible, nor traffic along it audible. Eventually, as the woods open up, the informal paths back to the pavement disappear as well.

The trail turns into a muddy area with some split-log bridges (known as puncheons) and planks in spots, then crosses one of the lake's unnamed feeder streams on a wooden bridge as it works its way east. You may see some snapping turtles here during breeding season. There are some forks where you may need to investigate both paths to find the white blazes and make sure you are still on the trail.

At a point where the canopy opens up as the understory becomes shrubbier, you can see the stand of pines to your left. Stop and consider that once these distinctive forests were extensive even here on western Long Island, as they still are far out east near the Hamptons. You may need to remind yourself that you are in the middle of an otherwise built-up area, so perfect is the sense of isolation.

Continuing north through some lowland woods, the trail reaches the intersection with the multiuse path you passed earlier. The sense of wilderness is harder to maintain here since the traffic on the highway is audible. The next section has some interesting passages and becomes increasingly shrubby as it follows some puncheons through an extensive wetland and crosses another tributary of Massapequa Creek. Turning eastward again, just when the trail seems about to reach Sunrise, it finally rejoins the multiuse path.

You can return to your vehicle or the station platform, secure in the knowledge that the primeval wildness still lingers even here.

MORE INFORMATION

There are no restrooms in the preserve. Massapequa Preserve does not have a website, but there is plenty of information at the Friends of Massapequa Preserve website—www.fdale.com/FMP/FMP.htm. The organization can be reached by phone: 516-541-2461.

TRIP 39
MUTTONTOWN PRESERVE

Location: East Norwich, NY
Rating: Easy
Distance: 1.5 miles
Elevation Gain: 30 feet
Estimated Time: 1.0 hour
Maps: USGS Hicksville; available at trailhead

Hike through woods, fields, and marshes in a remnant of the Long Island that once was.

DIRECTIONS
Take the Long Island Expressway to Exit 41 (Route 106/107). Follow the two highways north 0.5 mile into Jericho. Shortly after the Route 25 junction, the two highways split. Bear right onto Route 106 (Jericho-Oyster Bay Road) and follow it north approximately 3.5 miles to Route 25A (North Hempstead Turnpike) at East Norwich. Turn left on Route 25A. Look for the left turn to Muttontown Lane, a break in the center island, 0.1 mile west of the intersection.

Follow Muttontown through several blocks of a residential neighborhood to where it enters the preserve and becomes unpaved. A parking lot with space for about twenty vehicles opens up just short of the visitor center. *GPS coordinates:* 40° 50.241′ N, 73° 32.284′ W.

TRAIL DESCRIPTION
There are many parks and open spaces on Long Island today, but almost none in northern Nassau County that are open to the public. The vast wooded estates where F. Scott Fitzgerald imagined Jay Gatsby chasing Daisy still evoke the visions they did, but they have been subdivided into smaller estates today and are still as private.

In one place, however, that untamed Long Island that Fitzgerald saw in the closing passages of *The Great Gatsby* still exists. Three former estates have been combined into the 550-acre Muttontown Preserve, the largest nature preserve in the county.

Next to the parking lot is the Bill Paterson Nature Center, where you can pick up a trail map (the maps available at press time were not very reliable)

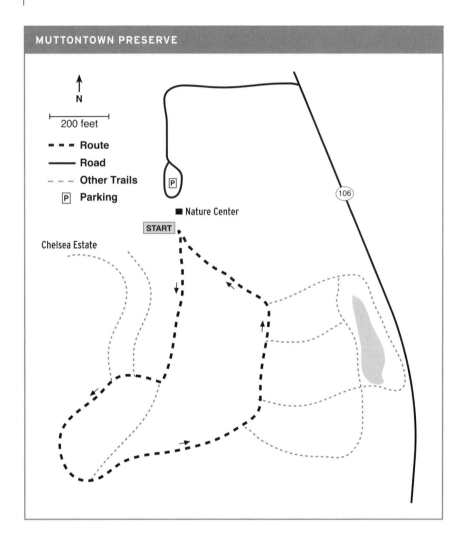

MUTTONTOWN PRESERVE

N

200 feet

- - - Route
——— Road
- - - Other Trails
P Parking

P

106

■ Nature Center

START

Chelsea Estate

and information about the preserve's wildlife from the many brochures and pamphlets available. There's also a register, so remember to sign in.

From the end of the lawn, take the wide bridle path off to the right. Within a few hundred feet you come to the first of several junctions, marked by a small post with metal "1 B" on it. This, like most of the other posts at trail junctions, bears no relation to anything on the map. It is the relic of a former system which has not yet been replaced with one consistent with the map.

Take a right toward a sometimes muddy area where the trees grow tall. You'll pass a path coming in from them on the right. Keep going as the trail bends to the left. This leads in a few hundred feet to another junction, with

Dogwoods overhang this tunnel-like country lane deep in Muttontown Preserve.

paths crossing on either side of a gate in a chain-link fence. Turn left on the path after the fence.

After 0.1 mile, you come to a field where another path comes in along the edge from the right. Turn left and follow around the field edge into the woods again to another fork. Bear left and follow the path along the chain-link fence, slightly uphill.

This area evokes the land's past. Most of it was originally part of the estate of Edgerton Winthrop, a prominent New York lawyer in the late nineteenth century.

Later the land belonged to Charles Hudson, a successful stockbroker. He built Knollwood, a castle-like mansion on the south end of the land. Benjamin Moore, a descendant of Clement Clarke Moore, author of "'Twas the Night Before Christmas," owned a section near the north end and built a mansion of his own on it in 1903. The deposed King Zog of Albania owned it for a few years in the middle of the twentieth century, but he never lived there and Knollwood began its descent into its present state of ruin then.

In 1968, Nassau County acquired the property through purchases from three different estates. Another donor gave 20 acres with traces of a pre-Revolutionary farm.

After going 0.3 mile, you pass through an area where dogwoods curve over the trail as it descends slightly, giving it a picturesque country-lane feel. The dogwoods lift again, the trail goes into an open area, and the soil gets sandier. Just after the field you reach a three-way junction. Turn left. Within 200 feet you reach another three-way junction with a 2 and 6 on the nearby post. This time continue as the trail passes between woods and marsh and the soil becomes noticeably sandier. When the marsh ends, you will pass another junction post with "6 A." The trail off to the right leads 100 feet to the top of a small kame, a hill created by the accumulation of sediment and debris left in a depression within a melting glacier. If you take the short detour to the top, you'll see that the soil still feels loose and sandy, somewhat like one left over from a fresh excavation such as Moses Mountain in the Staten Island Greenbelt (see Trip 3). There are also some small glacial erratics in the woods at the top.

Another 300 feet from the junction at the kame, you come to a fork with an East Norwich Fire Department sign. Take the left branch downhill, past another swampy area of dogwood on the left. The traffic on Route 106 is louder here, indicating your proximity to the preserve's eastern boundary.

Eventually the path picks up the eastern chain-link fence and you will find yourself back at the same junction where you started out just south of the nature center.

If you have time after you get back into your vehicle, consider taking the short drive over to see the other feature of this property, the Moore family's Chelsea estate. The main mansion, listed on the National Register of Historic Places, is eclectic in its architecture, inspired by a trip to China but incorporating several different cultural influences, and the grounds are delightfully landscaped as they were for the Moores.

MORE INFORMATION

Restrooms are available at the nature center. The preserve closes at dusk. Muttontown Preserve, 34 Muttontown Lane, East Norwich, NY 11732; 516-571-8500; www.nassaucountyny.gov/agencies/Parks/wheretogo/preserves/north_shore_preserve/Muttontown_Pres.html.

TRIP 40
MANETTO HILLS

Location: Plainview, NY
Rating: Moderate
Distance: 3.5 miles
Elevation Gain: 160 feet
Estimated Time: 2.0 hours
Maps: USGS Hicksville; Nassau–Suffolk Greenbelt Trail maps

Follow a loop through a little-known open tract on Long Island's central moraine in the corner between two major highways.

DIRECTIONS
Take the Long Island Expressway (LIE) to Exit 46. Follow Executive Drive, the LIE's service road, east almost 2 miles to the off ramp to Washington Avenue on the right. At the end, turn right again and go north on Washington to just past the overpass where the trail intersects (you will see the back of a sign on the right). Space is available along either side of the road to park. *GPS coordinates:* 40° 47.389′ N, 73° 27.326′ W.

The MTA N78 bus has stops nearby on both South Service Road and Bethpage Road. From them, walk west to Washington Avenue, where you will see the Nassau–Suffolk Greenbelt Trail's white blazes on the left side of the road, and can follow them north to the trailheads just past the overpasses.

TRAIL DESCRIPTION
Manetto Hills Park is the best-kept secret of Long Island hiking. Not just in the sense of not a lot of people knowing about it, but also in the fact that people pass by all the time and continue on with little, if any, awareness that it even exists. No signs announce its presence and no public entrance or parking is available. The county doesn't even have a webpage for it.

Yet this 138-acre tract is one of the best public places in Nassau County to appreciate the Ronkonkoma Moraine, the ridge of land pushed up by the glaciers that created the island. Its woods and terrain are similar in many ways to those in the larger and better-known West Hills Park (see Trip 41), a few miles to the east across the Suffolk County line.

An enjoyable loop hike can be made through the park by combining a section of the Nassau–Suffolk Greenbelt Trail that runs through a corridor of

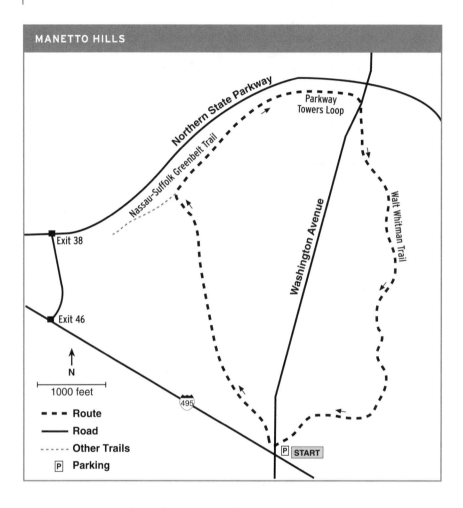

Trail View State Park on the east side of Washington Avenue, with a side trail called the Parkway Towers Loop. Start by crossing Washington Avenue (be careful; there is no crosswalk and traffic goes very fast). You may, in fact, want to park on the west side of the road in hot weather, as it is somewhat shaded.

The white blazes enter the woods at the south end of the chain-link fence. First, they go down to cross a small creek, with a separate bypass for mountain bikers, and then back up. The climb continues, with the LIE's traffic audible to the left, into an area with some white pine trees. There the trail turns right and starts moving away from the expressway.

The climb becomes a bit gentler, leveling out in a diverse forest where some sassafras grows by the side of the trail, along with the oaks and hickories. To the left you can see an office park, and to the right, backyards in the subdivision on the west side of Washington Avenue. Trail View, the 7.4-mile linear park

Manetto Hills Park is an oasis in this highly developed part of Long Island.

the Nassau–Suffolk Greenbelt Trail follows here, was originally condemned for use as a parkway right-of-way. Robert Moses, head of the Long Island State Parks Commission, had the authority to build parkways and planned to extend the Bethpage State Parkway north all the way to Caumsett State Park at Lloyd Harbor. However, he was unable to implement those plans, and in 2002 the state designated the land as a park all the way up to Cold Spring Harbor (see Trip 42), removing much of the Greenbelt Trail from local roads.

The trail goes up and down several bumps, with the woods widening out so no buildings are visible. At a low point before it approaches the Northern State Parkway, look for a tape flag hanging from a branch on the left side of the trail. Turn right on the path just opposite.

This is the north end of the Parkway Towers Loop. You will go about 0.1 mile before the first of its blue-dot-on-white blazes appears, but it is an obvious trail. It climbs to follow a narrow passage of wooded land between the parkway and the backyards on Harvard Drive, then descends via an old dirt road to come back down to Washington Avenue just south of where the parkway crosses on a pair of stone arch bridges.

Turn left and follow the blazes down the street another 0.1 mile to where the trail re-enters the woods just south of the church. You will have to cross the street to do this; be careful, as there is no crosswalk and traffic often goes through here at high speeds.

The trail turns right as it passes through a grove of Norway spruce, then follows a somewhat overgrown section to a crossing of a paved road to the nearby subdivision. It continues through another overgrown area with thorn bushes lining the trail and backyards in view on the right to another crossing, this time of a dirt road. A short distance past this it widens out and makes a couple of switchback turns into a shrubby area around a swamp.

From here it climbs into drier woods, ascending gently as it turns slowly eastward. Finally, it reaches a three-way junction where another trail that connects the loop to the Walt Whitman Trail in West Hills Park comes in from the left. Turn right.

You are now in Manetto Hills Park. The name "Manetto" for this area dates to colonial times and is probably a variation on an early settler's attempt at spelling the American Indian word now usually rendered as "Manitou." These woods were once the estate of Frank Shattuck, who owned and operated the New York–area restaurants in the now-defunct Schrafft's chain. The main house he built still stands, vacant, at the end of the dirt road you crossed.

After Shattuck's death in the 1960s, the land passed to the county, which wanted to make it available for development as housing or a golf course. A group of local activists fought these plans, and in 1972 they succeeded in getting the woods designated a park. One of the activists, Carl Ross, eventually moved to Washington, DC, and founded the advocacy group Save America's Forests as a result of the experience.

The trail continues to undulate through some sections with vines and tall trees that give it a slightly tropical feel, and then reaches the back fence of Crestwood Country Day School. For another 0.2 mile, it follows that fence, giving you an ample view of the school's extensive recreational facilities. There are a few entrances, all prominently posted as private property.

The trail returns to the woods, a mix of oak and hickory with some stands of immature maple and a few scrubby pines. Eventually it reaches the back fence of a large housing development, which it follows along for 0.1 mile. The trail then turns right back into the woods, having skirted a large section of private fields. It descends gently downhill, with the WLIW-TV broadcast towers that help give the trail its name sometimes visible through the trees to the left. After a level, sometimes muddy, section, it turns right at a junction with a former route of the trail and goes back out to Washington Avenue, right across from the trailhead where you started.

MORE INFORMATION

No restrooms are available. Dogs are permitted in Manetto Hills Park but not Trail View. Trail View State Park, 25 Lloyd Harbor Road, Huntington, NY 11743; 631-423-1770; www.nysparks.state.ny.us/parks/39/details.aspx.

TRIP 41
WEST HILLS COUNTY PARK

Location: Melville, NY
Rating: Moderate
Distance: 4.0 miles
Elevation Gain: 220 feet
Estimated Time: 2.5 hours
Maps: USGS Huntington; Long Island Greenbelt Trail Conference
West Hills; trail map available online at West Hills County Park website

Follow in the footsteps of Walt Whitman to the top of Long Island through this wild oasis in suburbia.

DIRECTIONS
From Northern State Parkway, get off at Exit 40N, for Route 110 north. Make the first left onto Gwynne Road. Follow it roughly 0.5 mile to Sweet Hollow Road and turn right. Turn right again into the dog-walk parking area at 0.1 mile, with space for 40 vehicles. *GPS coordinates*: 40° 48.050′ N, 73° 25.289′ W.

The MTA N79, Suffolk County Transit S23 and S29, and Huntington H4 bus routes serve the nearby Walt Whitman Mall. If coming from this direction, cross Route 110 to the Walt Whitman birthplace where the white-blazed Walt Whitman Trail begins, and follow it along the streets to Ridge Road.

TRAIL DESCRIPTION
Were he to return today to his old stomping grounds, the great American poet Walt Whitman (1819–1892) might not be amused to find that one of Long Island's shopping malls, not far from his West Hills birthplace, has been named after him. However, he surely would be pleased with the lands around it. Jayne's Hill, Long Island's highest peak, has remained as wild and undeveloped as it was when he was growing up in the vicinity.

This 854-acre section of West Hills County Park has plenty of trails, most of them wide bridle paths that serve equestrians from the nearby stables. There are also a couple of long-marked foot trails that follow the bridle paths. The Walt Whitman Trail makes a nice loop around the park to Jayne's Hill and back. Although we do not know which of these trails or old roads Whitman

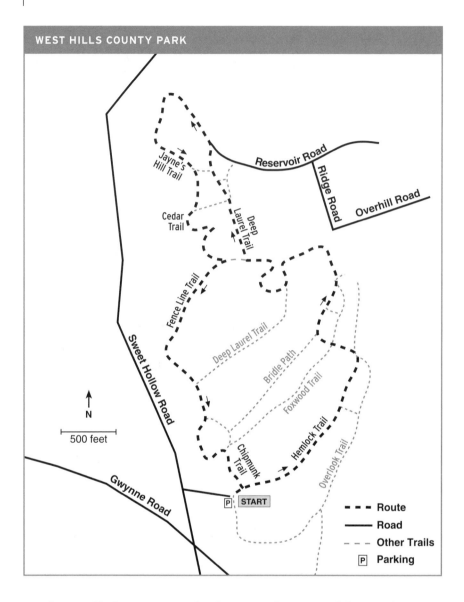

WEST HILLS COUNTY PARK

Jayne's Hill Trail

Reservoir Road

Ridge Road

Overhill Road

Cedar Trail

Deep Laurel Trail

Fence Line Trail

Sweet Hollow Road

Deep Laurel Trail

Bridle Path

Foxwood Trail

Hemlock Trail

Overlook Trail

N

500 feet

Chipmunk Trail

Gwynne Road

P START

- - - Route
—— Road
- - - Other Trails
P Parking

may have walked, it is certain that he wrote about one of them in his poem "Song of the Open Road." He mentions, "the long brown path before me leading wherever I choose."

A loop route around the park starts with the blue-blazed trail near the south end of the picnic area (east of the parking lot). It begins at a tree near a dirt road that curves around and into the woods. Pass through the fence and follow the blazes onto the road. Almost immediately after this, the blazes indicate a right turn off the road and onto a footpath that ascends gently, yet steadily, up the slope to the south through a birch forest.

The Walt Whitman Trail winds past twisted mountain laurels in the heart of Long Island.

The trail levels off and turns, eventually reaching another dirt road paralleling the park's southern boundary, where the blazes turn left. Traffic on the Northern State Parkway is audible in some places. There is one open area providing views over Melville to the Half Hollow Hills. The trail may be muddy in spots along this road

The road climbs gently and turns to the north. At one junction the blue blazes turn off the road to follow a short footpath uphill to connect with another road. The road continues past stables and backyards. At another junction, two paths fork without a blaze indicating which trail to follow—turn left here. The trail becomes a narrower path through some shrubbier areas and climbs up to the paved Reservoir Road, where another triad of blue blazes indicates the trail's end.

A sign opposite the trails maps the immediate vicinity. Turn left and follow the road 0.2 miles to the gate at the water tower. The trail becomes dirt once again. Continue past to the clearing, where you will see the white blazes of the Walt Whitman Trail enter opposite. Follow the blazes to the left along a wide path to an equally wide, yet unmarked, path on the left. Take the path 0.1 mile as it ascends the gentle slopes into a clearing.

This is the summit of Jayne's Hill. At 401 feet above sea level, it is the highest point in Suffolk County and, indeed, all of Long Island. There are two benches and wooden fences at the summit.

Whitman was here. In 1881 he wrote a letter to the *New York Tribune* describing the view: "thirty or forty, or even fifty or more miles, especially to the east and south and southwest: the Atlantic Ocean to the latter points in the distance—a glimpse or so of Long Island Sound to the north."

You can savor "Paumanok," Whitman's ode to Long Island, on a plaque affixed to a nearby rock, with the lines, *"One side thy inland ocean laving, broad, with copious commerce, steamers, sails, / And one the Atlantic's wind caressing, fierce or gentle . . ."* describing what he took in from this spot.

This is a good place to eat your lunch or snack. Once you are finished, you can continue along the Walt Whitman Trail, which leaves the clearing to the south, just opposite the way you entered it. It descends the log terraces, then levels out in a heavily shrubbed area with trees until it reaches another road for horseback riding.

The trail follows the road around a curve and turns left before descending into a broad ravine, after which it crosses the woods road again. These sections of trail are not supposed to be used by horseback riders and several of these trails are set off from the roads by offset wood fences. However, horseshoe prints and dropping piles can sometimes be seen, so watch your step.

There are a few more bridle-path crossings as the trail continues over gently rolling land. Just past one low, wet area, it turns away from the bridle paths for a long, unbroken stretch through dense stands of mountain laurel. Here it is easy to believe you are in some remote wilderness, especially as the trail continues up and down the gentle hills without any more junctions. This is the Long Island that Whitman knew.

Some cleared areas on Sweet Hollow Road become visible through the trees, and the trail descends to another bridle-path crossing. It climbs uphill and down again, reaching the fence at the north end of the picnic area on Sweet Hollow Road after passing through a small grove of rhododendrons and pines. The white blazes continue down the side to the beginning of the blue trail where you started, although you will probably head back to the parking lot, across the picnic grounds.

MORE INFORMATION

Restrooms are available at the trailhead. West Hills County Park, Sweet Hollow Road, Melville, NY 11747; 631-854-4423; www.co.suffolk.ny.us/departments/parks/West Hills County Park.aspx.

TRIP 42
UPLANDS FARM SANCTUARY
TO COLD SPRING HARBOR STATE PARK

Location: Cold Spring Harbor, NY
Rating: Moderate
Distance: 3.5 miles
Elevation Gain: 200 feet
Estimated Time: 2.5 hours
Maps: USGS Huntington; Long Island Greenbelt Nassau–Suffolk
Greenbelt Trail maps; Uplands Farm Sanctuary trail map available at
trailhead kiosk and online

**The northern end of the Nassau–Suffolk Greenbelt Trail offers
some of Long Island's most challenging hiking.**

DIRECTIONS
Get off the Long Island Expressway at the Seaford–Oyster Bay Expressway
(Route 135) and follow it north to where it ends at Jericho Turnpike (Route
25A). Take this route east to Woodbury Road and turn left.

Stay on Woodbury Road to the junction with Harbor Road (Route 108) at
the Cold Spring Harbor LIRR station, just inside Suffolk County. Turn left and
follow Route 108 north 2 miles to Lawrence Hill Road. Turn right and follow
it uphill until you reach the entrance to Uplands Farm Sanctuary at 0.5 mile,
on the right. Follow the signs to the end of a split rail fence and turn left just
before the barn into hikers' parking area on the left. There is space for approximately ten vehicles. The trailhead kiosk is 75 feet beyond the parking lot. *GPS
coordinates:* 40° 51.439′ N, 73° 27.197′ W.

If taking the LIRR to Cold Spring Harbor station, follow Route 108 north
to the Greenbelt Trail intersection, roughly 0.5 mile north of the station. Be
careful because there is limited space to walk and you will be vulnerable to
high-speed vehicles. From there you can pick up this hike where it intersects
the West Loop Trail.

TRAIL DESCRIPTION
With its highest point coming in at a mere 400 feet above sea level, Long Island
gets a bad rap from hikers who don't live there. How, they ask, can it really be
interesting and challenging to hike on such flat land?

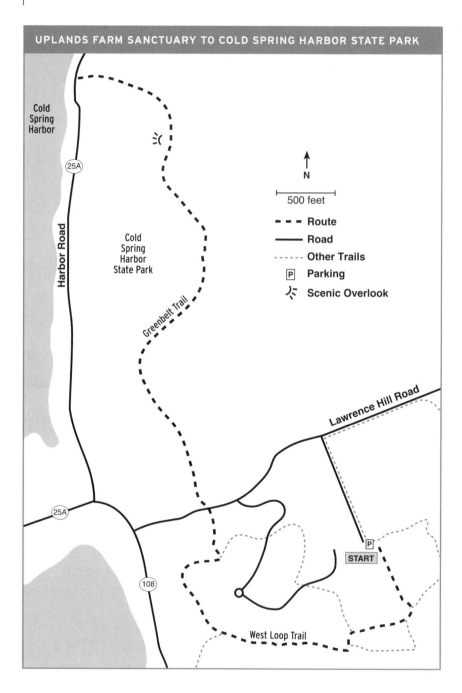

UPLANDS FARM SANCTUARY TO COLD SPRING HARBOR STATE PARK

Cold Spring Harbor

Cold Spring Harbor State Park

Harbor Road

Greenbelt Trail

Lawrence Hill Road

N

500 feet

- - - Route
—— Road
----- Other Trails
P Parking
⋏ Scenic Overlook

START

West Loop Trail

Consider heading to Cold Spring Harbor State Park for a few hours to find out. Located along the ridge overlooking the inlet that gave Cold Spring Harbor its name, it has the features of a moraine, the ridges pushed up by the ends of glaciers. You will find yourself hiking up and down the sometimes steep

This country lane runs through the woods at Uplands Farm.

bumps that occasionally require switchbacks, a feature not often seen on the trails of Long Island.

The best place to begin is just to the south of Cold Spring Harbor State Park, at Uplands Farm. The 97-acre sanctuary consists of a satellite research field and facility for Cold Spring Harbor Laboratories, the internationally renowned genetic research center. Here you will find some residential areas, the headquarters of the Long Island chapter of The Nature Conservancy, and the surrounding lands of a former farm that the conservation group manages.

The Nature Conservancy has laid out a trail system on the lands. The trails will allow you to get to the Greenbelt Trail with an easy warm-up for your legs as you enjoy the pastoral scenery. You may well see rabbits hopping across the grassy paths. Some grassland-dependent bird species can also be found here.

Start on the Daniel P. Davison Trail, which follows the path that goes to the right immediately after the trailhead. A sign indicates that this leads to the western loop. At the corner of the field, 0.1 mile from the start, it descends slightly into the woods, and then intersects an old field road where a sign tells you to turn right for the Greenbelt Trail.

This old road runs straight between two impressive rows of trees, and then up along the back of the residential area to a fork where only green-and-yellow markers indicate that either choice is a designated footpath. Take the left fork, which leads in shortly to another, similar fork. Here you will turn right and head west through the fields to a wooded area. About 0.2 mile from the second fork, you will leave the preserve for 0.1 mile and cross private land to Trail View State Park, where the white-blazed Greenbelt Trail comes in from the left. The combined West Loop and Greenbelt Trail curve along the hillside for another 0.2 mile back to the preserve boundary, where the West Loop re-enters as the Greenbelt Trail turns left.

From the junction, it re-enters the Trail View State Park, following a chain-link fence along Suffolk County Water Authority property to the northern end of Trail View State Park. This 7.4-mile, 400-acre linear park was originally planned as a northern extension of the Bethpage State Parkway to Caumsett State Historic Site. In 2002, with the road plans long since canceled, it was converted into a park built around the Greenbelt Trail.

Crossing Lawrence Hill Road, you see the sign for the southern end of Cold Spring Harbor State Park, a 40-acre tract across the top of the ridge on the east side of the inlet. The trail enters the park by ascending steeply up a section with several water bars. These small ditches across the trail divert runoff into the adjacent land, preventing trails that are routed up steep slopes from eroding into ditches. After a hundred feet the trail levels out again, keeping a tight course along state land between the lots on Harbor Road to the west and Seaward Court on the east.

The trail drops and then climbs again. In addition to the corridor it provides the northern end of the Greenbelt Trail, the park is an important habitat for migrating songbirds. Some of its oak trees are quite old, measuring three feet in diameter, and there are thickets of beautiful mountain laurel that bloom in June.

Dropping out of one of these thickets, the trail enters a narrow portion of the park with a view out to the harbor and its distinctive bar beach. Soon it reaches a junction with a short side trail, which goes down to Cold Spring Harbor's historic library building, where restrooms are available during operating hours.

The trail climbs again slightly through a forest with tall maple trees, and then begins its final descent. A series of switchbacks and steep sections with steps bring the trail to a large parking lot, where three white blazes mark the north end of the Nassau–Suffolk Greenbelt Trail.

Here you can stretch, relax, and take in the view of the harbor or the small park across the street. In the park is a plaque honoring Billy Joel, who posed here for a cover photograph of his first album, *Cold Spring Harbor*. If you have the time, check out the hamlet's quaint nearby Main Street, listed on the National Register of Historic Places in recognition of Cold Spring Harbor's past as a whaling village. Then turn around and head back to Uplands Farm.

MORE INFORMATION

Uplands Farm Sanctuary is open from dawn to dusk. Restrooms are available at the Uplands Farm trailhead, in the office, 9 A.M. to 5 P.M. Monday through Friday, and the Cold Spring Library near the northern end of the trail. Cold Spring Harbor State Park, Caumsett State Historic Park, 25 Lloyd Harbor Road, Huntington, NY 11743; 631-423-1770; nysparks.state.ny.us/parks/115/details .aspx. Uplands Farm Sanctuary, The Nature Conservancy on Long Island, 250 Lawrence Hill Road, Cold Spring Harbor, NY 11724; 631-367-3225; www .nature.org/wherewework/northamerica/states/newyork/preserves/art10995 .html.

TRIP 43
NISSEQUOGUE RIVER STATE PARK

Location: Kings Park, NY
Rating: Easy
Distance: 3 miles
Elevation Gain: 50 feet
Estimated Time: 2.0 hours
Maps: USGS Saint James; Long Island Greenbelt Nassau–Suffolk Greenbelt Trail maps

The grounds of a former state mental hospital offer a nice wooded shoreline for the northern end of the Long Island Greenbelt Trail.

DIRECTIONS
Take the Sunken Meadow Parkway to Exit SM4 for Sunken Meadow Road, the last exit before the entrance to Sunken Meadow State Park. Take that road east for 1.5 mile to a light at Old Dock Road, where it becomes St. Johnland Road. Continue down St. Johnland past the historic Obadiah Smith House on the left after 0.75 mile, and then cross over a stream. The parking area at Harrison Pond Park (a Smithtown Park) is just outside the state park on the right immediately afterward. There is room for five to ten vehicles. *GPS coordinates:* 40° 53.619′ N, 73° 13.657′ W.

TRAIL DESCRIPTION
In 1885, when Kings County was still the independent city of Brooklyn, it bought land along the North Shore of Long Island. A new psychiatric facility was to be built because those in the city were overcrowded. Within ten years the state took control of Kings County Asylum when it also became overcrowded. It was eventually renamed Kings Park and remained in operation for a century. Gradually, advances in treatment made it possible for most of the residents to leave the facility and live as outpatients. The facility closed in 1996.

Three years later, the state transferred 153 acres at the center to the New York State Office of Parks, Recreation and Historic Preservation for redevelopment as a state park. The property was named Nissequogue River State Park, a name that had previously been used for what is now Caleb Smith State Park Preserve.

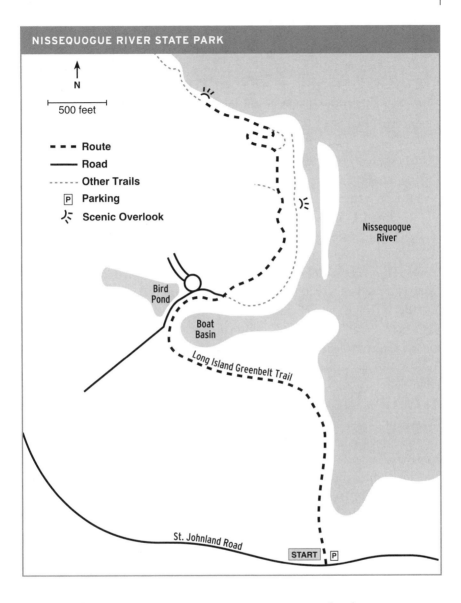

While the state government continues to entertain redevelopment proposals for the remaining property, the New York State Office of Parks, Recreation and Historic Preservation has ensured the protection of the scenic beauty of the Nissequogue estuary's wooded shoreline. The northern stretches of the 32-mile Long Island Greenbelt Trail, which connects nearby Sunken Meadow State Park with Heckscher State Park on the South Shore, can be found here.

This section of the Greenbelt begins near where you parked at Harrison Pond Park. White blazes are visible on one of the telephone poles. The trail enters the woods at an opening in the bushes on the north side of the road, just west of the small bridge over the pond's outlet stream.

The Greenbelt Trail descends slightly once it enters the woods to be almost level with the neighboring salt marsh at the inlet from the Harrison Pond outlet brook. Tall brushy shrubs crowd the trail, offering white flowers when in bloom. There are likely to be wet patches here in all but the driest times. Snapping turtles come ashore to lay their eggs during June and July. If you don't see the turtles, you can detect their presence by looking for the small holes they dig for the eggs.

Eventually the trail moves inland a little, into more wooded territory above the water, and it grows a little wider. The psychiatric center's vacant buildings and their fences are visible through the trees uphill to the left along this portion. When first opened, Kings County Asylum was meant to be a departure from previous institutions for people with mental illnesses. It was on a working farm, and residents could feed animals or grow food as part of their therapy.

After crossing another small brook next to its estuary, the trail forks without a blaze to indicate which direction it goes. The route to the left goes back toward the greenhouse and other developed areas; the Long Island Greenbelt Trail continues to the right, along the shoreline, and the white blazes soon reappear.

The trail stays inland this time, with the surrounding forest growing taller as oaks predominate. The trail's surface becomes more level, although there are still some wet spots. The trail bends westward and widens into an old road, its pavement decayed to gravel in some areas.

This section comes back out of the woods behind a large trash container near the parking lot for the state park marina. The white blazes lead you across a paved driveway and under some Norway spruces to the sidewalk along the main entry road. At an information kiosk, the trail turns right along the road for 200 feet, and then follows some steps back down to the water's edge.

Here you can enjoy the view of the small inlet, under a verdant canopy of maples and oaks with a thick green carpet beneath from a wide trail. It soon returns to the paved road via the edge of a picnic area and crosses behind a small concrete building next to the hospital's Colonial Revival–style main building before returning to the woods.

The trail remains as a wide path, but the woods have changed a little bit. They are taller and more mature, with some pines and birch mixed in. You are farther from the water here and higher up.

Paths come in from the rear of the hospital buildings, still visible, at first. Eventually, after some bushy passages, the woods are more pristine. The trail

The Nissequogue River estuary is home to many moored boats.

reaches a high point with a limited overlook where you can sometimes see ospreys. Then it drops into the low areas behind the dunes and bluffs, partly following an old rail spur, and continues with short paths leading out to the beach. The woods get a little shrubbier. Finally, it switches back up to the edge of one of the dunes, where a small bench allows you to rest while you take in the view of the Nissequogue estuary. There are often many moored sailboats and you can see Long Island Sound beyond, with Connecticut visible on clear days.

From here, the trail drops down to the beach, which you may want to explore. At this point, you could continue north up the Greenbelt Trail, but as that stretch is on a narrow beach and is sometimes underwater, this may be a good place to turn around and return to your vehicle.

MORE INFORMATION

Restrooms are located behind the former main building of the psychiatric center, where the trail crosses the paved road after the picnic area and returns to the woods. Dogs are not allowed. Nissequogue River State Park, 799 St. Johnland Road, Kings Park, NY 11754; 631-269-4927; nysparks.state.ny.us/parks/110/details.aspx.

SNAPPING TURTLES

The first thing to remember about snapping turtles is that they *do* snap—and quite viciously (enough to have severed a few human fingers). It's better that you avoid touching them entirely and leave that to properly trained and protected professionals.

A snapping turtle can coil its neck with its powerful teeth around to the middle of its carapace (the hard shell on its back). This snakelike capability led to the scientific name *Chelydra serpentina*. They also have powerful claws and hind legs, both of which are often wet and slimy with microbes you don't really want on your skin, much less in your bloodstream.

Now that we have that out of the way, let's learn a little about this ecologically important and vital creature. Schoolchildren across the state of New York voted to have it named the official state reptile, a designation formally adopted by the state legislature in 2006. Its habitat is wetlands, mostly east of the Rocky Mountains, ranging from Canada to as far south as Ecuador. It is the largest freshwater turtle species in the western United States, and in some areas, it is hunted and used in turtle soup.

Where snapping turtles make their home is often an indicator of the health of the area. If the habitat becomes polluted or otherwise unsustainable for them, snapping turtles have been known to travel great distances overland to find a new place to live.

Snapping turtles are omnivorous. They scavenge for plants and hunt by perching on rocks or logs, or sometimes on the bottom of shallow waters. Their prey includes fish, frogs, birds, and small mammals. In captivity they have been known to live for almost 50 years. Wild turtles are believed to have 30-year life spans.

In the New York metropolitan area, you are most likely to see them near wetlands during the females' peak laying season in June and July, roughly midway through their mating season. The females will crawl inland, crossing trails, roads, and backyards if necessary, to find a good dry place to dig a small hole and lay 25-80 eggs. After 9-18 weeks, the eggs hatch (late in the season, the hatchlings overwinter in the nest). Even if you do not see the turtles, you may see their telltale holes along trails and elsewhere.

TRIP 44
CONNETQUOT RIVER STATE
PARK PRESERVE

Location: Oakdale, NY
Rating: Moderate
Distance: 3.8 miles
Elevation Gain: 15 feet
Estimated Time: 2.5 hours
Maps: USGS Central Islip; Long Island Greenbelt Trail; trail map available at entrance gate

Follow the roads and paths of an old outdoorsmen's club that is now one of the largest protected areas in suburban Long Island.

DIRECTIONS

Take the Sunrise Highway east (Route 27) to Exit 46, Montauk Highway (Route 27A). Bear right at the end of the off-ramp and follow 0.2 mile to the area where parking for roughly 30 vehicles is available on either side of the road just below the West Brook Pond dam. *GPS coordinates:* 40° 44.684' N, 73° 09.376' W.

From the Long Island Rail Road station at Great River, turn right to go south on Connetquot Avenue. At the traffic light 0.1 mile down the road, turn left on Union Boulevard. Stay on the left side of that road and look for where the Long Island Greenbelt Trail crosses, marked by a white blaze near a speed limit sign. Follow the trail through the woods to Route 27A at Bayard Cutting State Arboretum and over the railroad tracks to where it enters the woods again near the sports complex. You will reach the dam in 0.3 mile.

TRAIL DESCRIPTION

Most of western Long Island's remaining open space has taken the form of small slivers of land here and there. Often they were preserved by accident, left over after other land around it was developed, or just in private hands so long as to have remained undeveloped when a large enough amount of public money was available to purchase it. A hundred acres of an old estate here or five hundred along a riverfront there are almost all we have to remind us of what western Long Island looked like even as recently as a century ago.

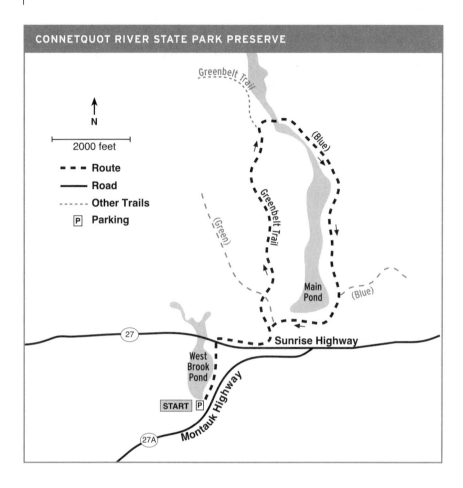

CONNETQUOT RIVER STATE PARK PRESERVE

N

2000 feet

- - - Route
——— Road
· · · · · Other Trails
P Parking

Greenbelt Trail

(Blue)

Greenbelt Trail

(Green)

Main
Pond

(Blue)

27

Sunrise Highway

West
Brook
Pond

Montauk Highway

START P

27A

There is, however, one notable exception. The 3,473-acre Connetquot River State Park Preserve, a former hunting and fishing preserve outside Great River in the Town of Islip, is the largest tract of wild land west of Brookhaven. It is even accessible via the Long Island Rail Road, via the Long Island Greenbelt Trail. All you need is a free permit that you can get in the mail by writing to P.O. Box 505, Oakdale, NY 11769.

From the public parking along Route 27A, pick up the Greenbelt Trail's white blazes and then turn right along the south side of the lake just before crossing the dam. Follow the trail along the lakeshore to the bridge that carries the Sunrise Highway over the water. A narrow, metallic deck allows foot traffic to pass under the bridge. Hikers around 6 feet or taller will have to duck down here—there isn't a lot of headroom.

Once across, turn right, climb up the stairs, which account for most of this trip's vertical ascent, and follow the blazes along the paved walkway alongside

West Brook Pond, formed by an old mill, is near Connetquot River.

the Sunrise Highway. So far you have been hiking through lands that are part of the Bayard Cutting State Arboretum. Now, by turning left and walking up the entrance road, you will be entering Connetquot State Park Preserve itself. Check in at the entrance booth and turn left with the blazes into the main parking lot.

This is a good place to stop and refresh yourself. There is water available, both at the outside tap and inside the large building to your left, part of the original club complex that now serves as the park's administrative offices. Restrooms and maps also are available.

Back on the trail, follow the yellow trail, the wide route marked with the preserve's yellow trail markers as well as the Greenbelt Trail's white blazes. It leads off to the left from the lot, and then turns north through some meadows into a few stands of pine barrens. The distinctive forest continues even where there are no pines.

There are benches for the occasional break, and interpretive plaques along the trail explain what you're looking at in the local ecosystem. You may also see some of the game animals that members of the Southside Sportsmen's Club hunted here for almost a century—deer and lowland birds are often dashing or flying away. While the hunters of that day might have pursued them into the woods, you must stay on the trail. As many signs remind you, especially at the long, open firebreaks, there are deer ticks and the attendant risk of Lyme disease in the grassy, brushy areas off-trail.

The trail parallels the paved Hatchery Road for almost a mile before finally crossing it just before reaching the trout hatchery complex itself. You may want to stop here, where the yellow trail ends at the red trail and the Greenbelt Trail continues northward through the picnic areas. Just aside it is a small wooden bridge over a fast-flowing, shaded section of the Connetquot River. It will cool you down just standing there, and there are nearby water taps if you'd like to refill your water bottle. Below the bridge is where the actual hatchery begins, with the river split into separate channels used to raise three different species of trout for anglers. Interpretive plaques explain this, as well as the importance of the river's watershed to Long Island's drinking water supply.

Follow the red trail markers for your return route to the entrance, across the hatchery. Turn right on the trail after you have crossed the last channel and follow alongside the ponds.

The landscape here is different from the yellow trail's on the route to the hatchery. The trail is narrower and the surrounding woods wetter. It curves back and forth through areas of skunk cabbage and sometimes through muddy stream crossings.

Eventually it reaches some drier areas where the tall oak and pines return. In a few places, the vegetation opens up to allow you to go to the edge of the Connetquot, wider here than at the bridge above the hatchery, and look it over from docks that are also designated angling spots (in many places there are trails to other such spots—please stay off them as the signs request).

The red and blue trails merge onto the same dirt road as they curve around the southeast corner of Main Pond. At an old pair of wooden gateposts, the trail turns right onto the original route of South Country Road, the road across the South Shore here displaced by the construction of the Sunrise Highway in front of the park.

Another 0.1 mile along, the woods end and you reach the dam that creates Main Pond. This is an excellent place to look over the buildings of the Southside Club and the mid-eighteenth-century mill that created the pond.

The club was originally the site of a popular inn on South Country Road. Wealthy men from New York City would frequently come out to hunt on the nearby land. When owner Eliphalet Snedecor retired in 1866, some of those guests pooled their resources and bought not only the inn, but also 879 acres of the surrounding land.

In 1870, they established the hatchery, which began successfully producing fish for stocking the river two decades later. The club continued to expand its holdings until it reached its present acreage by the middle of the twentieth century. In 1962, the club was sold to the state, with a provision allowing members to lease it back for another ten years.

When that time had expired, Connetquot River State Park was opened to the public for passive recreation, such as hiking, hunting, and birding. Six years later, the state legislature made it a state park preserve in recognition of its environmental resources. The entire property is also listed on the National Register of Historic Places.

Return to your vehicle on Route 27A the way you came. If you have time, you may want to check out the nearby Bayard Cutting State Arboretum, built around the only large South Shore mansion that survives.

MORE INFORMATION

Restrooms are available at the entrance complex and hatchery. No dogs are allowed. Free permit is required—request by regular mail at P.O. Box 505, Oakdale, NY 11769. Connetquot River State Park Preserve, 631-581-1005; nysparks.state.ny.us/parks/8/details.aspx.

TRIP 45
MIANUS RIVER PARK

Location: Greenwich and Stamford, CT
Rating: Easy
Distance: 2.2 miles
Elevation Gain: 140 feet
Estimated Time: 1.0 hour
Maps: USGS Stamford; trail map available at website for Mianus River Watershed Council

Loop through some old estates along the Connecticut panhandle's major river.

DIRECTIONS
Get off the Merritt Parkway at Exit 33. Follow Den Road 0.3 mile to Roxbury Road and turn right. In 0.4 mile, Roxbury Road reaches Westover Road. Turn left. Follow roughly 1.1 mile to Merriebrook Lane (just past Fort Stamford Park) and turn right. There is parking for about five vehicles at the end of Merriebrook Lane, where it reaches the river. *GPS coordinates*: 41° 04.850′ N, 73° 35.034′ W.

TRAIL DESCRIPTION
The Mianus River is not well known outside the small portions of Fairfield and Westchester counties it flows through, but it boasts some beautiful parks along the river in New York and Connecticut. Two of those parks are located right next to each other along the Greenwich–Stamford municipal boundary. Mianus River Park is a 220-acre former estate jointly managed by both municipalities. Just south of it is the 84-acre Mianus State Park, combined from sections of two other former estates. The two have a combined trail system. The parks have become popular with trout anglers, mountain bikers, and dog walkers. This short loop is an excellent introduction to these two parks for hikers.

From the parking lot, cross the bridge and follow the paved road through the gate uphill. You'll see a sign showing the trail system mostly in the state park, a section of which is called its local name, "Treetops State Park," from its past as the estate of controversial torch singer Libby Holman.

Turn right off the paved road and follow the blue-blazed West River Trail Spur, which runs alongside the Mianus, named for the area's last Siwanoy

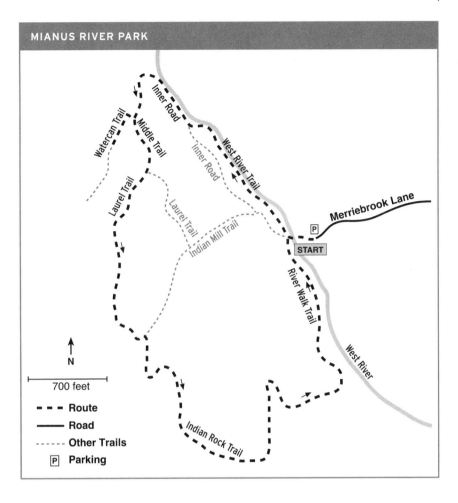

chief, for 0.1 mile before it joins the main West River Trail. After another 0.2 mile, the West River Trail merges into River Road.

You'll pass some fenced-off areas where plant communities have been protected. The parks are quite diverse despite their low relief from the river and wetlands, with upland species like mountain laurel and red oak on their low hills. An inventory by The Nature Conservancy has documented 100 tree species, 150 bird species, and 250 wildflower species. If you are the kind of hiker who enjoys identifying flora and fauna, you may want to bring a guidebook or two.

At 0.1 mile from the merger with River Road, you'll reach a kiosk with a trail map and other information where another old road splits off to the left. Take it. In barely 100 feet you'll see an unmarked trail going uphill to the left. Follow it up and around to a junction with the Middle Trail. Turn right and then almost immediately left onto the Watercan Trail and into the Town of Greenwich.

The trail goes over the top of the hill. There is no view, save into the nearby swamps with some glimpses of the woods beyond them, but there's a group of rocks just off the trail that makes a nice lunch or break spot.

From there, turn around and return to the Middle Trail and turn right. Continue 0.1 mile past the Ridge Run junction to the Laurel Trail and turn right. After another 0.1 mile, during which you cross into the state park, turn left at the Swamp Trail junction to stay on the Laurel Trail.

The trail descends slowly through an upland hardwood forest of oak and maple. As it does, you will see what appear to be the ruins of a stone oven in the woods to the right. A short spur trail, not on the map, leads to it. This structure is called the Creamery, although its exact purpose and origin are unknown. It is one of the few artificial structures in the park (despite its past as estate lands, no remains of houses have been found).

Return to the Laurel Trail, turn right, and descend gently another 0.2 mile to a paved cul-de-sac. This, the end of Indian Mill Road, is not an entrance to the park as prominently posted parking regulations leave no doubt.

Indian Mill Road continues into the park beyond a gate at the east end of the cul-de-sac. Just beyond it, turn right onto the Indian Rock Trail. This will be your route back to the parking lot unless you feel you've had enough, in which case you can just follow Indian Mill Road back across the park 0.3 mile to the trailhead.

Otherwise, take the Indian Rock Trail. It first descends to make a sharp turn around a swampy area redolent with ferns, and then climbs up past a rock with a hollow where rainwater often accumulates. As always, if you decide to take some for your own use, it is advisable to filter it.

The trail now heads across one of the most rugged sections of the park. In the next 0.2 mile, it goes up a couple of the small knobs, past some of the swamps, and over the hilltop with Indian Rock itself, a large group of split glacial erratics left behind at the end of the last Ice Age when the ice carrying them melted. Here red pines flourish alongside the trail.

Eventually the trail levels off and reaches the park's southern fence. It follows this closely for the next 0.5 mile, giving you a view of the sort of houses and backyards Greenwich and Stamford, which you return to along this stretch, are known for.

After a return to the north, the trail, now following an old road, turns sharply right to stay with the fence. Another old road, overgrown and blocked

This old stone oven is found at the Creamery, a ruin with origins that remain unknown.

off, turns left. It leads to private property, a small inholding within the state park, and should not be followed.

The woods grow taller as the ground begins to slope down toward the river again. After 0.2 mile more along the fence, the trail turns leftward and becomes the Riverwalk Trail. This last 0.3 mile of the hike gives you some nice views of the Mianus and the houses across it from the steep slope on the river's west side. At the end, you'll be back on the other side of the bridge you crossed to start the hike.

MORE INFORMATION

No restrooms are available. Dogs must be leashed, and they may not bathe in the Mianus River. Mianus River Park, Town of Greenwich Department of Parks & Recreation, 101 Field Point Road, Greenwich, CT 06836-2540; 203-977-4688; www.ct.gov/dot/LIB/dot/documents/dbikes/108.pdf.

TRIP 46
DEVIL'S DEN PRESERVE

Location: Weston, CT
Rating: Difficult
Distance: 7.0 miles
Elevation Gain: 450 feet
Estimated Time: 3.5 hours
Maps: USGS Norwalk North, Bethel; trail map available at trailhead

See gorges, reservoir vistas, and historic artifacts in this grand loop through one of Connecticut's most popular nature preserves.

DIRECTIONS
From Exit 42 on the Merritt Parkway, go north on Route 57 for 3.8 miles to the blinking light. Continue straight ahead onto Route 53 toward Redding. At the next traffic light, 1.7 miles ahead, turn left on Godfrey Road. Continue to Pent Road, 0.5 mile down (just before the bridge), and turn right. It reaches a dead end at the parking lot, with space for 35 to 40 vehicles. *GPS coordinates:* 41° 14.282′ N, 73° 23.851′ W.

TRAIL DESCRIPTION
Like most other protected woodlands of western Connecticut, the land now known as the Devil's Den was once used for the manufacture of charcoal. On their excursions through the woods, some of the nineteenth-century charcoal makers, climbing over the rocky ledges and outcrops, found a depression in one resembling a hoof print. They thought the print had been left by the Devil, and thus this patch of woods got its name. In the mid-1960s, a woman named Katharine Ordway began buying up the land. She eventually donated it to the state chapter of The Nature Conservancy (TNC), and today the 1,756-acre Devil's Den Preserve is the largest privately protected area in Fairfield County and the largest TNC property in Connecticut.

In addition to providing a large link in a chain of 15,000 forested acres and protecting the headwaters of the Saugatuck River's West Branch, the Den (as it's known) attracts thousands of hikers every year.

At the parking lot, pick up a free trail map and brochure. Make note that the key to navigating through the preserve is the numbered junctions indicated on the map. The trail blazes merely indicate whether skiing is allowed in

DEVIL'S DEN PRESERVE

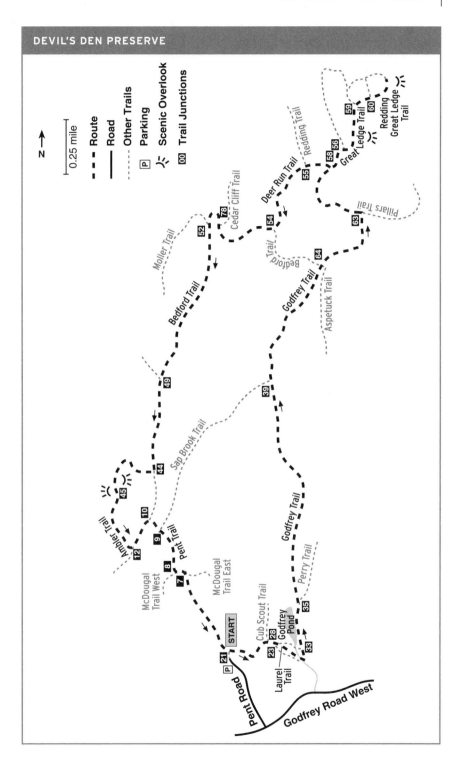

winter or just hiking (red for the former and yellow for the latter), and those trails that are part of the Saugatuck Valley system (white).

Start off on the Laurel Trail, which begins at junction 21. As the sign clearly indicates, this old road is the main route to Godfrey Pond. You'll pass a large mound in a cleared area, a legacy of the charcoal era, with an interpretive display, as the trail begins to wind down toward the pond.

At junction 23, leave the Laurel Trail for the unnamed footpath on the left. In 0.1 mile, it traverses down the steep slope, crosses a picturesque creek, and goes uphill again past two more junctions to the dam at the end of Godfrey Pond, an old mill pond that's a common destination for some of the preserve's more casual visitors. It takes its name from the family that ran a sawmill here for almost a century after the American Revolution.

You might want to pause and take in the scene, and perhaps look for some of the 145 species of birds that have been identified here. Once you're done, turn left at junction 33 and follow the old road alongside the pond 0.3 mile to junction 35. There, bear left onto another old road, the Godfrey Trail.

This trail follows Godfrey Brook, one of the pond's inlet streams, through a forest with a northern-hardwood feel, with plenty of birch, beech, maple, and ferns on the floor. Roughly 0.5 mile from the junction, the old road fords one of Godfrey Brook's tributaries. It then climbs slightly, once again passing through sections of forest where the trees seem to be afloat on a fog of fern.

Another 0.5 mile from the ford, you'll see a rusted metal tank and wheel in the woods off the trail, near an old stone foundation. A short spur allows you take a closer look at what an interpretive panel explains is the remnants of a "portable sawmill" used in this area when lumber and charcoal were its main industries.

Just afterward, the Sap Brook Trail comes in from the left at junction 39. If you want to shorten the loop, you can take this across the preserve to the Pent Trail and return to the parking lot that way.

If not, it's another 0.5 mile to junction 64. Stay on the Godfrey Trail another 0.3 mile to where it crosses into an area with state-land markers, part of nearby Centennial Watershed State Forest. Turn left onto the Dayton Trail at junction 63 and follow it back into the preserve. It loops around in 0.4 mile past junction 58 to the Great Ledge Trail at junction 56. Turn right and follow the yellow blazes to a rocky ledge on the preserve–forest boundary where you have a view over the nearby forest.

Continue along the trail and the ledge. You will pass a small stone marker, topped with yellow paint, with a "W" on one side and an "R" on the other. This is the Weston–Redding town line.

This rusted machinery provides a clue of the industrial history of Devil's Den Preserve.

In this section of the preserve, distant from the trailhead, the trails are lightly used. You may thus have to trust the blazes even though they don't seem to be on a well-defined path. But the junctions are still marked, and soon enough you come to number 59. Turn right and within about 200 feet you will reach junction 60. Continuing straight ahead will put you on the Redding Great Ledge Trail. At the rocky ledge ahead, you'll get your reward for following these trails this far: a nice viewpoint over part of Saugatuck Reservoir.

When you're done enjoying it, retrace your steps all the way back to junction 58 and turn right on the Deer Run Trail. Follow it 0.5 mile past junction 55 to the Bedford Trail at junction 54 and turn right.

You'll be following the Bedford Trail for 1.3 mile, through the switchback at junctions 78 and 52, past the swamps on the left, to junction 49 where it becomes the Den Trail. That trail, in turn, will take you 0.5 mile through higher and drier woods to the Ambler Trail at junction 44.

Turn right. This path leads you past some dramatic rock ledges with huge, dice-like boulders calved at their feet, into Ambler Gorge, a rocky ravine carved out by a small stream. In times of heavy rainfall, it makes a nice cascade looking up from the bridge you cross it on.

Past the gorge, the trail climbs sharply via switchbacks to an area of rock outcrops and ledges. There are few views, mostly over the surrounding forest, and the one on the spur trail from junction 45 seems to have grown in.

Continue along the Ambler to junction 12, in the middle of a grassy area, and turn left on the Saugatuck Trail. In 0.1 mile you'll be at junction 10, where another right turn takes you across a swampy section on the Pent Trail. Follow the Pent 0.2 mile past some rocky outcrops to junction 8. Turn left and then right shortly thereafter at junction 7. From here, the Pent Trail continues another 0.5 mile through declining junction numbers to the opposite side of the parking circle from where you started.

MORE INFORMATION

No restrooms are available at the trailhead. No dogs are allowed. Open sunrise to sunset. Groups of ten or more must register in advance. Devil's Den Nature Preserve, 33 Pent Road, Weston, CT 06883; 203-226-4991; theden@tnc.org; www.nature.org/connecticut.

TRIP 47
NAUGATUCK STATE FOREST

Location: Beacon Falls, CT
Rating: Moderate
Distance: 1.0 mile
Elevation Gain: 400 feet
Estimated Time: 1.0 hour
Maps: USGS Naugatuck

This short but challenging hike leads to a spectacular view of the Naugatuck River valley.

DIRECTIONS

From the south, take Route 8 to Exit 23. Turn right on Route 42 at the base of the off-ramp. Continue ahead on South Main Street into downtown Beacon Falls after Route 42 turns right on Bethany Road. About 0.3 mile north of that intersection (if you miss it, Main Street dead-ends after another 0.3 mile, allowing you to turn around), turn left onto Depot Street across from the old brick mill buildings and cross the bridge over the Naugatuck. At the end, turn right on Lopus Road. Follow over the tracks, and then turn right on Cold Spring Road. Follow it under Route 8 and along the railroad tracks (it will change to dirt, sometimes rough, and run very close to the tracks in some areas) to a large dirt parking area on the left with room for about 35 vehicles. *GPS coordinates:* 41° 27.234′ N, 73° 03.860′ W. If you pass this, you will reach a closed bridge where you will have to turn around.

From the Metro-North station at Beacon Falls, follow Lopus Road as described above. It is a walk of approximately a mile to the parking lot.

TRAIL DESCRIPTION

Twenty miles from suburban coastal Connecticut, the Naugatuck River valley is delightfully undeveloped—offering a sense of remoteness that belies its presence in a small, populous state—and easily accessible. The river is followed by the CT 8 freeway, the main north–south route in western Connecticut, and the Waterbury Branch of Metro-North's New Haven Line.

Between two of its stations, in the towns of Naugatuck and Beacon Falls, lies almost half of the 5,000-acre Naugatuck State Forest. Here road, river, and rail follow the narrow gorge between steep, rocky, dramatic peaks.

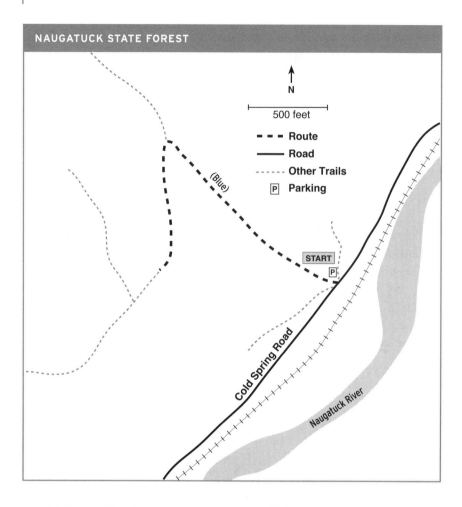

NAUGATUCK STATE FOREST

N

500 feet

- - - Route
——— Road
········· Other Trails
P Parking

(Blue)

START

P

Cold Spring Road

Naugatuck River

This hike will take you up one of those, Tobys Rock Mountain, a short distance north of Beacon Falls. From the trailhead, you may be able to see the viewpoint you will be heading for. It is not too far away, but you will have to work for it.

Three trails diverge from the northwest corner of the lot. You will take the middle one that climbs over some rocky steps to make a steady traverse of the side of the Spruce Creek gorge. It is marked by an occasional blue blaze.

It follows the old woods road steadily upward alongside the gorge. The ground on the downhill side slopes down steeply enough that you can easily see the rocky cliffs of the mountain on the other side. You can hear the creek below and its cascades. To your left, uphill, the terrain is just as steep but becomes increasingly shrubbier. You can see hemlocks rising higher up.

You can observe Route 8 in the Naugatuck Valley north of Tobys Rock Mountain.

After hiking about 0.3 mile from the trailhead, as the trail keeps rising and curving around the side of the mountain, another trail forks off sharply to the left. Turn and follow it uphill through what is at first a green tunnel created by the surrounding shrubbery.

The trail climbs a little more steeply here, eventually emerging into more open forest after several hundred feet. The blue blazes, sometimes very faint, return and the trail traverses upward along a steep slope through a mountain slope forest of maples and hemlock.

The trail then turns more directly uphill, becoming steeper. This stretch ends at a wide area with a stone fire ring and ashes in the middle, evidence of past use as an informal campsite. From here the blue blazes indicate the trail continues slightly uphill into an area where the hemlocks give way to a more open mountain forest of scrub and chestnut oak with a grassy floor.

Just above the campsite there are open rocky areas to the right. These are the overlooks you have come to take in. (If you reach an area where the blazes change to white and use tape wrapped around the trees, you've gone a little too far.) The view is excellent but limited. Short side paths lead in both directions to better, less obstructed lookouts. The one on the right is the viewpoint you saw from the parking area. The one on the left has a sweeping view to the north up the valley. Be very careful at both overlooks—the drop off the edge is steep.

To the north road, river and rail compress themselves through the passes between the mountains on up to the town of Naugatuck, the next settlement between here and Waterbury in that direction. Off to the south, the landscape becomes more open as the Naugatuck River flows farther toward the Housatonic River at Derby. In summer, look across the valley at an area of darker green in the middle of the hillside of High Rock Grove to the northeast (in colder weather it will be obvious).

This is an area where hemlock was replanted in the 1930s to reforest the area, which had been heavily logged. The forest was created a decade earlier with purchases by Harris Whittemore, a Naugatuck industrialist and railroad magnate known chiefly today as an art collector. He was also a member of Connecticut's State Forest Commission and, in 1921, began purchasing tracts of land in and around this valley with the intent of eventually assembling a large tract to give to the state.

He died in 1928, not having been able to make his donation. His family continued his mission, however, and in 1931 was able to give the state most of the land around Tobys Rock and High Rock Grove that you're hiking on. The reforestation and restoration efforts began almost immediately, reversing more than a century of heavy logging for the charcoal industry.

Later purchases have expanded the land to include separate tracts elsewhere in the region, more than doubling the Whittemore family gift. It has become a popular spot for local birders and mountain bikers, and, to the west of this section, home to the reservoirs that supply water to the town of Seymour to the southwest.

However, it has not yet become a major destination for hikers. As the experience of getting here may suggest, the state has not developed it for extensive use and other groups have taken it upon themselves to maintain and develop the trails; thus, there is no map of all of them. Fortunately in this little section, it is easy to get to this viewpoint.

Return the way you came. At the bottom, given the brevity of this trip, you may find yourself with the time and inclination to go farther along Cold Spring Road, over the bridge (still passable on foot), and to the small grassy area on the other side of Spruce Creek.

There you will find interpretive displays on the history of the area, from the heavy logging to its use as a picnic area and resort around the turn of the twentieth century. You may wish to explore the path up to Spruce Creek and take in some of its picturesque cascades and rapids.

MORE INFORMATION

No restrooms are available at the trailhead. Connecticut Department of Environmental Protection, Western District, 230 Plymouth Road, Harwinton, CT 06791; 860-485-0226; www.ct.gov/dep/site/default.asp.

TRIP 48
LOWER PAUGUSSETT STATE FOREST

Location: Newtown, CT
Rating: Moderate
Distance: 2.0 miles
Elevation Gain: 270 feet
Estimated Time: 1.0 hour
Maps: USGS Southbury

Enjoy this walk through the hemlocks along the Housatonic River.

DIRECTIONS

Get off Interstate 84 at Exit 11. At the end of the off-ramp, turn right on Mile Hill Road to Route 34. Turn right and follow south roughly 4.5 miles to Great Quarter Road. Turn left. Follow Great Quarter 1.3 miles to its end at a gate, with parking for about twenty vehicles. *GPS coordinates*: 41° 24.132′ N, 73° 11.290′ W.

TRAIL DESCRIPTION

There are many hikes that will take you on a walk along a flowing stream. However, there aren't too many where you get to enjoy the undeveloped shoreline of a major river, without even picnic groves or baseball fields.

Four streams north of Pittsfield, Massachusetts, merge into the Housatonic River. By the time it reaches the Connecticut border, it becomes the second longest river in southern New England after the Connecticut, with its watershed taking in some portions of Columbia and Dutchess counties in neighboring New York.

Like most large rivers, the shore of the Housatonic, from the Mohican for "beyond the mountain place," is mostly industry or private residences. But just above 1,063-acre Lake Zoar, a 1,157-acre tract has been preserved as Lower Paugussett State Forest.

That tract of land is what's ahead of you at this parking lot. Take the trail that leaves the lot from the right, toward the river, with a light blue blaze, indicating it is part of the statewide scenic trail system. It passes under some hemlocks, and then settles in between the river and the continuation of Great Quarter Road.

This is very gentle, level walking near the top of the low bluff at river's edge. There are a few occasional breaks along the sides if you want to get down to the

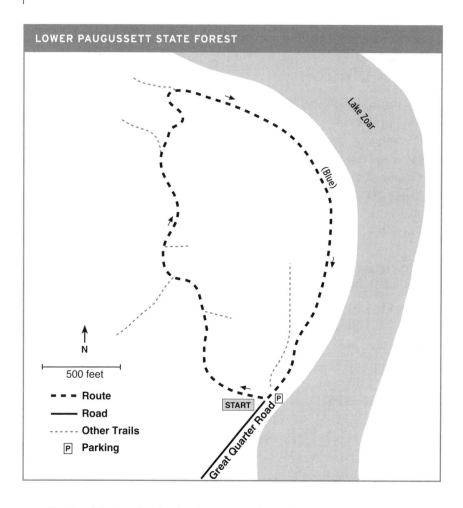

LOWER PAUGUSSETT STATE FOREST

Lake Zoar

(Blue)

N

500 feet

- - - Route
—— Road
----- Other Trails
P Parking

START
P

Great Quarter Road

river level safely. Don't take drinking water from the Housatonic—because of past industrial pollution from as far north as Pittsfield, the state's Department of Environmental Protection has given this section of the river a "D" grade, which means neither it nor its fish are recommended for human consumption. However, if you want to clean up some of the waste at these spots and pack it back out, go ahead. It makes the river more beautiful for everyone.

Most of the time, the river is best enjoyed from the trail, through the trees and occasional gaps. Its mood varies with the season—still and mirror-like on lazy summer days; gently white capped on fall days, brilliant with orange and yellows of the maples and oaks in these woods; and gray and stony on overcast winter days when ice rims the broad channel.

Lake Zoar, which you're walking alongside, is one of three along this section of the Housatonic created by the three dams built by Connecticut Power

Lake Zoar, seen here, was created by damming the Housatonic River.

and Light along the river early in the twentieth century. It takes its name from the community of Zoar that was lost when the land was flooded. Some of the land acquired was set aside to become the state forest by mid-century.

The view is enhanced by the mostly undeveloped landscape opposite, broken by just the occasional house and a small town park. After 0.7 mile, the trail reaches a large clearing with a well-used fire ring in the middle. The dirt road that runs parallel to the trail ends here.

Continue along the blue-blazed trail. The woods ahead get taller and denser, the bluff is higher above the river, and the landscape gets more rugged. The trail gets rockier in some places, and sometimes runs close to the bluff edge, so put your feet down carefully. You'll see more and more hemlocks in the woods to the left as the trail follows the river's curve to the west. A large hill also rises in that direction, with tiny needles of sun coming through the dark green hemlocks.

At some points the path widens, following old charcoal roads. It gets farther away from the river. After crossing a creek, it climbs up a 0.1-mile rocky stretch shaded by hemlock. At the top, you will reach a junction with an unmarked trail on the left at a large split rock.

Take the turn. The trail is light at first, but later as it makes left and right turns, mountain-bike tracks appear, helping to guide you along. After 0.2 mile and a return across the creek, you will reach an old dirt road. It, too, is unblazed. Turn left and start going uphill.

After 0.3 mile, you will reach the top. A small side road branches left to a crude camping area, but there is no view. The road you've been walking on continues downhill another 0.1 mile to where old, battered pavement begins. At this point, you should see a crude trail created, apparently, by mountain bikers, sloping directly down into the woods on the left. Follow it downhill, then right at a fork with another, less-used trail, to a traverse that then bends downhill and comes out at a stand of red pines overlooking a large, sandy pit that shows evidence of heavy use by stunt-happy bikers. Paths around the edge of the pit lead to a road at the far side, which leads 100 feet down to the pavement along Great Quarter Road.

Turn left and it's a leisurely 0.2 mile road walk back to where you parked.

MORE INFORMATION

No restrooms are available at the trailhead. Connecticut Department of Environmental Protection, Western District, 2340 Plymouth Road, Harwinton, CT, 06791; 860-485-3000; www.ct.gov/dep/site/default.asp.

THE THREATENED HEMLOCK

The skeletal and spiky remains of hemlocks you see in many of the forests of the lower Hudson Highlands are a sobering reminder of how nature can consume itself.

The eastern hemlock (*Tsuga canadensis*) is a tree that well deserves its popularity. Under cultivation as an ornament, it makes a beautiful tree. In the woods, the shade in the groves where it grows offers a cool spot for hikers passing beneath, accentuated by the soothing scent of its needles. Hemlock needles are flat and stick up from the branch, unlike the sharp, droopy ones on Norway spruces, which can sometimes be confused with hemlocks.

At one time, the hemlock's bark proved a rich source of tannin, a material used for the tanning of leather. For much of the nineteenth century, any hemlock more than a foot wide that was near a road was stripped of its lower bark and left to die.

The invention of a process for synthesizing tannin after the Civil War put an end to the stripping of hemlock bark. Around the same time, the conservation movement was beginning to protect many of the areas described in this book. The hemlock recovered and flourished anew.

Unfortunately, at the end of the twentieth century, a new threat appeared in the form of the hemlock woolly adelgid (*Adelges tsugae*). This aphid-like pest invades hemlocks and sucks out their sap. Its presence can be spotted easily in outwardly healthy hemlocks by the white woolly growth on the underside of branches.

Once infected, a tree usually dies within nine years (even faster in the southern states). The death of large hemlock stands leaves many bird and animal species with fewer habitats and subsequently warms the streams that flow near them. This has an impact on other animals and fish, as well.

Scientists are not sure if the northward surge of the adelgids is related to climate change or not, although the pest does not thrive in cold winters. Fossil records show a similar disappearance of hemlock 5,000 years ago, when the Earth was colder than it is today.

Some solutions have been proposed and are being tested. Fungi that poison the adelgid have been isolated. Beetles that prey on the adelgid have also been released in some areas. You can learn more at www.saveourhemlocks .org.

TRIP 49
UPPER PAUGUSSETT STATE FOREST

Location: Newtown, CT
Rating: Moderate
Distance: 2.4 miles
Elevation Gain: 450 feet
Estimated Time: 2.0 hours
Maps: USGS Newtown

Follow this trail on a roller-coaster course through varied and scenic terrain and then loop back through a working forest.

DIRECTIONS

Get off Interstate 84 at Exit 10. Make a left at the end of the ramp onto Church Hill Road (Route 6). Follow 0.3 mile to The Boulevard and turn right. At 0.6 mile, turn right at Hall Lane to stay on The Boulevard. At 0.4 mile from this turn you will go under I-84.

Shortly afterward, The Boulevard becomes Hanover Road. Bear right onto Echo Valley Road 0.5 mile from the underpass. Bear left at the intersection with Sanford and Alberts Hill roads at 0.5 mile from Hanover, and then follow the gravel continuation of Echo Valley into the woods 0.1 mile to two small dirt lots with room for ten to fifteen vehicles. *GPS coordinates:* 41° 26.961′ N, 73° 18.427′ W.

TRAIL DESCRIPTION

Some trails are hiked because of what they lead to: a summit, an overlook, or a natural feature such as a waterfall. Other trails are hiked because of what they go through or past: a particularly interesting forest, swamp, or creek. And many other trails are hiked simply for the pleasure of experiencing those very trails. These are trails that feel like they should be in an amusement park instead of a protected area. They eschew the monotonous and level and seek out the up, down, and around, with variable and changeable surroundings along the way.

Those trails are rare, since the terrain's just not available. But not at Upper Paugussett State Forest, where the southwest section of the 6.5-mile scenic loop around this 1,200-acre parcel has no views, yet is more memorable than many trails to some of the most sweeping views in the region.

The "ride" begins at the southwest corner of the parking lot. Follow the blue blazes, indicating a scenic trail as they do all over Connecticut. They go

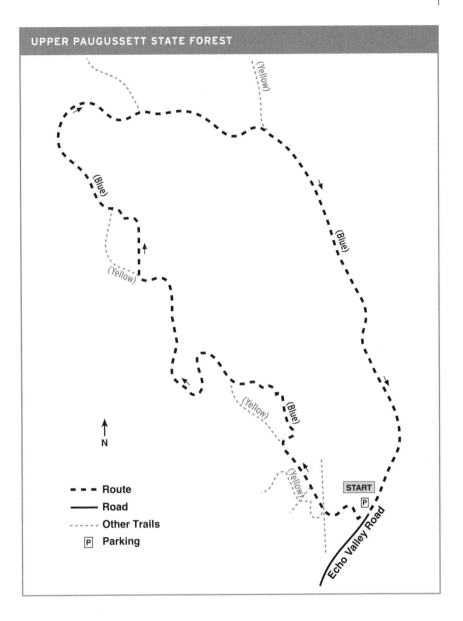

UPPER PAUGUSSETT STATE FOREST

(Yellow)

(Blue)

(Yellow)

(Blue)

(Yellow)

(Blue)

(Yellow)

START

N

- - - Route
—— Road
----- Other Trails
P Parking

Echo Valley Road

through second-growth woods over a gentle rise with nearby houses and their backyards in view to the left. After crossing an old dirt road flanked by two stone walls, the trail abruptly climbs up the short, steep face of another rise. Here you may see a paralleling, sometimes intersecting unofficial route blazed in yellow or orange. Stay on the blue trail.

The trail descends gradually off the rise into a vast bowl-like area, trending to the north as it does. About 0.2 mile from the rise top near the old road, the trail reaches another old road (from the nineteenth-century charcoaling operations that dotted Connecticut's woods for most of its history, as in other state forests) and turns right.

The trail follows a level course between rises on either side for roughly 0.1 mile, and then curves rightward past a stand of immature birches to a muddy area around a stream. You can see where the original course of the road continued ahead to an area now almost a quagmire. Follow the blazes rightward and up the stream a hundred feet to the new crossing, less muddy but still likely to wet your footwear. You will notice that this crossing is amid a small yet picturesque rocky ravine. Admire and photograph it if you would like, but there's more of this ahead.

Indeed, in another 0.1 mile, you'll reach a junction of deeper ravines where a yellow-blazed trail leaves to the left as the blue trail continues into a narrow ravine with impressive rocky walls, then climbs up the opposite side past large slabs. It tops out on a knob with a predominantly hemlock forest, more open than those below, gradually descending after 0.1 mile back into dense, immature hardwoods.

This section ends with a turn downhill near another junction with the yellow trail. From here the trail drops into a small bowl with cavernous tall trees above. It reaches a stone wall, crosses, and descends alongside the wall. It leaves the wall and reaches a dirt road after 1.0 mile.

The light blue blazes turn left; you'll turn right. The hike's roller-coaster-ride section ends here, but the hike back is not without interest. From the trail the road curves up around the north side of the hill. After 0.2 mile, the forest around it becomes dominated by beech, birch, and maple trees, with tall oak trees remaining alongside the road. This is an instance of the sort of northern hardwood forest more common in the Berkshires and Catskills at this elevation.

On some maps, this dirt road has been named after Polly Brody, the chairwoman of the state Conservation Commission who took the lead in protecting the land. In the mid-1960s, the original 880 acres of the state forest were up for development. She and her fellow commissioners paid for an appraisal that led one local official to describe the land as "a worthless goat pasture." Later they were able to persuade the state to buy it.

As the trail reaches the hike's highest point, it curves back along toward the south. On clear enough days, you can see the waters of Lake Lilinonah, another dam-created wide spot in the Housatonic, similar to Lake Zoar at Upper Paugussett's southern cousin, through the woods to the left. A road from the lake comes in from the left.

About 0.2 mile from the high ground you reach what seems like a junction. Cleared tracts of land, with thick, tall grass, run off to the left and right of the

The trail at Upper Paugusett State Forest climbs through varied and challenging terrain.

trail. This is an area where the state has been actively logging. Signs explain how the culling helps maintain the forest's diversity and long-term ecological health. Connecticut residents are also allowed, with permission, to take some trees for their own use as firewood.

Outside a small buffer, the logged areas continue for some distance on the right. A stone wall gives this section a picturesque quality. You can see how the state has carefully selected the trees to stay and those to cut, and how the forest is beginning to come back.

About 0.3 mile from the first cut junction, the woods finally return in full. The trail crosses a large brook that drains the cut area, then climbs upward gently back to the parking lot.

MORE INFORMATION

No restrooms are available at the trailhead. Connecticut Department of Environmental Protection, Western District, 230 Plymouth Road, Harwinton, CT 06791; 860-485-0226; www.ct.gov/dep/site/default.asp.

TRIP 50
POOTATUCK STATE FOREST

Location: New Fairfield, CT
Rating: Moderate
Distance: 3.1 miles
Elevation Gain: 600 feet
Estimated Time: 2.5 hours
Maps: USGS Pawling, New Milford; trail map available at website for Squantz Pond State Park

Go down to a beautiful cascade, then up to spectacular views over Connecticut's largest lake.

DIRECTIONS
Get off Interstate 84 eastbound at Exit 5 near downtown Danbury. Follow Downs Street to the traffic light at Main Street (Routes 39/53) and continue ahead onto North Street (Route 37). After 0.5 mile, it goes under I-84 and becomes Padanaram Road. Bear right at the fork 2 miles to the north where Route 37 becomes Pembroke Road. You will pass Margerie Lake Reservoir and then through downtown New Fairfield at the junction with Route 39 in another 1.5 miles. Another 1.5 miles from that junction, look for Pine Hill Road and turn right. Follow uphill 2.0 miles and bear left at a fork where both branches are signed as Pine Hill. The road dead-ends at an unpaved parking area with room for approximately ten vehicles. *GPS coordinates*: 41° 30.929′ N, 73° 30.242′ W.

TRAIL DESCRIPTION
Just north of Danbury is Candlewood Lake, Connecticut's largest. Besides the usual attractions for boaters and anglers, there are some parks along its shores. Most popular is Squantz Pond State Park. It's next to Pootatuck State Forest, the best place for hiking in the Candlewood Lake area. The largest of three parcels of this 1,155-acre wooded tract has a nice trail system that makes for a pleasant loop.

From the parking lot, follow the dirt road past the gate. About 250 feet in, it forks. Bear left and go downhill. It levels out at a junction with a yellow-blazed road to the right. On the trees nearby you will see the diamond-shaped metal markers that indicate state-land boundaries. Stay on the old road as you cross

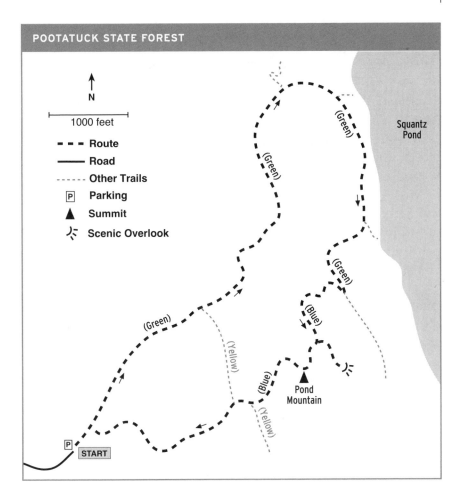

private land. It curves around the sides of a steep valley. At a small cascade on the left, it re-enters state land and then curves along the other side of the valley.

After another short descent, the old road levels off again. It slowly drops into a ravine where a small stream drains the depressed area to the right. Across it a high, rocky ledge rises.

Where the ledge ends, the old road turns right and descends again. Tall hemlocks shade the steep slope to the right; on the other side more hemlocks cover the mossy ground where the brook finally flows through a culvert under the old road.

Soon, you can hear the sounds of running water off to the left. Another 0.1 mile farther down the trail turns right, going more steadily downhill, and comes alongside the source of the sounds—Worden Brook. For the next 0.2

mile, cascades tumble to your left as the brook flows toward Squantz Pond, visible ahead through the trees.

This scene evokes the name of the forest. "Pootatuck" was the name of the local band of Mahican, whom European settlers met on the banks of the Housatonic River to the east. Pootatuck, their name for the Housatonic, means "river of falls" in the Mahican language.

Near the bottom of this, turn right onto another old road. Your descent has brought you to this, the lowest point on the hike. The old road stays mostly level at first, paralleling the edge of the pond. To your right is the other side of the ridge you saw coming down to Worden Creek, showing impressive cliffs with broken boulders (talus) below.

The road climbs some more, then bends to the right into another valley. It pools up at a stream crossing, and if you have a filter and pump you can top off your water bottle. This is a good place to do it. Immediately afterward, the old road starts to climb more steeply. At this point, it starts to run along the boundary between the state forest and the state park. It crosses another wide ravine and stream before leveling off. At that point, you'll see a gold-and-brown sign with the hiker symbol. Just opposite it a trail with a light blue blaze leaves to the right. Follow it.

A genuine footpath as opposed to the old roads you have been hiking on up to this point, this trail immediately establishes itself as the greatest challenge of the hike. For the next 0.4 mile it climbs more steeply than anything you have followed here, with only a short level break in the middle. In the dense woods around it you'll find a few trembling aspens.

The path ends at a junction in a draw between two rises. Turn left and follow the other path 100 feet up some rocky steps to its end at an overlook surrounded by scrubby chestnut oak and pines. Here you can easily see the state park and its beach. To its south are those sections of Candlewood Lake you can see, and Bethel and Newtown beyond.

Pootatuck and Candlewood Lake were created around the same time. In 1926, the Connecticut Light and Power Company began acquiring the land for the first large-scale pumped storage power-generating facility in the United States. Water from the Housatonic was pumped over to the lake, created by damming the Rocky River and its tributaries, then letting it descend down a large pipe to power a generator. The lake, at first called Danbury Lake, ultimately took its name from Candlewood Mountain in New Milford.

At the same time, the state of Connecticut began acquiring land on the mountains northwest of the lake, where charcoal making, the most common

Look for cascades along Spruce Brook near its entrance into Squantz Pond.

use of Connecticut's forests since colonial times, had ended. By 1929, it had acquired 960 acres, most of which was eventually covered by Squantz Pond.

Return to the blue trail and follow it up the steep section. It passes another overlook as it works its way through pines across the 1,400-foot summit of Pond Mountain. After descending, it passes a swampy area on the right, and then climbs again to a junction. Turn right and then bear left at the fork 250 feet ahead. This road winds past a couple of other small bumps, climbing slightly and then descending after 0.4 miles to the fork where you began the loop. Return to the parking lot from here.

MORE INFORMATION

No restrooms are available at the trailhead. Connecticut Department of Environmental Protection, Western District, 230 Plymouth Road, Harwinton, CT 06791; 860-485-0226; www.ct.gov/dep/site/default.asp.

THE MOUNTAIN LAUREL

Hiking in the woods of the New York area in late May and June often offers the reward of seeing flowering patches of mountain laurel. The shrubby plants frequently wall the trails in effusions of pink and white. In the mountains of the Carolinas, the laurel grows as a full tree, making the displays even more spectacular and visible from a distance. The mountain laurel is the state flower of both Pennsylvania and Connecticut.

The plant grows primarily on rocky mountain slopes, hence the name. In winter, mountain laurel patches stand out because the leaves not only remain on the plant but also remain green, one of the few broadleaf species in America to do so.

The mountain laurel is one of the earliest American species discovered and identified by European scientists. The first description of it dates to 1624. It gets its scientific name, *Kalmia latifolia*, from the Swedish botanist Pehr Kalm, known for being the first person to write about Niagara Falls. On an early eighteenth-century trip to the North America colonies, he collected some specimens and then sent them to his countryman Karol Linnaeus, who was in the process of developing the taxonomic system and Latinate binomial nomenclature for all living things that we still use today. Linnaeus, who had been Kalm's teacher, named its genus after him out of gratitude. Later, the plant found all over the eastern United States was able to establish itself in Europe as a popular ornamental, planted in gardens and yards.

American Indians used the plant's wood to make spoons, which is why it is sometimes called spoonwood. Much of the plant is actually poisonous (especially to horses). Early colonists also used the wood to make arbors, the spindles for their clocks, in the absence of worked metal.

Although the mountain laurel is not a timber species in the Northeast, New York has designated it an "exploitably vulnerable" species due to its desirability in landscaping. This means that while it is not currently threatened, it could be in the near future if certain trends continue. Mountain laurel may not be harvested in New York without permission of the landowner.

APPENDIX A: CRITICAL TREASURES OF THE HIGHLANDS

Critical Treasures, or areas in the Mid-Atlantic Highlands region threatened by development and sprawl, offer green getaways that are a stone's throw from many metropolises. These areas are also focal points for the Appalachian Mountain Club's conservation work in the Highlands. For more information, visit www.outdoors.org/hikethehighlands.

NEW JERSEY

Hunterdon County
Musconetcong Mountain
Musconetcong River Valley
North Branch Raritan River
 Watershed
Ramapo Mountains and Ramapo
 River Watershed
Upper South Branch Raritan River
 Watershed

Morris County
Farny Highlands
Musconetcong River Valley
North Branch Raritan River
 Watershed

Pequannock Watershed
Rockaway River Watershed
Schooley's Mountain
Sparta Mountain Greenway
Upper Passaic River
 Headwaters
Upper South Branch Raritan
 River Watershed

Passaic County
Pequannock Watershed
Ramapo Mountains and Ramapo
 River Watershed
Wyanokie Highlands/Wanaque
 Watershed

Somerset County

Upper Passaic River Headwaters

Sussex County

Hamburg Mountain

Rockaway River Watershed

Sparta Mountain Greenway

Wallkill River Valley

Warren County

Musconetcong River Valley

Pequest River Valley

Pohatcong Creek Valley

Pohatcong Grasslands

Pohatcong Mountain

Scotts Mountain

NEW YORK

Dutchess County

Fishkill/Beacon Ridge

Great Swamp

Quaker Brook–Haviland Hollow
  Watershed

Taconic Ridge

Orange County

Fort Montgomery Gateway

Goosepond Mountain Link

Greater Sterling Forest

Pochuck Mountain

Ramapo Mountains and Ramapo
  River Watershed

Schunnemunk Mountain/
  Moodna Creek/
  Woodcock Mountain

Wallkill Valley Farmland

Putnam County

Fishkill/Beacon Ridge

Great Swamp

Hudson Highlands/Fahnestock Link

New York City Croton Watershed
  Lands

Northern Putnam Greenway

Quaker Brook–Haviland Hollow
  Watershed

Rockland County

Ramapo Mountains and Ramapo
  River Watershed

Torne Valley

Westchester County

New York City Croton Watershed
  Lands

CONNECTICUT

Fairfield County
Candlewood Mountain/Vaughn's
  Neck
New Fairfield Agricultural Area
Quaker Brook–Haviland Hollow
  Watershed

Hartford County
Farmington River Canal
Farmington Valley Agricultural
  Area
Nepaug River Watershed
Salmon Brook Watershed
Traprock Ridges

Litchfield County
Bald Mountain
Blackberry Watershed
Boardman Bridge Scenic Area
Bull's Bridge Scenic Area
Canaan Lime Cliffs
Canaan Mountain

Candlewood Mountain/Vaughn's
  Neck
Farmington River Wild and Scenic
  Area
Furnace Brook Watershed
Goshen/Litchfield Agricultural
  Area
Highland Lake Watershed
Housatonic River Greenway
Kent Falls Watershed
Lake Waramaug Watershed
Macedonia Brook Watershed
Nepaug River Watershed
Robbins Swamp
Schenob Brook Watershed
Sharon/Salisbury Agricultural Area
Shepaug Watershed
Skiff Mountain Wildlife
  Management Area
Stanley Works Scenic Area
West Aspetuck Aquifer
Winchester Lake Watershed

APPENDIX B: RESOURCES

RECREATION AND CONSERVATION ORGANIZATIONS

Appalachian Mountain Club
www.outdoors.org
www.amc-ny.org

Adirondack Mountain Club
www.adk.org

Connecticut Forest and Park
  Association
www.ctwoodlands.org

Long Island Greenbelt Trail
  Conference
www.ligreenbelt.org

The Nature Conservancy
www.tnc.org

New York–New Jersey Trail
  Conference
www.nynjtc.org

PUBLIC AGENCIES

New Jersey Department of
  Environmental Protection,
  Division of Parks and Forestry
www.state.nj.us/dep/
  parksandforests/

New York City Department of Parks
  and Recreation
www.nycgovparks.org/

New York State Office of Parks,
  Recreation and Historic
  Preservation
nysparks.state.ny.us

New York State Department of
  Environmental Conservation
www.dec.state.ny.us

Palisades Interstate Park
  Commission
www.njpalisades.org/pipc.htm

Connecticut Department of
  Environmental Protection
www.ct.gov/dep

APPENDIX C: FURTHER READING

Adams, Arthur G. *The Hudson Through the Years*. Westwood, NJ: Lind Publications, 1983.

Albert, Richard C. *Damming the Delaware: The Rise and Fall of Tocks Island Dam*. State College, PA: Penn State University Press, 2009.

Appalachian Trail Conference. *Appalachian Trail Guide: New York–New Jersey*. Harpers Ferry, W. VA: Appalachian Trail Conference, 2007.

Barnard, Edward Sibley. *New York City Trees: A Field Guide for the Metropolitan Area*. NY: Columbia University Press, 2002.

Caro, Robert. *The Power Broker: Robert Moses and the Fall of New York*. NY: Vintage Books, 1975.

Charkes, Susan. *AMC's Best Day Hikes near Philadelphia*. Boston, MA: Appalachian Mountain Club Books, 2010.

Chazin, Daniel. *The New Jersey Walk Book*. Mahwah, NJ: New York-New Jersey Trail Conference, 2004.

Chong, Herb, ed. *Guide to the Long Path*. Mahwah, NJ: New York-New Jersey Trail Conference, 2005.

Colson, Ann T., ed. *Connecticut Walk Book West: The Guide to the Blue-Blazed Hiking Trails of Western Connecticut*. Rockfall, CT: Connecticut Forest and Park Association, 2006.

Daniels, Jane, and Walt Daniels. *Walkable Westchester*. Mahwah, NJ: New York-New Jersey Trail Conference, 2009.

Kenley, Kathy. *Quiet Water New Jersey and Eastern Pennsylvania*. Boston: Appalachian Mountain Club Books, 2010.

Kick, Peter. *AMC's Best Day Hikes in the Catskills and Hudson Valley*. Boston, MA: Appalachian Mountain Club Books, 2006.

Kick, Peter. *Catskill Mountain Guide, 2nd edition*. Boston, MA: Appalachian Mountain Club Books, 2009.

Laubach, René, and Charles W. G. Smith. *AMC's Best Day Hikes in Connecticut*. Boston, MA: Appalachian Mountain Club Books, 2007.

Myles, William. *Harriman Trails: Their History and Guide.* NY: New York–New Jersey Trail Conference, 3rd edition, 2010.

New York–New Jersey Trail Conference. *The New York Walk Book.* Mahwah, NJ: New York–New Jersey Trail Conference, 2005.

Pawloski, John. *Connecticut Mining.* Mount Pleasant, SC Arcadia Publishing, 2006.

Ransom, James M. *Vanishing Ironworks of the Ramapos.* New Brunswick, NJ: Rutgers University Press, 1996.

Reed, John. *The Hudson Valley.* New York, NY: Bonanza Books, 1960.

Rosenszweig, Roy, and Elizabeth Blackmar. *The Park and the People: A History of Central Park.* Ithaca, NY: Cornell University Press, 1998.

Scherer, Glen, *Nature Walks in New Jersey.* Boston, MA: Appalachian Mountain Club, 2003.

Sibley, David Allen, *National Audubon Society: The Sibley Guide to Birds.* New York, NY: Knopf, 2000.

INDEX

A

Abraham S. Hewett State Forest,
    xii–xiii, 142–145
Ambler Gorge, 221
American Revolution, 54, 55–57,
    98, 175
Appalachian Mountain Club
    (AMC), 244, 254–255
    Highlands conservation and,
    141, 241
Appalachian Trail, 37, 41–44, 52,
    55–59, 77–80, 91–95
    in New Jersey, 123–125,
    128–131, 140
Assiniwikam Mountain, xii–xiii,
    147–150

B

Bayard Cutting State Arboretum,
    211, 213
Bearfort Mountain, xii–xiii,
    137–140

Bear Mountain, x–xi, 55–59
Bear Mountain Inn, 56
Bear Mountain State Park, 55–59.
    See also Harriman State Park
Bellvale Mountain, x–xi, 41–44
Bill Paterson Nature Center,
    187–188
birding, 115, 168, 185, 213, 215
Black Rock Forest, xii–xiii, 102–106
Blue Mountain Reservation, x–xi,
    64–67
Breakneck Ridge, x–xi, 98
Buchanan Hill, 109–110
Bull Hill, x–xi

C

Caleb Smith State Park Preserve.
    See Nissequogue River State
    Park
campfires, xxx
Candlewood Lake, 236, 238
Canopus Lake, x–xi, 93–95

Castle Rock, 47–48
Cat Rocks, 44
Central Park, viii–ix, 3–8, 9
chestnut oaks, 81
Clarence Fahnestock State Park,
    x–xi, 91–95
Clinton Road, 146
Cold Spring Harbor State Park,
    xiv–xv, 199–203
Connecticut, hikes in, 214–239
Connetquot River State Park,
    xiv–xv, 209–213
Consolidated Edison, 101
Critical Treasures, 241–243
cross-country skiing, ix, xi, xiii, xv

D
Devil's Den Preserve, xiv–xv,
    218–222

E
Eastern Border Fault, the, 181
Eastern Pinnacles, 43

F
Fitzgerald, F. Scott, 182, 187
floodplain forest, 168

G
Great Swamp National Wildlife
    Refuge, xii–xiii, 166–169
Greenwood Lake, 137, 139

H
Harriman State Park, x–xi, 37–40,
    50–53
Hemlock Falls, 177
hemlock trees, 231

Hempstead Plains, 182
Highland Lakes State Park,
    xii–xiii, 117–120
Highlands. *See also* Hudson
    Highlands; New Jersey
    Highlands
    conservation of, 101, 141
    Critical Treasures of, 241–243
Highlands Conservation Act,
    141
Highlands forest, 42, 47, 66, 81,
    104, 124, 129, 231
Highlands Trail, 104, 133, 141
High Line, viii–ix, 10–14
High Point, NJ, xii–xiii, 123–126
Hobart Gap, 175
Hook Mountain State Park, viii–ix,
    32–35
Housatonic River, 227
Hudson Highlands, history of, 2,
    47, 54, 100, 101
Hudson Highlands State Park,
    x–xi, 47, 96–100
Hudson River, 2
hunting, xxvii, 44, 110, 213

I
InterActive Building, 14

J
Jayne's Hill, 195, 198

L
Lake Zoar, 228
LaTourette House, 16
Leave No Trace ethics, xxix–xxx
Long Island, hikes on, 183–213
Long Island Greenbelt Trail, 205

Long Mountain, x–xi, 50–53
Long Path, 52, 118, 162
Lower Paugussett State Forest, xiv–xv, 227–230

M

Mahlon Dickerson Reservation, xii–xiii, 133–136
Manetto Hills, xiv–xv, 191–194
Manitoga, x–xi, 60–63
Maple Falls Cascades, 178
maps, regional locator, iv
Massapequa Preserve, xiv–xv, 183–186
Mertz Library, 27
Mianus River Park, xiv–xv, 214–217
Mianus State Park, 214
mid-Atlantic Highlands. *See also* Highlands; Hudson Highlands; New Jersey Highlands
conservation of, 141
Critical Treasures of, 241–243
Monroe, William, 148–149
Moses, Robert, 9, 30, 182
mountain biking, 64, 90, 154, 214, 226
mountain laurel, 240
Mount Defiance, 153–154
Museum of the Hudson Highlands, 102
Muttontown Preserve, xiv–xv, 187–190

N

Nassau-Suffolk Greenbelt Trail, 184, 191, 202

The Nature Conservancy (TNC), 218
Naugatuck State Forest, xiv–xv, 223–226
Newark Basin, 121, 165
New Jersey, hikes in, 123–183
New Jersey Highlands, 121–122, 133
conservation of, 141
Critical Treasures of, 241–242
New York Botanical Garden, viii–ix, 24–27
New York City
hikes within city limits of, 3–32
natural history of, 1–2
Nimham Mountain State Forest, x–xi, 87–90
Nissequogue River State Park, xiv–xv, 182, 204–207

O

oak trees, 81
Orchard Beach, 29

P

Palisades Cliffs, 165
Palisades Interstate Park, xii–xiii, 160–164
geology of, 165
Paugussett State Forest. *See* Lower Paugussett State Forest; Upper Paugussett State Forest
Pawling Nature Preserve, x–xi, 77–80
Pelham Bay Park, viii–ix, 28–31
pine barrens, 183
Pootatuck State Forest, xiv–xv, 236–239

Pound Ridge Reservation. *See* Ward
    Pound Ridge Reservation
public land-management agencies,
    244
public transportation, hikes
    accessible by, ix, xi, xiii, xv,
    xxii
    in Connecticut, 223
    on Long Island, 183, 191, 199,
        204, 209
    in New Jersey, 137, 160, 175
    in New York City, 3, 10, 15, 20,
        24, 28
    in upstate New York, 37, 41, 45,
        55, 60, 64, 73, 77, 82, 96
Pyramid Mountain Natural
    Historic Area, xii–xiii,
    156–159

R
Rattlesnake Swamp Loop, xii–xiii,
    127–131
recreation and conservation
    organizations, 244
Revolutionary War. *See* American
    Revolution
Ringwood-Ramapo Trail, 153–154
Ringwood State Park, xii–xiii,
    151–155
Rockland Lake, 32, 34–35
The Russel Wright Design Center,
    x–xi, 60–63

S
safety considerations, xxv–xxviii
Shawangunk Grasslands National
    Wildlife Refuge, xii–xiii,
    111–115

Sheep Meadow, 6
Shepherd Lake, 152–154
short-eared owl, 115, 116
snapping turtles, 208
snowshoeing, ix, xi, xiii, xv
South Mountain Reservation,
    xiv–xv, 175–179
Standard Hotel, 12
Staten Island Greenbelt, viii–ix,
    15–19
Stewart State Forest, xii–xiii,
    107–110
Stillman, Dr. Ernest, 102
Storm King Mountain, 100, 101,
    102
Sugarloaf South, x–xi, 45–49
Sunset Pond, 142
swamp chestnut oak, 81
swimming, 32, 151–155

T
Teatown Lake Reservation,
    x–xi, 69–72
Terrace Pond, xii–xiii,
    143–144
Terrapin Nesting Area, 22
Tobys Rock Mountain, 224
Torrey, Raymond H., 51–53
Trail View State Park, 202
Treetop State Park, 214
Tripod Rock, 158–159
trip planning, xxv–xxviii, xxix
trip ratings, explanation of,
    xxiii–xxiv
turkey, wild, 68
Turkey Mountain Nature P
    reserve, x–xi, 73–76
Tuxedo Loop, x–xi, 37–40

U

Uplands Farm Sanctuary, xiv–xv,
    199–203
Upper Paugussett State Forest,
    xiv–xv, 232–235

W

Ward Pound Ridge Reservation,
    x–xi, 64, 82–86
Washington Rock, 177
waste disposal, xxx
Watchung Reservation, xiv–xv,
    170–174

waterfall hikes, 177–178
Welch, William A., 57–58
West Hills County Park, xiv–xv,
    195–198
West Pond Loop, viii–ix, 20–23
white-tailed deer, 36
Whitman, Walt, 195
Wildflower Island, 70–71
wildflowers, 215
wild turkey, 68
Wyanokies, 147

ABOUT THE AUTHOR

DANIEL CASE, a native of New Jersey, has written for a variety of publications, from the Sun Newspapers of suburban Cleveland to Kaatskill Life magazine. He has served on the board of the Catskill Mountain 3500 Club, and hikes extensively in New York and New Jersey. Currently, he works in secondary education. He lives in the Hudson Valley with his family.

Appalachian Mountain Club

Founded in 1876, the AMC is the nation's oldest outdoor recreation and conservation organization. The AMC promotes the protection, enjoyment, and understanding of the mountains, forests, waters, and trails of the Appalachian region.

People
We are more than 100,000 members, advocates, and supporters; 16,000 volunteers; and more than 450 full-time and seasonal staff. Our 12 chapters reach from Maine to Washington, D.C.

Outdoor Adventure and Fun
We offer more than 8,000 trips each year, from local chapter activities to major excursions worldwide, for every ability level and outdoor interest—from hiking and climbing to paddling, snowshoeing, and skiing.

Great Places to Stay
We host more than 140,000 guests each year at our lodges, huts, camps, shelters, and campgrounds. Each AMC destination is a model for environmental education and stewardship.

Opportunities for Learning
We teach people the skills to be safe outdoors and to care for the natural world around us through programs for children, teens, and adults, as well as outdoor leadership training.

Caring for Trails
We maintain more than 1,500 miles of trails throughout the Northeast, including nearly 350 miles of the Appalachian Trail in five states.

Protecting Wild Places
We advocate for land and riverway conservation, monitor air quality and climate change, and work to protect alpine and forest ecosystems throughout the Northern Forest and Mid-Atlantic Highlands regions.

Engaging the Public
We seek to educate and inform our own members and an additional 2 million people annually through AMC Books, our website, our White Mountain visitor centers, and AMC destinations.

Join Us!
Members support our mission while enjoying great AMC programs, our award-winning *AMC Outdoors* magazine, and special discounts. Visit www.outdoors.org or call 800-372-1758 for more information.

APPALACHIAN MOUNTAIN CLUB
Recreation • Education • Conservation
www.outdoors.org

About the AMC in New York

THE APPALACHIAN MOUNTAIN CLUB has two active chapters in New York. The AMC New York–North Jersey Chapter offers more than 2,000 trips per year, ranging from canoeing and kayaking, to sailing, hiking, backpacking, and social events. The chapter is also active in trail work and conservation projects and maintains a cabin at Fire Island. The AMC Mohawk–Hudson Chapter serves residents of Albany, Columbia, Fulton, Greene, Montgomery, Rensselaer, Saratoga, Schenectady, Schoharie, Warren, and Washington counties, and offers a variety of outdoor activities for all levels of ability. You can learn more about these chapters by visiting www.outdoors.org/chapters. To view a list of AMC activities in New York and other parts of the Northeast, visit trips .outdoors.org.

AMC Book Updates

AMC BOOKS STRIVES TO KEEP OUR GUIDEBOOKS AS UP-TO-DATE as possible to help you plan safe and enjoyable adventures. If after publishing a book we learn that trails are relocated or route or contact information has changed, we will post the updated information online. Before you hit the trail, check for updates at www.outdoors.org/publications/books/updates.

While hiking or paddling, if you notice discrepancies with the trail description or map, or if you find any other errors in the book, please let us know by submitting them to amcbookupdates@outdoors.org or in writing to Books Editor, c/o AMC, 5 Joy Street, Boston, MA 02108. We will verify all submissions and post key updates each month. AMC Books is dedicated to being a recognized leader in outdoor publishing. Thank you for your participation.

AMC BOOKS & MAPS

**EXPLORE THE
POSSIBILITIES**

More Books from the Outdoor Experts

AMC's Best Day Hikes in the Catskills and Hudson Valley

BY PETER W. KICK

This guide leads hikers along 60 of the region's most spectacular trails, from short family nature walks to long day hikes. Each trip description includes a detailed map and a summary of the trip time, distance, and difficulty.

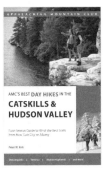

ISBN: 978-1-929173-84-6
$16.95

AMC's Best Day Hikes in the Berkshires

BY RENÉ LAUBACH

Discover 50 of the most impressive trails in the Berkshires, from short nature walks to long day hikes. Each trip description includes a detailed map, trip time, distance, and difficulty. Includes tips on area snowshoeing cross-country skiing, and nature notes.

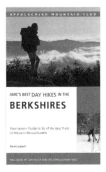

ISBN: 978-1-934028-21-6
$18.95

Quiet Water New York, 2nd Edition

BY JOHN HAYES AND ALEX WILSON

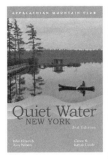

From clear and quick-flowing waterways to picturesque ponds surrounded by mountain peaks, this guide allows paddlers to explore the great variety of water adventures New York has to offer with 90 spectacular quiet water destinations.

ISBN: 978-1-929173-73-0
$19.95

Quiet Water New Jersey and Eastern Pennsylvania

BY KATHY KENLEY

Great for families, anglers, canoeists, and kayakers of all abilities, *Quiet Water New Jersey and Eastern Pennsylvania* features 80 trips, covering the best calm water paddling in the region.

ISBN: 978-1-934028-34-6
$19.95

Get Ready for
Adventure.

Appalachian Mountain Club's southernmost destination for lodging and outdoor adventure.

Located on a beautiful glacial lake in the 70,000-acre Delaware Water Gap National Recreation Area and close to the Appalachian Trail, the Mohican Outdoor Center is an ideal retreat for groups and families. Year-round outdoor recreation opportunities abound in this unique natural area, including hiking, paddling, climbing, and skiing.

Just a 90-minute drive from New York City and less than 3 hours from Philadelphia, Mohican Outdoor Center offers an accessible base for outdoor exploration

Call 908-362-5670 for reservations or visit www.outdoors.org/lodging

Mohican Outdoor Center • 50 Camp Road • Blairstown, NJ 07825-9655 • 908-362-5670 • www.outdoors.o